TOMMY'S WAR

A FIRST WORLD WAR DIARY

1913-18

Thomas Cairns Livingstone

Edited by Ronnie Scott
Foreword by Andrew Marr

Harper
Press

HarperPress
An imprint of HarperCollinsPublishers
77-85 Fulham Palace Road
Hammersmith, London W6 8JB
www.harpercollins.co.uk

Visit our authors' blog: www.fifthestate.co.uk

First published in Great Britain by HarperPress in 2008

9 8 7 6 5 4 3 2 1

A catalogue record for this book
is available from the British Library

ISBN 978-0-00-728067-4

Typeset by **'OMEDESIGN**
Printed and bound in Italy by L.E.G.O SpA

In memory of
Thomas, Agnes and Wee Tommy.

CONTENTS

About the diaries

Thomas Cairns Livingstone began writing his diary shortly before 'flitting' from 20 to 14 Morgan Street, Govanhill, Glasgow in 1913. Just why he started his diary has been lost to the annals of time, but a clue surely lies in his grandfather's and father's need to record their daily lives and their love of writing. Thomas' grandfather was a teacher of English in Lurgan, Northern Ireland, his father, Joseph, kept an exquisite hand-illustrated journal of events deemed important to the Livingstone family. Perhaps Thomas was simply keeping up a family tradition he enjoyed, as well as marking the time that he first moved into his own home with his new family.

He had married Agnes Smart Cook (thinking that marrying A. Smart Cook he would never starve…) three years before moving to Morgan Street. The first few years of the diaries record – at the foot of each page – events of each day ten years earlier, when they were courting. Their son, Thomas Cairns Livingstone junior – invariably known as 'Wee Tommy' – joined the family in 1911 and was a toddler at the time of the move and the diaries' commencement.

The diaries reveal how very well suited Thomas was to his job as a mercantile clerk. He had a pressing need to record all sorts of detail even, in many entries, the precise hour that he awoke and went to bed, with the discipline to maintain this long after most would have given up. Thomas never missed his daily entry for over twenty years, loyally filling each dated page of his clothbound diaries with his signature dry, humorous notes, observations and wonderful drawings, summarising the day's events at home and further afield. Often a drawing is more telling than the words themselves, and he clearly meant one to be read against the other. From the accounts of other relatives, they were seen as something of a family treasure, and a list of each family visit is included in most volumes. In later years, Thomas enjoyed showing them off to his nephews and nieces.

After 1918 the diaries continue in their fine characteristic vein over the course of a further decade and a half, providing a very special snapshot of the post-war world and the unfolding Livingstone family pocket saga. Thomas ended his epic in 1933 as Wee Tommy started his working life at Glasgow University and old age caught up with Thomas senior. A very poignant last entry, dated 1950, records the death of his beloved wife, Agnes.

Upon Thomas' death in 1964 the diaries passed to a less-than 'wee' Tommy, who remained his only child. He kept them until his own death in 1995, by which time he was living in Northumberland. The diaries were entered into a local county auction house in 2005 which, as a local antiques dealer, I happened to attend. There was something compelling about these twenty-odd little volumes nestled together in a shoebox, and I was able to secure them for the princely sum of £300.00.

That very weekend Thomas and his diaries quickly began to become part of my life. I read them cover to cover – including Joseph's own volume of family records – utterly absorbed by the lost life stories spilling out from their pages of hand-written words and pictures. Some pages even had stamps from Thomas' collection stuck on to them. It was like opening a time capsule. Every facet of life seemed to be recorded there, from glorious summers, heart-rending sadness of losing loved ones, frustrations with work, to his enduring love for Agnes. What seemed particularly special was being able to witness daily life and Wee Tommy growing up against the backdrop of the Great War, together with a chronicle of all the events in Glasgow and the rest of the Empire. As the war progressed, the bottom portion of every page – after tales of jam-making, walks in the park and seemingly constant redecorating of the front room (presumably because of the sooty fire) and blacking of the grate – sombrely lists the loss of life that each day's newspaper had announced, together with any notable gains or military achievements.

Soon I found myself on the road in a quest to explore the life and discover more about this remarkable man from Glasgow and his family.

I'm extremely grateful to Dr. Irene O'Brien and the wonderful staff at the Mitchell Library in Glasgow, and all the Livingstone relatives, Helen Carlyle, Ella Brown and Colin Brown, who have helped me in my quest, and with whom I've been delighted to share the details I've found about their 'lost' relative.

If you know more about Thomas than I have been able to uncover already, then I look forward to hearing from you – you'll find the contact details at the back of this book.

When the BBC's Antiques Roadshow rolled in to Alnwick Castle in July 2007, I couldn't resist taking the diaries along. I found myself pulled out of a queue and ended up being filmed with books expert Clive Farahar. The episode was broadcast that autumn and caused a lot of interest from publishers and literary agents keen to bring the diaries to the nation's attention. It was thrilling that in the end they were taken on by HarperCollins, themselves of Glasgow descent, and in whose blank diary pages Thomas Cairns Livingstone left his enduring mark.

At last, some of the best of the private diaries of Thomas Cairns Livingstone are ready to be enjoyed and treasured by everyone. A lot of people have worked on bringing this to fruition, but I'd like especially to thank my partner Joan for her patience and support; Gordon Wise of Curtis Brown for offering to take on their representation; Michael Morrison, whose mother was 'wee' Tommy's great friend and heir; John Bond and Arabella Pike and all the team at HarperPress for all the hard work in assembling this edited volume of the years 1913-1918 and sourcing such suitable photographs to complement Thomas' illustrations and stories; Dan Cruickshank, for his early enthusiasm; and Ronnie Scott, for bringing those stories to life for the uninitiated, picking out storylines and providing background notes to enable us to understand Thomas Cairns Livingstone's world more than a little better.

Shaun Sewell
Northumberland, June 2008

Foreword

A small man in a badly made suit, a hat jammed on his head and an empty pipe between his lips, is walking down the street towards the tram, with a small boy attached to one hand, in turn clutching a mouth organ. Around him are men in uniform, loud gossipy women on the corner, the rattle of horse-drawn carts, the smells of sulphur, oil, coal and sweat. On the walls as he passes, lurid recruiting posters urge him to join the lads in France, to fight to save his women from the Hun, or simply exclaim that his country needs him. Head down, fingering his last stiff collar, he disappears into the crowd gathering by the tram stop. The streets are shabby and the war news is terrible. There is a faint sound of the mouth organ being played. Who is he, this man? What does he do? Does he have a wife at home, her hands coarsened with heavy washing and scouring, but her bread smelling sweet? Will he soon be wearing a khaki uniform, and die choking in French mud thinking of the small boy; or will he survive this so-called Great War? Does he like cards? What does he think of Germans, and this throbbing, clattering city where he has spent his life? But he has gone, vanished into time like the millions upon millions who lived through momentous times but who were not Lloyd George, or Haig, or even Harry Lauder.

Well, by extraordinary luck and chance, he has not gone. Back from the dead, Thomas Cairns Livingstone of Rutherglen, a clerk, married to Agnes, who was often ill, and the proud father of Wee Tommy, is returned to life through handwritten diaries and drawings discovered in an auction in Northumberland in 2005 and bought for £300. So now we know what he thought, who he was and what happened to him later. It is a story extraordinary in its ordinariness; it is good to have him back. For in general, history is owned by those who record it. Only a handful of truly powerful people were recorded by others at the time. Mostly, historians have depended on autobiographies, property records, diaries, letters, newspapers and account books. So 'history' has too often been that of those at the top of the pile, the politicians, writers and professional leaders; and it has been a hard task to disinter the lives of millions who left no written trace. It was not until 1937 that 'Mass Observation' began to accumulate the diaries and thoughts of ordinary Britons. Before that, the voices of the majority had been heard through snippets in newspapers, court reports or in rare sociological exercises, like Charles Booth's studies of the London poor. There were a few memoirs by people further down the tree, clerks and governesses; some of the working-class Suffragettes and trade unionists left written records, for instance. There was the knowledgeable mimicking of working-class and lower-middle-class life by novelists – the clerks and shopkeepers of H. G. Wells, or the miners of D. H. Lawrence. But the material was always scanty.

During the First World War there was much recording of the lives and heroism of the men at the front, who wrote letters back home. Some retold their stories much later to historians. Little by comparison was written about the home front, where, of course, the vast majority of British people were living their lives. Oral historians like Richard van Emden and Steve Humphries have done much to salvage material from those they could find who were still alive; numerous local historical societies have done the same. But the diary of Thomas Livingstone is a rare thing. Here is the Great War as it was seen by an ordinary man, no hero, living in the backstreets of Glasgow. You might call him a Scottish Pooter, except that his drawings and humour are more self-knowing. He was no special rebel, indeed no special anything. But that is the point. As with family history, the stories of plain people upend and challenge the stories told by historians. For instance, I had no idea just how near the trenches seemed until learning that my family, also from Glasgow, got laundry back from sons in the trenches every week, and sent the clean underclothes back, along with cakes, chocolate and tobacco. The fast train service made Flanders seem very close. Thomas' story is family history, except that his immediate family has long gone and it has been returned as a family story for all of us.

These were momentous times, and Glasgow in 1913–18 was a city at the edge of turmoil, seen by some as the next Bolshevik Petrograd. Yet as Auden famously pointed out while contemplating a painting of the fall of Icarus, great events take place in the middle of ordinary ones, 'while someone else is eating or opening a window or just walking dully along'. Tommy's War is a war in a world of dull work, shortages, crying children and everyday diseases. He is not much concerned with high politics, though he has a shrewd and cynical take on government and its wartime propaganda: 'This is SOS Week in Glasgow. Save our souls. Sink or swim. Stew or sausages. Steal or starve. Save or starve. Sew our shirts. Have your choice …' He has a rebellious streak, but his rebellion is more directed at the hated factor, or rent-collector, than the government itself. In that, as in so much, he was pretty typical. The revolt which is remembered as 'Red Clydeside' was a series of disputes, starting with one over rent controls. The vast majority of Glaswegians rented their homes and when 20,000 munitions workers arrived in the city, the shortage of rooms was quickly exploited by the private landlords. Rents went up by more than a fifth. Factors were attacked by women, pelted in the street and went in fear. People refused to move or pay up. Placards reading 'Rent Strike' and 'We are Fighting Landlord Huns' went up in the windows and when, by May 1915, around 25,000 tenants were refusing to pay, ministers started to panic. Thomas, surely, would have sympathised but at the time he was much more interested in a huge rail crash at Gretna, which killed around 227 people but which has been largely forgotten by history. And this, too, is part of the appeal. The 'story' of those times that has been smoothed into predictability by historians is constantly disrupted by small surprises.

Thomas had no desire to be a soldier. In that, too, he was typical. After the great torrents of excited volunteers in the early days of the war, when patriotic enthusiasm had been dampened by stories of the reality of trench warfare, millions of men tried very hard not to serve their country, at least not in France or in khaki. We remember the 'white feather' campaigns and the famous Kitchener recruitment posters, and indeed huge citizen armies were created. But the feathers and the posters were needed because of widespread reluctance, particularly as a sense of the length and grimness of the fighting settled in people's minds. As the war advanced, reflected in newspaper stories about victories and defeats, the pressure piled on. Like Thomas, it became impossible to be both patriotic and a quiet civilian. He is darkly humorous about his dilemma. When the Derby scheme was announced, offering men the chance of volunteering in return for a delay in being actually called up, he reports, 'Got a love letter from Lord Derby egging me on to enlist before they make me.' And later: 'Recruiting sergeant up at night to assist me in making up my mind. I did not go away with him.' Finally, on a snowy December night in 1915, he gives way: 'Could resist no longer. Joined the army today … God save the King.' In fact, Thomas never did have to become a soldier. For him the war is always just off-stage, as in a classical tragedy, a succession of liners and battleships being sunk, poison gas used, terrible losses reported, revolutions erupting and aircraft raiding. We must remember, this is how most people would have experienced it. And most, too, would have been more immediately concerned, as Thomas was, with the small things of life – rain, wind, coughs, shortages, chores, food and family.

As with Pepys or Boswell (admittedly, greater diarists) we enjoy the constant rub of the ordinary against the 'historic'. Given that some historians have insisted the general public was fairly ignorant of the war it is interesting that Thomas, from his Glasgow flat, pretty accurately records each major event as it happens. Thus he is fully aware of the first day of the Battle of the Somme, even recording that it started 'at 7.30 a.m. today'. But with 67,000 British casualties on the first day alone, a third of them killed, he quickly moves on, so that two days later, his main worry is that his young son Tommy is being teased by another boy: 'Nice warm day. Tommy getting abused by the young microbe next door called Alec Gray. So I spoke severely to the aforesaid young microbe surnamed Gray. His ma then abuses Agnes.' It is a moment to be compared with Pepys' worries about the fate of a cheese during the Great Fire of London. Sometimes the juxtapositions are cheerily surreal: 'The King doing Glasgow this week and round about. I saw him today. Agnes made plum jam at night.' Or, from 16 March 1917: 'Doctor up in the forenoon. Tommy has the German measles. Doctor says it is a mild case … Revolution in Russia. Czar dethroned. The Duma are in full power. The Czar and Czarina are prisoners.' This, we all know, is how things are, the pattern of life. Great events occur. We note them. Meanwhile we have to cope with German measles, or a local lout.

Thomas is not given to rhetorical flourish or overstatement. He is a brisk, tart, dryish writer, who presents himself as put-upon and henpecked and whose drolleries are the more striking for their rarity. Yet he is, in his way, a good writer, too: he has a distinct voice and it is impossible to spend an hour with his diaries without having a clear impression of the man. No diarist who is disagreeable will keep our attention long: Thomas Livingstone is, we come to understand, a thoroughly likeable man whose love for his wife and son and growing horror at the scale of the slaughter shine through the laconic and self-mocking entries. What I find makes this book particularly touching are the illustrations, the quick pen-and-ink sketches, carefully coloured, of Thomas and the cast of characters, wife, son, recruiting sergeant, chimney-sweep, soldiers and the rest. They have a humorous immediacy and artlessness which is very winning, and go perfectly with the tone of the written diary. In the end, the best test of a book like this is whether one wants any more of it or not: I for one ended it in 1918 with a feeling of frustration. If the diaries continue to 1933, what happens next? Let us hope we find out, but meanwhile a little more about the city where Thomas lived, and the times he lived through, may be helpful.

Glasgow is special, was special and always will be. I should know. During the late nineteenth and early twentieth centuries, my family were solidly Glasgow. They were of a higher social class than Thomas, though they yo-yoed with the fortunes of the city itself. Various branches went from farm labourers to quarrymen to quarry owners during the great days of the Victorian expansion; the owners of floridly posh new houses – a window for every day of the year in one of them, apparently – and proud members of the middle-class clubs and societies. One was a Unionist Lord Provost, the last of his political line. Others became losers in the years of depression that followed the Great War, when a pie factory, for instance, lost its shipyard worker customers. But they all belonged to the tight, self-confident world of the Second City of the Empire, remembering its glory days when much of the world's shipping tonnage had been built on the Clyde, and further back when the 'tobacco lords' who had established the wealth of the new trading city were laying out grand new squares and crescents. It was a city, like Chamberlain's Birmingham or the 'Cottonopolis' of Manchester, with a very strong sense of itself and its history, utterly unconnected to the airs of the formal capital, London. My own father vividly remembers being shown by his father the sight of the *Queen Mary* lying half-built and silent in the yards when bad times had arrived; and the veteran soldiers, with waxed 'Kitchener' moustaches and empty sleeves or trouser legs pinned up, employed to brush clean the points for Glasgow's famous trams.

His city, and that of his forebears, was based on technological experiment, audacity in business and a ready supply of cheap labour, coal, steel and water. In 1840, Glasgow was a textile town of some 250,000 people, a vast increase on the previous decades. But by 1900 she was more than three times as big, and surrounded by booming satellite towns. Iron smelting and steel-making combined with the deep estuary connected to the booming Atlantic and imperial trade routes made Glasgow a perfect industrial revolutionary capital. Steamships were built on the Clyde from mid-Victorian times but the rival yards produced competitive pressure which gave Glasgow a world lead in techniques such as screw propulsion, triple and quadruple expansion, high-pressure boilers, turbines and diesel engines. For a century, 'Clyde-built' was a global byword for reliability and skill – a memory which lingered on long enough for the engineer on the Starship Enterprise to be 'Scotty'. This expertise in turn led to other engineering successes, from locomotives and machine tools to sewing machines, bicycles and cars: in the pre-1914 Glasgow of Thomas' world, the Singer factories were world innovators and the Argyll Motor Works was turning out cars which seemed as likely to dominate world markets as anything made in America. Glasgow was an innovative, aggressive, roiling and cocky place, thick with smoke, noise, the smell of oil and the raucous boasts of chisel-faced city fathers in their stock exchange and their new, grandly built churches. Govanhill, his part of the city, around a mile south of the centre, was one of the poorer districts but far from slum-ridden. Its industry included important locomotive and iron works and its red sandstone apartments were by Edwardian standards relatively spacious as working-class housing. It boasted a fine new Carnegie Library and much admired public baths.

This is not surprising. Glasgow industry sustained a cultural and intellectual self-confidence that has been all but forgotten. Glasgow has always felt oddly American, in the heavy, steel-framed structures and the shape of its public buildings – and still does. The revival churches of 'Greek' Thomson are one thing, but the greatest glories of the city for anyone with a taste for the daring are the buildings of Charles Rennie Mackintosh, the nearest Britain has ever had to a Gaudí, and a man who made corners of Glasgow as exotic as Gaudí's Barcelona. Glasgow University never achieved quite the Enlightenment status of

Edinburgh but it was a close thing. Glasgow was ancient enough, dating back to a college founded in 1451, and the city had a formidable roll-call of philosophers, scientists, doctors and religious scholars. By the early twentieth century, bright Glasgow students would no more have thought of going south to Oxbridge for their learning than of sailing to Mars. Glasgow, with her Gilbert Scott spire rising high, was as exciting a university as any in the country. Then there were the great institutions, the Mitchell Library and the riotously Spanish Baroque Kelvingrove Art Gallery. The 'Glasgow Boys' were a school of painters unlike any group elsewhere; and they were followed by Colourists who brought the brightness of the French Fauves to the north, as no English painters of the time quite achieved. All this was going on around Thomas, a mile or two to the west, the cultural life of a city which allowed him, at least, to visit art galleries and carefully laid-out public gardens. Among the smoke and the dirt, there were bright things gleaming.

Glasgow had her own novelists, her own songs, her own orchestral and music-hall traditions, her own favoured holiday resorts, in the southern Highlands or 'doon the watter' on the banks of the Clyde estuary. She had her famous and excellent High School for the middle classes and distinctive political traditions. These included, sadly, a vicious sectarianism. For Glasgow was a migrants' city. She had been little more than a large village before Atlantic trade, and then shipbuilding caused mushrooming growth; so almost every Glaswegian had come from somewhere else. Many, of course, had arrived from other parts of the Scottish lowlands, from labouring, merchant or professional families established earlier in Edinburgh, or the smaller burghs of the country. They would be overwhelmingly Presbyterian, either loyal members of the national Church of Scotland, or members of rival churches which had broken away during the great disruptions of the mid-nineteenth century. Their traditions of serious book-learning and disputation would feed many later politicians, including some of the Marxists for which Glasgow also became famous. Another great migration came from the Highlands, the 'Teuchters' much ridiculed by city humorists and on music-hall stages, though the mockery was intermingled with sentimental claims about Hielan' hames and aboriginal 'but-and-bens' (small cottages) in songs by the likes of Harry Lauder. These Highlanders, Macleans, Camerons, MacDonalds and Campbells, were again mostly Protestant but included a sprinkling of Roman Catholics from those islands and small outcrops which had stayed with the old faith.

The third great migration, however, was Irish, mostly Catholic but including – as with Thomas' family – Protestants who had been 'settled' in the north of Ireland but who had returned. Thomas' father was from Lurgan, not far from Belfast, and he carried his sectarianism to Glasgow where he worked as a railway clerk. He joined a Loyal Orange Lodge. His views are not hard to guess. For the Protestant majority in Glasgow, of all classes, the Catholics were seen as credulous Papist peasants, 'bog-trotters' whose loyalty to Scotland or the Empire could never be assumed and whose priests, taking their orders from the Vatican, led them by their whisky-inflamed noses. The 'Papes' did not use proper lavatories, had recklessly large families which they could not feed, and were in general treated as a lesser breed. This sectarianism was as poisonous as anything expressed by apartheid-era Boers for black Africans, and just as sharp-edged as the near-identical feelings in Ireland itself. There were Orange Order marches, complete with bowler hats and gloating banners, well into the sixties. In return, the Catholic migrants forged and defended a militant identity of their own, initially based in poor enclaves such as Cowcaddens and Maryhill, with their own football club (Glasgow Celtic was founded in 1887), a disciplined church structure and increasingly assertive membership of the trade union movement. They tended to regard their Protestant fellow workers as deferential fools, dupes of the ruling order, and terminally dull.

So Glasgow was a city divided by religion, as it still is, though less violently these days. It was also, of course, a city divided by class and wealth. The great engineering and factory-owning dynasties, plus their lawyers, doctors and stockbrokers, lived in genuinely grand style in the West End. A mile or two to the east were scattered some of the foulest slums in Europe. The world is still thus divided, but while today's hedge fund managers, city stars and footballing plutocrats live behind high walls, or in country estates, then Glasgow's rich and poor literally rubbed shoulders in the streets, cramming the city centre where most of the business was done, and the gossip passed on. It was not the grand terraces, though, but the Glasgow slums, especially the tenement flats of the Gorbals, that have been remembered. In many ways rightly so: these were the dark and dangerous cave-dwellings of razor-wielding gangs and heroically drunken drunks. In fact, the tenement was a sensible and popular style of housing and is still used across much of Scotland. With between three and four storeys, a common stair and flatted apartments, it offered warmth and communal living with enough space for family privacy – well suited to the wet climate and long winters of the country. A good tenement is as intelligent a housing style as a terrace, or a row of semis. What made the Glasgow tenements notorious was simply lack of hygiene and intense overcrowding as the city expanded. Conditions by the mid-nineteenth century were terrible, though no different from the slums of Manchester, Sheffield, Leeds or Birmingham. Yet the large immigrant families, working in industries with terrible safety records, and against the hard-drinking, heavy-smoking culture of the Scots and Irish, resulted in child and adult mortality rates which were shocking even by Victorian and Edwardian standards.

Out of this grew a militant socialism which touches Thomas' life at key moments, not least when he witnesses the Marxist agitator John Maclean, a man admired by Lenin and made a Communist commissar, returning in triumph from prison. Being Thomas, he is not, of course, much impressed: 'Saw a most unholy mob of Bolsheviks in town today. It was a procession of some of our enlightened citizens welcoming home [Maclean] (from jail). He is standing for Parliament for the Gorbals. Heaven help us all!' Most historians believe the stories of Red Clydeside have been exaggerated by later socialists with pickaxes to grind, and it is surely true that Glasgow was never really on the edge of social revolution. But at the time, it was taken very seriously: the war-leader Lloyd George was famously heckled and abused when he addressed trade unionists about letting in less well-qualified labour. Maclean, and some others, had openly opposed the war and been removed from the city to prisons in the east of Scotland. After the war was over, troops and tanks were indeed ordered north at a time when Westminster was jittery about the prospect of British Bolshevism.

Yet the biggest story of Glasgow during the war was the recruitment, maiming and deaths of huge numbers of her citizens. Scots volunteered quickly and in great numbers: Edwardian Scotland was still a comparatively militarised country, with strong regimental traditions and a general pride in the record of Scottish soldiers in the Napoleonic and Crimean wars. As a result, with some crack regiments, Scotland lost a disproportionately large number of her men. By one estimate she lost 110,000 in all, a fifth of total British losses, rather than an eighth, as her size by population would have suggested. Glasgow herself lost 20,000 men, often soldiers from the slums who formed much of the Highland Light Infantry, though nearby coal-mining and rural areas suffered even more. As in England, the upper and middle classes volunteered early and were cut down early too: Glasgow University lost one in six of her graduates. The pressure on Thomas must have been intense. Yet it was quickly realised that if Britain was to fight and win a long war, she needed her mines and industries, shipyards and offices, to continue to function and a complicated system designed to keep vital workers in place was established. Armbands and badges were provided for key employees so that they would not be harassed in the streets by women bearing white feathers; other badges were produced for those (like Thomas) who had offered to fight but were not yet needed. It was a time of sidelong glances and offensive muttering about slackers and cowards: for Thomas it was a matter of some importance that 'I have now got my khaki armlet to let folk know I have attested and await the call.'

Unlike the Second World War, this was not really a people's war – not at least for the British, though it was for many Russians and Germans. The Zeppelin and Gotha raids and the occasional bombardments by German warships against east coast towns are recorded by Thomas but direct danger reached little of the civilian population. In this war, only around 850 civilians died in Britain, as compared to 60,000 in the later conflict. Yet the war affected Thomas and his family, and every other family, in multiple less dramatic ways. It was not simply the friends who left for the fighting, or the growing evidence that the Empire was not performing as well as people had expected. Britain herself rapidly became shabbier, duller and hungrier. Famously, Lloyd George insisted on weaker, more watery beer and introduced tough pub licensing hours to try to deal with the (very real) problem of low productivity caused by drunkenness. Tobacco, as Thomas finds, becomes harder to obtain. Unlike the later world war, this one passed mostly without rationing. Until halfway through it, the Liberal government remained wedded to small-state, free market beliefs and tried hard not to interfere too much. The result was a life of unpredictable shortages, fast rising prices and adulterated food, which provoked riots in some parts of Britain, though not Glasgow.

Yet when Thomas notes in the spring of 1917 that the Germans are trying to starve Britain he is quite right: he may not have known just how close they were coming to success. The U-boat campaigns in the Atlantic had been devastating and Britain came within weeks of having to sue for peace simply for lack of food and oil. It was only a late directive to try the convoy system which saved the day. Meanwhile government action would eventually result in rationing by 1918, while strenuous efforts were made to increase agricultural production at home. In the country, people turned back to snaring rabbits, raiding birds' nests and growing their own vegetables but in the towns the population struggled with meagre, dull diets featuring the much-hated National Loaf, a soggy, greyish concoction which nevertheless contained more nutrition and fibre than the white loaf everyone preferred. Shortages were everywhere, from coal to clothing. To save energy, street lighting was conserved, theatres closed early and entertainment much restricted; it is notable that Thomas' most frequent references to entertainment seem to be dubious books from the library, games of cards and walks in the park, rather than nights out in bars or at the cinema.

Women, meanwhile, got their first chance to break into male trades, whether they were the tartan-uniformed bus conductors on the Glasgow trams, or women police officers patrolling parks in search of vice, or female munitions workers. This clearly affects Thomas, as it did most traditionally minded men, though he rarely voices derision and seems to accept that the world is changing fast around him. His wife is often sick, as is his son, and he clearly has few domestic skills, but it is a small, tight, traditional family in which he does his best. Glasgow was notorious for its drunkenness and domestic violence, and indeed across Britain battered women rarely complained to the police about drunken husbands: when they did, they got little sympathy. By those admittedly low standards, Thomas seems to have been a good husband. His wife Agnes' ill health was again typical. Ill health and medicines, mostly ineffective still, feature heavily in these diaries. Mortality rates, particularly in urban Scotland, were shocking. The ravages of so-called Spanish Flu, which took a huge toll of the world just after the war, are well known; but it was a time still when less exotic infections, from measles to whooping cough, killed many. Agnes struggles with mysterious internal pains, lumbago and toothache so excruciating that she talks of killing herself. That was life – sorer, rougher and more dangerous by a country mile than it is today. Thomas notes her troubles and does the heavy lifting, and the cleaning, and does not complain. He is hardly romantic or gushing in his descriptions of Agnes but that is not his style. It is eloquent that his diary suddenly ceased when she died. These were two undemonstrative people who needed and loved one another very much.

So here is a slice of Britain from below, during some of her darkest years, and seen through the prism of the empire's Second City, and the pen of one of the countless millions who mostly went unrecorded, unsung and unremembered. The message is an individual, human one, the more moving and memorable because it does not fit neatly into a historian's grand narrative. Here, amid the malfunctioning chimneys, boat excursions, bad food and worse news, the little domestic feuds and distant echoes of hectoring from politicians, is the story of one undistinguished, shrugging, perky, rather loveable man who just wanted to get on with his life, be kind to those around him and – if pushed – 'do his bit for the Flag' but please, not something too dangerous and please, not quite yet. Here clear and unmistakable is the voice of that fabled abstraction, the man on the street – not the man on the Clapham Omnibus, as it happens, but the mannie on the Kelvingrove Tram. He isn't easily taken in. He is only a little sorry for himself. He is not noticeably religious or political. He stands aside from the great enthusiasms and lunacies around him; in his sensible, defiant ordinariness, he is almost Charlie Chaplin-esque. He is the man the rest of them are fighting for. And, luckily perhaps, I for one closed his diary realising that I liked him rather a lot.

Andrew Marr, June 2008

People and places

Thomas Cairns Livingstone had a wide social circle and spent many of his evenings and holidays in the company of relatives, friends and neighbours. As well as writing about them by name, Thomas often uses their location as a shorthand way of referring to them. This guide to the people and places in Thomas' diary should help untangle Ina from Isa, and Lily from Wee Lily.

200 Main Street, Rutherglen
Thomas lived here before he was married. During the years of the diary it was the home of Thomas' Uncle Willie.

Alexander Baxter
Proprietor of Paterson, Baxter and Company, which employs Thomas. Their premises were at 170 Ingram Street, in the warehouse district of central Glasgow. They had other offices in Leeds, London, Cape Town, Oslo and Copenhagen.

Mary Carlyle (née Livingstone)
Sister of Thomas, born in Balmoral Terrace, Hill Street, Lurgan, County Armagh, in the north of Ireland, on 27 September 1884. Her mother died two weeks after her birth. Mary married Thomas Carlyle on 16 July 1904; he was 34, some 14 years older than her. He was a shirt-cutter, she was a shirt-fitter. None of the family witnessed the marriage, and the couple moved to Edinburgh shortly afterwards. They had four children: Thomas, Helen (or Ella), Jane (or Jean) Weir, and Dorothy. We know from Ella's recollections that Mary and her family remained relatively close to their Glasgow relations well into Tommy Livingstone Junior's adulthood.

Mr and Mrs Carmichael
Neighbours of Thomas and Agnes at 14 Morgan Street.

Clydebank
Home of Jenny Roxburgh and her family.

Coatbridge
Home of Agnes' family, and also of the Crozier family.

Henrietta ('Hetty') Cook
Cousin of Agnes. She married Gordon Mossman in Glasgow on 18 December 1918 at the age of 23 (he was 26). They were married 'by declaration' (a civil ceremony) in front of witnesses, and by warrant issued by the Sheriff Substitute of Lanarkshire, a form peculiar to Scotland, regulated by the Marriage (Scotland) Act 1916. She was described on her marriage certificate as an engineer's 'clerkess', living at 11 Leven Street, Glasgow. She was usually known as Hetty.

James Cook
Nephew or cousin of Agnes. Shot in the hand during the First World War, and nursed in the Victoria Hospital, a military hospital in Bellahouston Park, Glasgow. He was a witness to the marriage of Hetty Cook in December 1918, described on the certificate as 'mercantile clerk; sapper, Royal Engineers'.

James Crichton
Private James Crichton (41152) of the Scottish

Rifles, Cameronians was killed in action on 21 March 1918. He was aged 21 and buried in the Poziers graveyard. James worked with Thomas at Paterson and Baxter and was one of the first of the company to join up. Thomas would have read the account of his death through the Glasgow newspapers as they usually printed Rolls of Honour about four weeks after the death.

The Crozier Family
Agnes' Aunt Agnes married Robert Chapman Crozier in 1881. The Crozier family lived in the Blairhill area of Coatbridge. Robert or 'Uncle Bob' ran a grocers and spirit shop at 142 Bank Street, Coatbridge and then moved into the hotel trade, managing the Royal Hotel in Coatbridge after the war until his death in 1921. Robert and Agnes had four daughters, Margaret (possibly known as Daisy), Mary (May), Jeanie (Jean) and Henrietta (Hetty). Sadly, May died whilst on holiday at Rothesay from the Spanish 'flu in 1918 at only 24.

Donald Ferguson
Married to Josephine, Thomas' sister. He died of epilepsy and heart failure on 19 October 1916, at Beracah, Paisley Road, Barrhead, in what was probably a private nursing home, although his usual residence was 3 Greenlodge Terrace. On his death certificate, the occupation of his late father Samuel is given as 'shepherd'.

Isabella McArthur Ferguson
Daughter of Donald and Josephine Ferguson. Thomas' niece. Born 20 October 1900 at 204 French Street, Bridgeton, Glasgow. Also known as Isa.

Josephine Ferguson (née Livingstone)
Sister of Thomas, born in Silverwood, near Lurgan, on 13 August 1874. First born of Joseph's children with Mary Cairns. First worked as a shirt-maker. Married Donald Ferguson in Glasgow on 10 June 1898 and honeymooned in Belfast. At the time of their marriage, Donald was living at 175 Gallowgate, Glasgow, and Josephine at 10 India Street, Rutherglen. Both Josephine and her husband worked in a grocery shop, possibly the Bridgeton branch of Cochrane's, a Glasgow chain. They had three children, Isabella, Lily and Jack. Donald died of epilepsy in 1916, and Josephine continued working in the grocery business.

Jack Ferguson
Son of Donald and Josephine Ferguson. Thomas' nephew.

Lily Florence Livingstone Ferguson
Daughter of Donald and Josephine Ferguson. Thomas' niece. Born 4 May 1899 at 204 French Street, Bridgeton, Glasgow. Worked as a clerkess. Also known as Wee Lily.

The Gordons
Relatives of Agnes living in the Ibrox area of Glasgow.

Greenlodge
Thomas' father Joseph lived at 3 Greenlodge Terrace, Greenlodge Street, Bridgeton, Glasgow. His daughter Josephine and her husband Donald Ferguson also lived there with their children, a fairly usual arrangement at the time.

Andrew Hamilton

Former office boy in Paterson and Baxter. Married Nellie Pettigrew in July 1915, lived in Hickman Street in Govanhill, and had a son in 1918.

Ibrox

Home of Agnes' family, and also of the Gordons, close family friends to Thomas and Agnes.

Agnes Smart Livingstone (née Cook)

Born in Braid Street, Glasgow (near St George's Cross) on 10 November 1879 to James and Agnes Cook (née Henderson). Her parents were married on 7 November 1879 (three days before she was born) in the St Rollox district of Glasgow. Her father was a lithographer, and Agnes herself was a cardboard cutter at the time of her marriage to Thomas in 1910.

Duncan Graham Livingstone

Brother of Thomas, born in Balmoral Terrace, Lurgan, on 2 June 1880. Worked for Anchor Line Cruises and sailed the Glasgow-New York route aboard the TSS (twin-screw steamship) Columbia from 1908 to 1910. Fought in the Army Service Corps from 1918 to 1919. Lived between Belfast and Glasgow.

Joseph Livingstone

Father of Thomas, born in 1847 in Lurgan, County Armagh, in the north of Ireland, the son of John Livingstone, a teacher of English, and Mary Ann Livingstone (née Hare, she died near Rutherglen in March 1881). Lurgan is 19 miles south-west of Belfast, and was known as a centre of the linen industry. He was married three times: to Sarah Gilpin in 1867 in Seagoe Parish Church (she died in January 1873); to Mary Cairns on 3 October 1873; and to Jane Weir in January 1885 (she died in 1909). All of his children were with Mary Cairns, whom he married in Maralin (or Magheralin) in County Down in the north of Ireland. She had previously been married to a Mr McKinlay. She died in October 1884 shortly after the birth of her youngest daugher, Mary Livingstone, while still at the Lurgan residence of her father, Thomas Cairns.

Joseph Livingstone worked as a clerk for the Caledonian Railway Company from 1876, and later as a mercantile clerk. He moved to 10 India Street, Rutherglen, in the 1880s, then lived at 3 Greenlodge Terrace, Bridgeton, Glasgow. He was a member of the Ancient Order of Foresters, a friendly society, and the Carnbroe Loyal Orange Lodge, a Loyalist and Unionist 'secret society' with its origins in the north of Ireland. Carnbroe is a village to the south of Coatbridge.

Josephine Livingstone

Daughter of Samuel and Nellie Livingstone. Thomas' niece. Born 28 April 1902 in Glasgow. Also known as Ina.

Mary Ann Livingstone (née Hare)

Mother of Joseph and paternal grandmother of Thomas. Died of chronic bronchitis on 7 March 1881 at 3 George Gray Street, Eastfield, Rutherglen.

Nellie Livingstone (née Muir Meikleham)

Married to Samuel, Thomas' brother. Her parents were James Meikleham and Elizabeth Meikleham (née Muir).

Samuel John Livingstone
Brother of Joseph and uncle of Thomas. Born 1856 and worked as a railway clerk and as a coal merchant. He was married to Mary Elizabeth McColl, a draper's assistant, in 1883 by a Church of Scotland minister at their home at 543 Dalmarnock Road, Glasgow.

Samuel John Livingstone
Brother of Thomas, born in Balmoral Terrace, Lurgan, in 1878. Worked as a grocer's assistant, then a grocer's manager, in a branch of Cochrane's. He was married to Nellie Muir Meikleham on 28 January 1902 at 217 Broad Street, Mile-End, Glasgow by a minister of the United Free Church. They had two children, Josephine (also known as Ina) in 1902 and Samuel John, in 1919.

Samuel Livingstone Junior
Son of Samuel and Nellie Livingstone. Thomas' nephew. Born 1919.

Thomas Cairns Livingstone
Born 4 June 1882 at 10 India Street, Rutherglen, the only one of six children of Joseph and Mary Livingstone to be born in Glasgow. Josephine, Lily, Duncan, Samuel and Mary were born in Lurgan, County Armagh, in the north of Ireland. Thomas' mother died in 1884 when Thomas was aged two, and he was raised by his father, his older siblings and his step-mother Jane. The family moved to 4 French Street, Bridgeton around 1900. He was schooled in Rutherglen and took extra classes in English and French.

Thomas started work in 1895 and began courting Agnes Smart Cook in 1903. They were engaged on 19 December 1908 and married on 10 June 1910 in Agnes' home at 37 Whitefield Road, Ibrox, by the Reverend John Tarish of the Tron United Free Church.

Their first home was at 20 Morgan Street in Govanhill, where their son Thomas Cairns Livingstone Junior was born in 1911. They moved to a tenement house at 14 Morgan Street in 1913.

Thomas worked as a mercantile clerk at 170 Ingram Street in central Glasgow in the offices of the firm of Paterson, Baxter and Company, which manufactured linen and sailcloth. Given that this address was in the heart of the warehouse district of the city, manufacturing may have taken place at different premises.

Thomas Cairns Livingstone Junior
Born on 9 August 1911, the only child of Thomas and Agnes. Attended Victoria Primary School in Batson Street, Govanhill. At the time of his birth, it was the custom in Scotland to give a first son his paternal grandfather's first name and his mother's maiden name as his middle name. This happened with Thomas Senior in 1882, but when it came for him to name his son, he broke with tradition, choosing to continue his own mother's maiden name rather than that of Agnes' mother. Generally known in the diaries as Wee Tommy.

Claude Maxwell
Brother of Miss Maxwell, Wee Tommy' teacher in Victoria Primary School. He joined the Royal Highland Regiment (the Black Watch) as a Private and was commissioned as a Second Lieutenant in the Durham Light Infantry. He was wounded but served the full term of the First World War.

Jenny and Kate Roxburgh

Sisters who lived in Radnor Street, Clydebank. Agnes probably knew Jenny through her earlier employment as they were both in the stationery trade, Agnes a cardboard cutter and Jenny as a stationery assistant. Later Jenny worked as a nurse on Maryhill.

Ruglen

The local pronunciation of Rutherglen.

John White

Married to Lily, Thomas' sister. A telegraphist, he worked for the General Post Office.

Lily Florence White (née Livingstone)

Sister of Thomas, born in Hill Street, Lurgan, on 15 May 1878. She worked as a power loom weaver and on 9 November 1911 was married in Trinity Church, Anderston, Glasgow to John White. At the time, her address was 3 Greenlodge Terrace, his was 1054 Argyle Street, both Glasgow. She died on 28 October 1914 of uterine septicaemia, pleurisy and pneumonia, at her father's home on Greenlodge Terrace, although her married residence was 44 Clincarthill Road, Rutherglen.[1] She was buried in Rutherglen Cemetery.

[1] Lily's death certificate lists three causes of death, in order of likelihood. Doctors at the time tended to do this in the absence of a post mortem examination.

North Glasgow

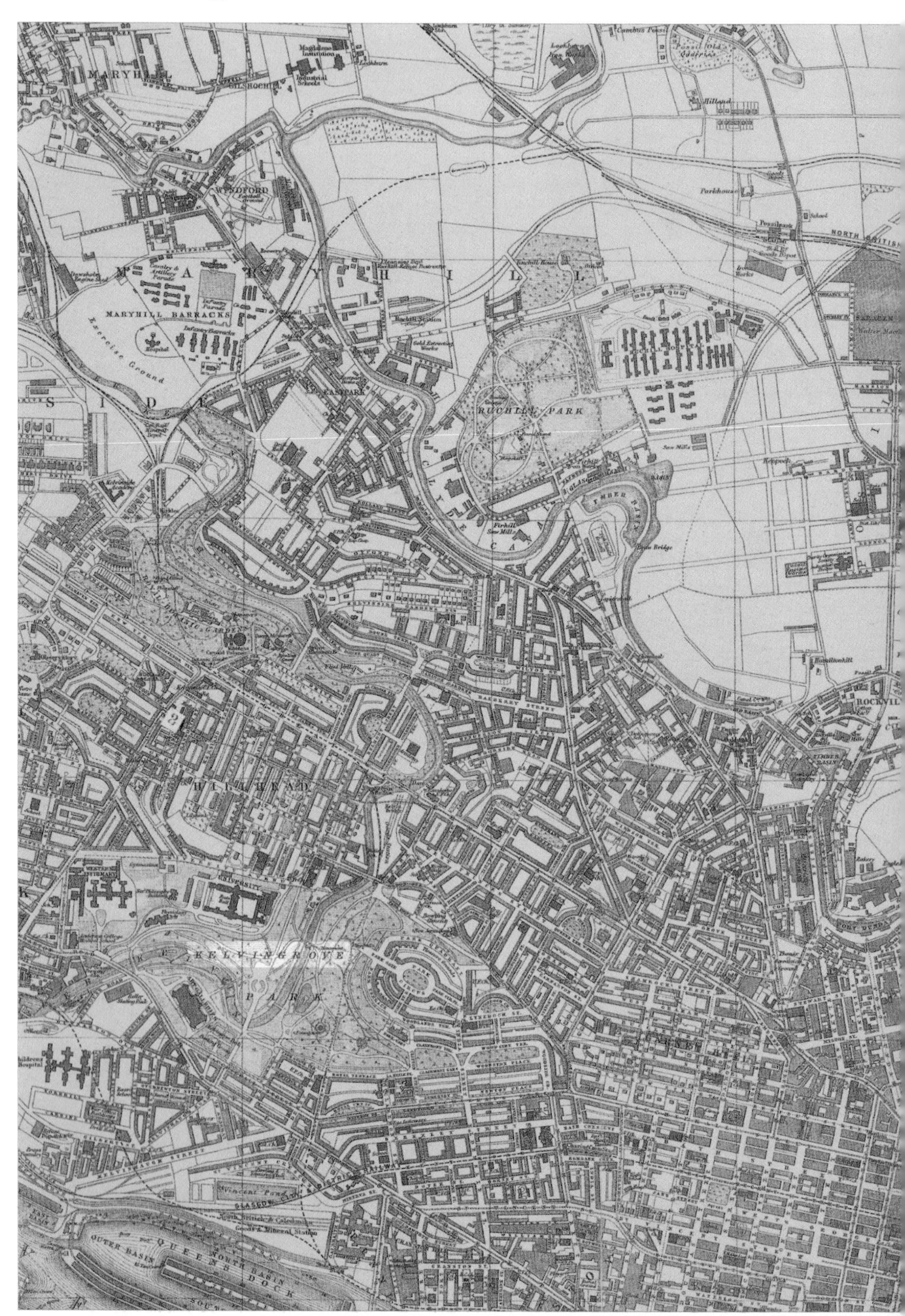

Municipal Boundary
STOBHILL GENERAL HOSPITAL
SPRINGBURN PARK
SPRINGBURN
SPRINGVALE
SIGHTHILL CEMETERY
Barnhill Poorhouse
CALEDONIAN RAILWAY
NORTH BRITISH RAILWAY
Sighthill Station
Corporation Gas Works
St. Rollox Depot
MONKLAND CANAL
ALEXANDRA PARK
MILNBANK
NECROPOLIS
High Balornock
Low Balornock
Barmulloch
Balornock House
Petershill
Blochairn Steel Works

South Glasgow

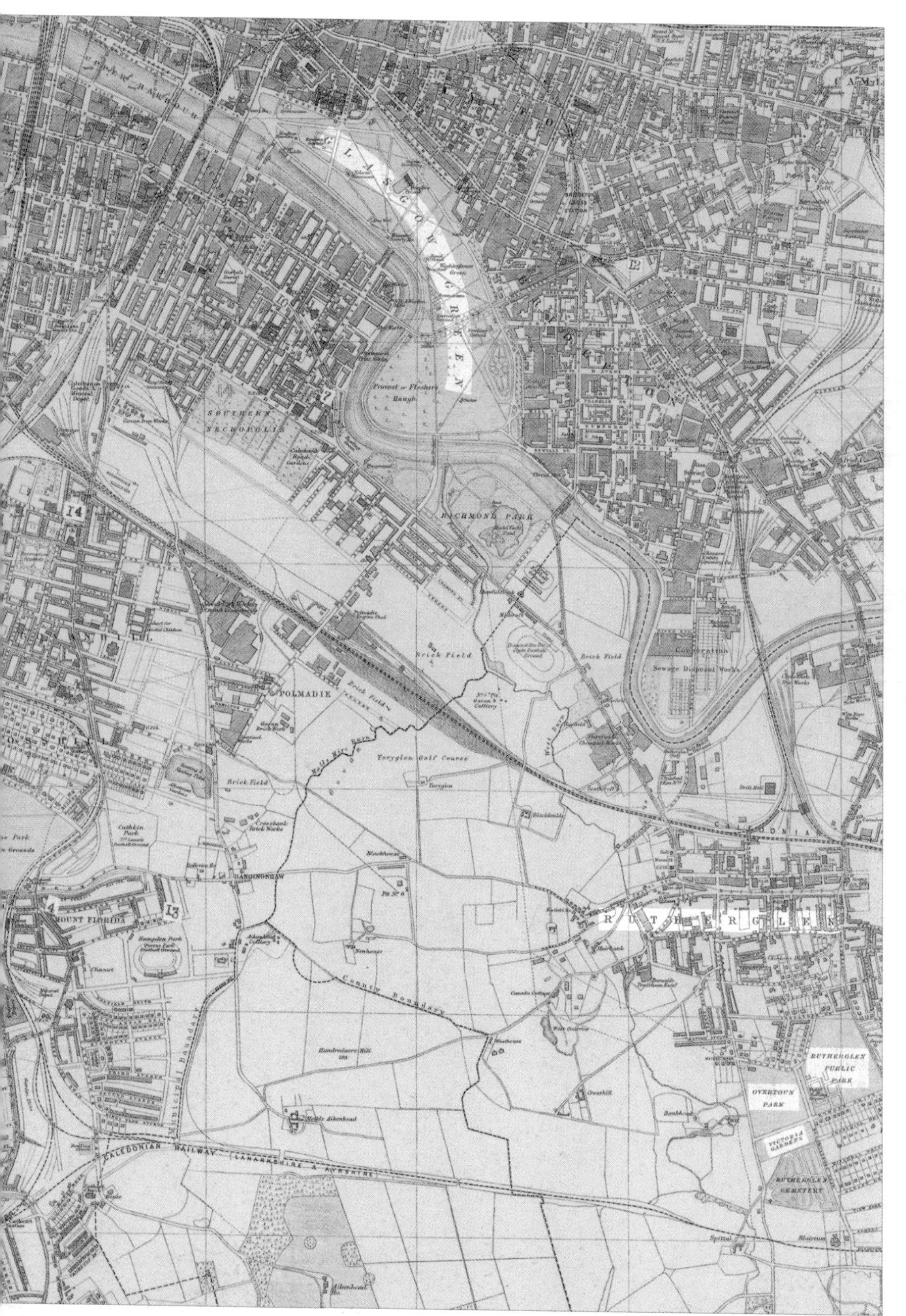

GLASGOW GREEN
RICHMOND PARK
SOUTHERN NECROPOLIS
POLMADIE
Brick Field
Toryglen Golf Course
Sewage Disposal Works
BANGINGSHAW
MOUNT FLORIDA
Hampden Park
Cathkin Park
Hundredacre Hill
County Boundary
RUTHERGLEN
RUTHERGLEN PUBLIC PARK
OVERTOUN PARK
VICTORIA GARDENS
RUTHERGLEN CEMETERY
CALEDONIAN RAILWAY
LANARKSHIRE & AYRSHIRE

1913

The great War may have begun with 'the shot heard around the world' when the Serbian nationalist Gavrilo Princip assassinated Archduke Franz Ferdinand, heir to throne of the Austro-Hungarian Empire, on 28 June 1914, but the roots of the conflict lay in the previous century. In broad terms, its origins involved the national politics, culture and economies of the combatant states, and a web of alliances struck between the leading European nations during the nineteenth century, following the defeat of Napoleon Bonaparte in 1815 and the Congress of Vienna in 1814-5. In response to the murder, the Austro-Hungarian Empire declared war on Serbia on 28 July, which put into action a web of treaties that brought Germany and the Ottoman Empire into the war on the side of the Austro-Hungarian Empire, and France, Belgium, Britain, Russia and Japan behind Serbia.

In 1913, when Thomas' diaries begin, there were clear signs that the great European powers were preparing for war. In April he saw 'the Great Territorial March Out' and on 5 May he noted that Earl Roberts of Kandahar, a distinguished former military commander, was on a recruiting visit to Glasgow. The Territorial Force was formed on 1 April 1908, with a strength of around 269,000 men organised into 14 infantry divisions and 14 mounted yeomanry brigades. The force was set up by Secretary of State for War, Richard Burdon Haldane, under the terms of the Territorial and Reserve Forces Act 1907.

[1] Langloan was a village in Old Monklands.
[2] See 'People and Places', pp.18-23
[3] Dinner was the midday meal. The car was a tramcar, rather than a motor car.
[4] Until around 1920, young children of either sex wore dresses over their nappies.
[5] Thomas detested the factor, who represented the owner of the property. Tenants paid rent to the factor, and relied on him for repairs. The 'whirly' was a metal cowl on the chimney pot, with small 'sails' that spun in the wind and drew smoke up the chimney. If it malfunctioned,

Wednesday, 1 January

Got 11.29 train from Glasgow Cross to Langloan[1] and spent the day in the bosom of the Crozier family. Very nice day. We went out for a walk in the afternoon. Jean, Hetty, Meg, Agnes, Baby and I.[2] Hetty and Meg saw us off by 10.9 train (Caledonian). Were home at 11 p.m. Some little showers fell but on the whole good weather.

Sunday, 5 January

Fine day though dull. After dinner I took car to Cathcart and walked from there to Clarkston and on to Giffnock, through by the quarries to Cathcart again and car home.[3] Wee man sneezing all day. Agnes not well at all. Wee man very cross in morning. Did not go to church.

Monday, 6 January

Cleaned the range tonight, including the flues. Dirty job. Agnes washed the floor after. Wee man still sneezing. Wee man got a new frock.[4]

Tuesday, 7 January

Lit the kitchen fire this morning, but it was a failure. Called at the factor and cussed him, so the men put a new 'whirly' on today.[5] 13 public houses in Ward 21 (Govanhill).[6] 19 licensed grocers.[7] Population 35,082. Municipal electors 7,813.[8]

Wednesday, 8 January

Knocked the kitchen blind down, so had to knock it back up again. We are going to flit.[9]

---

the whirly could force smoke and soot back down the chimney and into the house.

[6] Govanhill was one of the wards, or electoral districts, of the city.

[7] Licensed grocers were the only businesses, except public houses, that were allowed to sell alcoholic drinks for use off the premises.

[8] In 1913, the parliamentary voters' roll was made up of men aged 21 or over who either owned or lived in property with an annual rental value of £10 or more.

[9] Flitting is a Scottish word for moving house.

Thursday, 9 January

Agnes out in forenoon looking for a new house. Out again after tea time to see one in 14 Morgan Street. I was not out. Agnes doing a washing tonight. I minded wee Magintey.[10]

Friday, 10 January

Cold east wind today. Factor here in afternoon to see about a house we wanted. Agnes ironed tonight, I cleaned the brass rail and jelly pan.

Saturday, 11 January

Cold disman day of sleet and rain. We went househunting in afternoon but didn't find a good enough house.

Sunday, 12 January

Rain and snow all day long. Went and saw Dr Gardiner at 5 p.m. and made him my doctor, to fulfil the requirements of the law.[11] Agnes not very well today.

Monday, 13 January

Went and saw the factor at 5.30 and booked a new house at 14 Morgan Street, 2 up left.[12] Got my boots mended today for a bob. Nobody came tonight to cheer our loneliness.

---

[10] An affectionate name for a child. Its use may come from Thomas' Irish relatives, or his own upbringing in Scotland by an Irish immigrant family.

[11] The National Insurance Act 1911, which took effect on 13 January 1913, provided insurance for workers against ill-health and injury. Registration with a family doctor was compulsory. Thomas appears to have beaten the deadline for registration by seven hours. Under the scheme, each worker contributed 4d a week, his employer added 3d and the state 2d.

[12] The apartment on the second floor, with the door on the left of the second floor landing.

1913

Tuesday, 14 January

Horrid cold frosty day. Not out at night. Youth up today putting a board up at our window.[13]

Anderston Library reading room.

Wednesday, 15 January

Went to library tonight for my usual volume of sermons.[14]

Friday, 17 January

Lifted the room carpet tonight and the waxcloth around thereof.[15] Agnes did a big ironing.

Tuesday, 21 January

Agnes met me at 170 Ingram Street[16] and we went to Brigton.[17] Sam and Nellie and the weans[18] there. Got home at 11.40. Got the keys to our new house in the letter box.

---

[13] The board advertises a 'room and kitchen to let'. This type of house, typical for a tenement, consisted of a front room or parlour, which was for entertaining guests, and a kitchen, which had one or more bed recesses, curtained areas that contained the household's bed or beds. The Livingstones' new house had an inside toilet; many were less fortunate and had to share a toilet on the landing between floors. [14] Thomas is probably being ironic.

[15] The front room would have been floored with waxed cloth, a type of linoleum, with a carpet in the centre. [16] Thomas' work address. [17] Bridgeton. [18] Thomas' brother and sister-in-law.

Thomas and his family - and indeed everyone in the United Kingdom until 14 February 1971 - used a monetary system based on pounds, shillings and pence. A pound was worth 20 shillings, and a shilling or 'bob' was worth 12 pence. The sum of one pound, three shillings and sixpence was written as £1 3s 6d, with the letters 's' and 'd' derived from Latin. Sums of money were also given in shillings, with a 'solidus' (forward slash) after the number of shillings, such as 3/6 (three shillings and sixpence) or 30/- (thirty shillings, with the hyphen used to indicate that there were no pennies).

Thomas' wallet and Agnes' purse would have held farthings (there were four farthings to a penny), half-pennies, pennies, three-penny bits, sixpences or 'tanners', shillings, florins (two-shilling pieces) and half-crowns (worth 2/6). They would also have notes valued at 10/- and £1 and, on rare occasions, £5 and £10. In broad terms, we can multiply any prices mentioned by Thomas by 83 to arrive at a modern equivalent.

Wednesday, 22 January

Took a turn up to our new house in the morning. Mr Gordon up at night and fitted up kitchen and room gas in our new mansion.[19] All the Ibrox crowd up. Mr McCort did the whitewashing for 30 pennies.[20] Bought three new mantles for 9 pence. Heavy snow at night.

"Dis-ordered order is the
active cause of

Thursday, 23 January

Got away today at 11 a.m. to flit myself and family. Called in at Bow's Emporium[21] and arranged for a man to fit in the room grate. Went up to the new house in afternoon and whitewashed the kitchen press and bunker. The flitting starts tonight. To help we had Sam and Donald, Mr McCort, Mrs and Miss Gordon and Josephine.[22] We ceased operations at 10.30 and had supper.

[19] Mr Gordon extended the house's gas supply to the lighting fixtures in both the front room and the kitchen. The Ibrox relatives were members of Agnes' extended family .

[20] Probably Daniel McCort, a decorator who lived at 20 Morgan Street.

[21] Bow's Emporium was a department store on the corner of High Street and Bell Street, just north of Glasgow Cross.

[22] Sam and Donald were Thomas' brother and brother-in-law, respectively. Josephine was Thomas' sister.

Friday, 24 January

Putrid wet day. Man came up and fitted in room grate. It was a hard job and he lost his chisel, so Agnes gave him a 'tanner'. Cost of grate fitted in was 4/6. The piano was removed for 4/-. The plaster men [came] in the morning. Man up to measure us for a gas stove. Agnes got a gas stove from her aunt.

Saturday, 25 January

Agnes at the painter in the forenoon arranging about our kitchen. Went up to the old house in the afternoon and took off the Yale lock, name plate and letter box. Man here sorting the kitchen gas. At night whitewashed ceiling and walls of the closet and put up the kitchen pulley.

Saturday, 1 March

Out at the Barrows[23] before tea and bought an awl and a wee wally bow-wow[24] for the cherub.

Wednesday, 12 March

Today's advertisement: 'Children's Fancy Dress Ball. Mr J. B. McEwen's Juvenile Pupils, St Andrew's Halls, Granville St, at 5 p.m. Carriages at 9.30 p.m. Spectators' tickets 1/6. Tickets to be had at 29 St Vincent Crescent.'[25] I did not manage to the above.

[23] The Barrows was an open air market where people could hire static barrows on which to sell everything from fresh food to household ornaments. It was to the east of the city centre, it later became formalised in roofed enclosures known as Barrowland.

[24] A wally bow-wow was a ceramic ornament in the shape of a dog. Many city mantelpieces were adorned by a matching pair of wally dugs (china dogs).

[25] Thomas has evidently seen a newspaper advertisement for a children's entertainment. St Andrew's Halls, to the west of the city centre, were among the most prestigious public halls.

Monday, 24 March
'Men must either be the slaves of duty or of force.' (Or the wife.)

Tuesday, 25 March
Was at library at night for my usual good moral book.

Monday, 14 April
Cold, wet day. National strike started in Belgium today.[26] *King of Spain shot at yesterday.*[27] *He was not hurt.*

Wednesday, 16 April
Got a note from the factor. Cuss him that the rent is raised 22/- in the year. Now we'll starve.

Monday, 21 April
Telephoned the factor about the rent and found to my delirious joy it was only advanced 4/- in the year, to wit £3 15s 3d per quarter.[28]

Friday, 25 April
Fresh sort of day. National strike in Belgium fizzled out. Agnes still got toothache. Poor Agnes. Her bottom teeth are up the pole.[29]

Saturday, 26 April
Very cold and windy. Wet. In the afternoon I went to the Stirling's Library[30] and on my way back saw the start of the Great Territorial March Out. I went into a doorway and saw it all. Rain coming down in buckets. Poor 'sojers'. They were wet.

[26] The national strike, which lasted until 24 April, was called to demand the vote for all adults.
[27] José Sancho Alegre, a young Spanish anarchist from Barcelona, shot King Alfonso XIII of Spain at a military parade in Madrid. He was found guilty of the attack, and sentenced to death. The king commuted the sentence to life imprisonment,
[28] Thomas presumably telephoned from work, since he does not have a phone at home. The rent is expressed quarterly. See 'Housing and Factors', pp. 207-209.
[29] 'Up the pole' is a quaint term for being out of order or beyond use.

Monday, 5 May

Lord 'Bobs' in Glasgow today to make us all 'sojers'.[31]

Wednesday, 7 May

Paid the cussed factor his cussed rent. Cussed cold and cussed windy.

Saturday, 10 May

Took the wife of my bosom and my son also heir out for a walk by Hangingshaws and back by Mount Florida. Saw the Boys' Brigade inspection on our way home.

Friday, 16 May

Beautiful summer day. Took the wee man a walk to Queen's Park at night. Agnes met us there. Saw the recruits drilling in the recreation grounds.

Sunday, 18 May

Played hymns on the piano and amused our good selves in divers ways.

Sunday, 25 May

Broke the clasp of my wally teeth today.[32]

[30] Stirling's library was the main public library in the city centre.

[31] Lord Roberts of Kandahar was a distinguished Anglo-Irish soldier, who had made his name in India, Africa and Afghanistan. He was commonly known as Lord Bobs. He was a prominent advocate of conscription, and was head of the National Service League from 1905 until his death in 1914. 'Sojers' is how the word soldiers is often pronounced in Glasgow.

[32] Thomas evidently has a set of false teeth, known as wally (ceramic or china) teeth.

Tuesday, 3 June

I went straight from my work to the man who pulls teeth and got my renovated set. Seeing it was my first offence he charged me nothing. I did not press the good man.

Wednesday, 4 June

Lost my usual bob on the Derby.[33] Got my hair cut. This is my birthday.

Thursday, 5 June

'Every step of life shows how much caution is required.'

Tuesday, 10 June

This is the anniversary. 'Marriage notice. 10 June 1910. At 39 Whitefield Road was spliced Agnes Smart Cook, spinster, to Thomas Cairns Livingstone, bachelor. MOSC.56 SCA. 7,053. God save the King. Ora Pro Nobis. Let Glasgow Flourish.'[34]

Thursday, 26 June

[On holiday in Rothesay.] We saw two blessed warships, one of which anchored in Sweet Rothesay Bay.[35]

As well as the war clouds gathering over Europe, in 1913 there was another battle raging in Britain as the supporters of equal votes for women staged spectacular protests to win publicity for their cause. On Wednesday 2 June, Emily Wilding Davison ran onto the racecourse at Epsom during the Derby and was struck by Anmer, King George V's horse, and its jockey Herbert Jones. The seasoned campaigner may have intended simply to disrupt the race and to unfurl the banner of the Women's Social and Political Union, but she died of her injuries and became a Suffragette martyr.

[33] The Derby Stakes, run in the first week of June each year at the Epsom Downs Racecourse in Surrey, is one of the most prestigious flat races for thoroughbred horses in the world.

[34] Thomas seems to be making fun of wedding notices, either on church noticeboards or in the press. The Latin phrase means: 'Pray for us.' The final sentence is the motto on the coat of arms of the city of Glasgow.

[35] The warships in the Clyde would appear to be an omen of the coming war. The phrase 'Sweet Rothesay Bay' is from the sentimental traditional song 'Rothesay Bay'.

Friday, 27 June

Rothesay's full of sailormen now.

Saturday, 12 July

This is the Glorious 12th.[36]

Saturday, 9 August

The wee man's birthday. Two years old now, bless his little heart.

Thursday, 14 August

Dull sort of a day, cooler.

Not out a night. Agnes' eyes annoying her. Gave my music stand a coat of varnish.

[36] The anniversary of the Battle of the Boyne is celebrated each year on 12 July by members of Orange Lodges and other Protestant and Loyalist groups in Scotland and the north of Ireland. The phrase 'the glorious 12th' is usually applied to 12 August, the opening of the grouse-shooting season.

Friday **15**
(227-138)

7. 11.30

We went to Library tonight, up Victoria Road & back by Cathcart Road
Home 9. p.m.

Dull day but very very warm.

Sir Walter Scott born 1771
J. C. L. born 1882

Thursday, 21 August

Wet all day and extra special wet at night. The doctor got paid tonight (12/-).[37] *Got myself a new pair of boots today (10/6).*

Monday, 25 August

Bought a book tonight called *The Evolution of Man* for some deep study.[38]

Friday, 24 October

Got a notice from our beloved factor raising our rent 6/- in the year. Heard two revolver shots about 11.30 p.m. A man round the corner shot his girl and then committed suicide. Foolish fellow.

Saturday, 25 October

Man that shot himself last night is dead. Girl is not dead.[39]

---

[37] Before the National Health Service was founded in 1948, people paid doctors for health care, and doctors or pharmacists for medicines. The National Insurance system, which came into effect in 1913, only covered the insured worker.

[38] This is likely to have been *The Evolution of Man*, by Ernst Haeckel, written in German and published in English in 1905 and often reprinted. Haeckel was a German biologist and naturalist who championed the evolutionary theories of Charles Darwin.

[39] The confused reports of the shooting show the speed at which gossip travels in close communities.

Wednesday, 5 November
This is Guy Fawkes day. The factor was here for his rent. Not having any gunpowder handy, he got it.

Monday, 10 November
Agnes' birthday.

Saturday, 15 November
At library in afternoon for an 'Annie S. Swan'[40] and a book for myself.

Wednesday, 19 November
Working late, home 9.30 (stocktaking). New carpet for kitchen tonight (5/11).

Sunday, 23 November
Wet forenoon, cleared up in the afternoon. After dinner, just to enliven up proceedings, we took the car to Cathcart Cemetery and admired the tombstones etc., and came back in the car.

Wednesday, 3 December
Rained in buckets all day long. Think I'll make an ark.

[40] Annie Shepherd Swan (1859-1943) was a Scottish romantic novelist who wrote around 200 popular books. She also contributed to women's magazines. Book titles included: *A Lost Ideal*, *Thankful Rest*, *The Guinea Stamp: A Tale of Modern Glasgow* and *A Divided House*. The book was presumably for Agnes.

1913

Wednesday, 10 December

Agnes and Tommy at Ibrox.[41] They got home at 10.15 p.m. I sat in and enjoyed myself in divers ways.[42]

Monday, 22 December

Nice day. Addressed all the Christmas cards tonight.

Thursday, 25 December

A Merry Christmas. Got away [from work] at 12.35. Took Agnes and Tommy into the town and admired the shops.

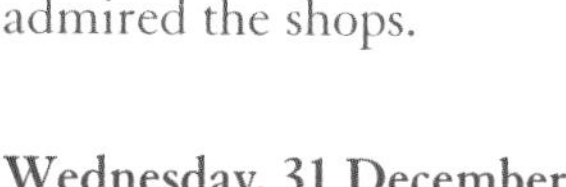

Wednesday, 31 December

On holiday today. After dinner we took 3.22 train to Coatbridge via Blairhill, and spent the time in the bosoms (collectively and allegorically) of the Crozier family. I went down to the hotel and had a glass of milk? with Mr Crozier.[43] Tore ourselves away in time for the 10.12 train via Glasgow Cross. Sat up and saw the New Year come in, and so ends this year.

---

[41] Agnes' family, the Gordons, lived in the district of Ibrox on the south side of Glasgow.

[42] We know that Thomas enjoyed reading and smoking his pipe. However, this is the first reference to alcohol.

[43] Tommy's 'glass of milk' may well have been something stronger.

1914

The war makes its first appearance in Thomas' diary on the day Austria and 'Servia', as it was sometimes written, were first at war, followed by reports of the armies of Russia, then Germany, then 'all Europe' mobilising. Britain entered the war when Germany invaded Belgium, since Britain and Belgium had a mutual defence treaty. On 4 August 1914, the British government declared war on Germany, King George V called out the Territorials and the government nationalised the railways. As the year progresses, Thomas charts the actions that made this 'world' war different from any other conflict. In August he notes that this is 'the biggest war in the world's history' and that 'a few million men' are taking part in a battle in Belgium; in September he writes that British shipping is falling prey to German submarines but that British aviators have 'fried' a Zeppelin shed in Cologne; in October, he sees crowds of Belgian refugees in Glasgow and records 'fighting by earth, air, water and under the water'; in November he notes that the war is costing Britain £1 million a day; and in December records the first of the German air raids on the east coast of England.

Thursday, 1 January

A Happy New Year to you. On holiday today. All of us at Greenlodge Terrace.[1] *There at 6 p.m. John and Lily*[2] *also there. Home 11.30 p.m.*

Monday, 5 January

Our 'lum' makes the most unholy noise when the wind blows, and the man below came up about 10 p.m. and said he couldn't sleep for it.[3] *My oh my.*

Tuesday, 6 January

Wrote a love letter to the factor about the lum. This is Epiphany.

Friday, 9 January

Man up today greasing the 'whirly' on our lum.

Saturday, 10 January

Went to the library for some moral books in the afternoon. Wrote Duncan tonight.[4]

---

[1] Thomas' father, Joseph Livingstone, lived at 3 Greenlodge Terrace, Bridgeton.
[2] Lily was Thomas' sister, married to John White.
[3] Lum is a Scottish word for chimney.
[4] Duncan was Thomas' brother, who lived between Belfast and Glasgow.

JANUARY, 1914.

7.10 Monday 12 ○ 12.30

(12-353)

Tommy kept us waken a bit during the night.

Lily John & Pa here 6 to 9 50 pm.

Tommy still got a Cough & ear-ache

Cold frosty day.

JANUARY, 1914.

7.20. Tuesday **13** (13-352) 12.25.

Very cold day

Entertaining tonight
All Greenlodge here
6 to 10.15 pm.

Tommy not so bad now

for ~~Thursday~~
Wed see next
saturday

10.20
pm

Friday, 16 January

Very foggy and frosty. Not very well myself at night. Took some castor oil, so help me bob.[5] Sat in front of the fire all night and made myself comfortable.

Wednesday, 21 January

Agnes very ill at night. Bathed her feet, gave her a hot drink and put her to bed.

Thursday, 22 January

Agnes in bed as much as possible today.

Saturday, 24 January

Went to the library in the afternoon and for 'messages'.[6]

Sunday, 25 January

Wild, stormy day. Agnes worse again today. Lily came in for a little in the afternoon to see her. Third Sunday after Epiphany. First Sunday after pay day.

Thursday, 29 January

Tommy not well at all, so I went for the doctor at night. Doctor came, took his temperature, which was 101° [Fahrenheit][7], shook his head and looked serious. May develop into quite a lot of other things. Got a new hygienic pipe (6d).

[5] Castor oil was used to ease constipation and induce vomiting. 'So help me bob' is a bowdlerisation of the Christian oath 'So help me God.' Usually rendered in Scotland as 'Help ma boab.'

[6] 'Going for the messages' is a Glasgow expression for going out for grocery shopping.

[7] The equivalent temperature in Celsius is 38°.

Friday, 30 January

Doc up again seeing Tommy. His temperature still 102°. Got him a bottle to reduce same. Doctor puzzled. Wee man cheerier at night.

Saturday, 31 January

Doctor up today. Wee man just the same. Doctor can't tell what's wrong. We are getting a bit anxious about Tommy. Poor wee man.

Sunday, 1 February

Doctor up again. Tommy's temperature down to 100°. Doctor doesn't know yet why he is not well, but says it isn't measles, fever, diphtheria or pneumonia. Sam up, Lily up, and Mrs Carmichael in to see the young man.[8] Gave Tommy an extra large dose of castor oil.

Monday, 2 February

We did not sleep much during the night. The oil did its duty right nobly and we were kept on the hop. I was at work early, to wit 6.45 a.m. to let some engineers in. Wee man much better, temperature down to normal. Doctor was here. Agnes about pegged out now.

Tuesday, 3 February

Wee Tommy up for an hour and a half at night. Quite shaky on his feet. He was very cross all day. Agnes' patience exhausted by night. Sad times.

Wednesday, 4 February

Doctor up. We are to get Tommy's tonsils cut. Holy Moses.

---

[8] Mrs Carmichael was a neighbour in the same tenement as the Livingstones.

Saturday, 7 February

Hetty came here shortly after 3, so we all had a pleasant evening. Saw her away by 9.12 from Central.[9]

Tuesday, 10 February

Chased a mouse at night. Nobody hurt but myself.

Wednesday, 11 February

Agnes at doctor with Tommy arranging about the amputation of his tonsils. He is coming on Sunday to do the dismal deed. Agnes bought a mousetrap so set it at night with great expectations.

Thursday, 12 February

Looked at the trap this morning. The mouse had eaten the bait but left the trap as it couldn't eat it also. Better luck next time.

Friday, 13 February

A small mouse was in the trap this morning. Agnes most melancholy. Sad times. It's getting near Sunday. Poor wee man.

Saturday, 14 February

Caught another mouse. Weeping skies today. Doctor up at night saying he could not come tomorrow as his assistant doctor would be away, so we have put it off for a week. Another weary week. This is St Valentine's Day.

[9] Tommy usually walks his visitors to their tram or train, often travelling long distances. In this case, he and Hetty presumably walked from Govanhill to Central Station, in the centre of town, so that she could catch her train home. Hetty was Agnes' cousin.

[10] Nell Ruth was probably the wife of Frank Ruth who lived at 20 Morgan Street.

Sunday, 15 February

Nell Ruth up for a little, also Lily and John.[10] Agnes just about done up, with the anxiety and worry, and then to wait another week. Still sad times.

Thursday, 19 February

Stuffed up the hole where the mice come in to see us, in case we are devoured.

Friday, 20 February

Wee man very restless during the night, so we slept not, perchance a flea was chewing him, or perhaps it is some new trouble. 'Mon père' here at dinner time, and Mrs and Miss Gordon in the afternoon.

Saturday, 21 February

It's getting nearer tomorrow. My hair is getting grey.

Sunday, 22 February

Wild morning and wet. Mrs Gordon came up about 10.45. Doctor Drevor came up about 11.30 and then Dr Gardiner shortly after. We got shaky then. Poor Wee Tommy stretched on the table, chloroformed, and his tonsils cut and adenoids removed. It lasted about 10 minutes but left a poor wee sick sore boy. Mrs Gordon went away about 4.15. Andrew came in for a little, also Mrs Cormack, then Lily and Mrs Carmichael. Mrs Brown came to the door and wee John McCort was up.[11] Sad times.

[11] Andrew Hamilton was a former office boy in Paterson and Baxter, where Thomas worked. John and Margaret Carmichael lived at 14 Morgan Street and were neighbours and good friends of the Livingstones. Mrs Brown was likely to be Catherine or Charlesina Brown who lived at 14 Morgan Street. John McCort was the son of the painter, Daniel McCort (see 23 January, 1913).

Monday, 23 February

Wee man had to be nursed all day, his throat very sore. Nell Ruth up in the morning. Mrs Gordon and Nannie here in the afternoon.[12] Josephine here at night.[13] Wee man a little cheerier at bedtime. Mrs Cormack came up for a little at night. Agnes nearly all out.

Wednesday, 25 February

Wee man still finds it difficult to swallow and has a stiff neck.

Thursday, 26 February

Mrs Gordon up in the forenoon, also the doctor. Tommy got a very bad cold and his neck has to be rubbed with olive oil. Lily up for a little in the afternoon. Tommy very wretched at night. Not well at all.

Friday, 27 February

Agnes washed the stairs. Tommy's cold much the same, but he is fearfully cross. Agnes 'fed up'.

Saturday, 28 February

Doctor up in the forenoon. Thinks Tommy all right now except for his cold. He is not coming back 'grâce à Dieu'.[14] Went to the library in the afternoon. Pouring wet day. Tommy behaving like a little fiend. Agnes got a sore back and shoulders. She is having her doubts about the operation now. Extra melancholy.

[12] Nannie Gordon.
[13] Josephine was Thomas' older sister.
[14] 'Thanks be to God'.

Sunday, 1 March

Very wet day (of course). Tommy seems in better spirits. Poor Agnes in a state of collapse today. Took a walk around the '100 Acre Dyke' after dinner.[15] Agnes had to lie down for a little today.

Monday, 2 March

Cold, windy, wet day (again, of course). Wee man fine today. Did a little joiner work at night. Got my hair cut. Trout fishing begins today.

Tuesday, 3 March

Weather same as yesterday, only worse. Agnes washed the stairs. Tommy's neck seems to have more joints in it now.

Thursday, 5 March

Weather beastly, heavy rain, the quintessence of cussedness. Tommy quite well now.

Tuesday, 10 March

Chased a mouse in the scullery last night, but caught it not.[16]

Wednesday, 11 March

Agnes very ill during the night and not at all well today.

Thursday, 12 March

Agnes in the wash-house in the afternoon.[17]

---

[15] The Hundred Acre Hill, also known as the Hundred Acre Dyke, was a hill in Cathcart, now part of King's Park.

[16] The scullery was a small area off the kitchen generally used for washing and storing dishes and kitchen equipment.

[17] The wash-house was a stone or brick structure at the rear of a tenement, used by all of the tenants in rotation. It contained a boiler, a number of sinks and a wringer or mangle.

Saturday, 14 March

Agnes very ill at night, sick and vomiting and wild sort of pains inside. Am greatly alarmed.

Sunday, 15 March

Agnes very ill during the night and vomited a lot. It is the bile. Feeling a little better during the day. Jenny Roxburgh here about 2 p.m.[18] She brought Agnes a nice white shawl. Jenny left about 8.30 p.m. and I saw her on to a Dalmuir car at Glasgow Cross.[19]

Wednesday, 18 March

Agnes in good form today. She broke the teapot and broke a bowl at night when she was baking, and spilled treacle all over the carpet. Glad I didn't do it.

Sunday, 22 March

A very nice day. Tommy got a bad cold and Agnes got a very sore head. Before dinner I took a long walk. Pollokshaws, Cowglen Road and Crookston. Took the car back from there as I was late.

Monday, 23 March

We got no sleep all last night. The wee man saw to that. He complained of a sore head, a sore tooth, a sore belly, a sore ear, a sore knee.

Saturday, 28 March

Slave trade abolished 1807.
I entered into bondage 10/6/10.

---

[18] Jenny Roxburgh was a family friend who lived in Clydebank and worked as a nursing sister in Maryhill.

[19] Dalmuir is to the west of Glasgow, on the River Clyde near Clydebank.

Sunday, 29 March

All of us at Clydebank, nestling in the bosom of the Roxburgh family.

Tuesday, 31 March

Nannie Henderson here in the forenoon, saying goodbye as she is going to Australia.[20] I did not see her, so I shed tears (je ne pense pas).[21]

Wednesday, 1 April

Agnes has got a very sore head. I have got a most cussed cold in my head. I want to kill somebody.

Saturday, 4 April

This is the 'International', so in the afternoon I took the wife and family to the vicinity of Mount Florida and watched the folk coming away from the match.[22] I counted about three million of them. England 1, Scotland 3.[23]

Friday, 10 April

Cleaned all the windows tonight, and Agnes polished the marble staircase.

Saturday, 11 April

Dull sort of day. Coldish. Took Agnes and Tommy in the afternoon to see the Barrows and then we went to Bow's and bought a new pot (2/3).

---

[20] Nannie Henderson was probably one of Agnes' aunts.

[21] 'I don't think so'.

[22] Hampden, the Scottish national football stadium, is in the district of Mount Florida in south Glasgow. It had the largest capacity of any ground in Scotland, and one of the largest in Europe.

[23] The game was one of six in the British Home Championship, which was won by Ireland.

Monday, 13 April

This is the spring holiday, so it rained and it rained and it stormed. John came about 10 a.m. to take me a walk of about 30 miles.[24] Being quite 'compos mentis' I firmly but gently declined.[25]

Wednesday, 15 April

Agnes cleaned out the room and we rearranged the furniture and shifted the piano to make folk think we had a lot of new stuff.

Thursday, 16 April

Agnes at Ibrox and then at Kingston Halls with the Gordons to a 'Kinderspiel'.[26] She got home 11 p.m.

Saturday, 18 April

Delightful day. After dinner we took car to Pollok Estate and recreated ourselves and then walked to Dumbreck Terminus and got car home.[27] Took a walk out myself at night and bought myself a new pipe (1/-).

Sunday, 19 April

Took a walk this morning to Queen's Park before breakfast. After breakfast had a seat in Toryglen Golf Course. After dinner had Tommy out for a brace of hours in Queen's Park. Mrs Livingstone not out at all. Weather couldn't be better.

---

[24] Thomas' brother-in-law.

[25] 'Of sound mind'.

[26] Kingston Halls was a public hall in the Kinning Park district of Glasgow. The German word 'Kinderspiel' means children's games.

[27] Pollok Estate was owned by the Maxwell family for more than 700 years. It was gifted by them to the city of Glasgow in 1966. Part of the estate is now known as Pollok Country Park. The estate also contains the Burrell Collection gallery, opened in 1983.

Walking routes

Walking has long been a Glasgow way of life. Car ownership has always been lower within the city boundaries than in the richer suburbs and countryside beyond. Even today, the 2001 census shows that Glasgow has the highest percentage of car-free households of all local authority areas in Scotland. This is partly because of the high levels of public transport in the city and partly because of the high levels of relative poverty. Neither of these factors has changed significantly since Thomas' day.

Necessity aside, most Glaswegians enjoy the communal aspects of public transport and the street, where chance encounters and opportunities for conversations and exchanges of news abound. Just as Glasgow in the early twentieth century was a great city for teashops and public houses, it was also a great city for 'windae hingin', the practice of leaning out of tenement windows, forearms crossed on a blanket or pillow, taking part in the life of the street from one's window on the world. Times have changed, but Glasgow remains a friendly city - this aspect of city life has even been enshrined in a tourist marketing slogan - and life in the fresh air, however bad the weather, seems to encourage and nurture this.

Thomas seems to find solace, strength and inspiration in his walks. When his family are away from him, he writes that he feels unsettled, then takes to the open countryside. He walks to visit his father in Bridgeton, his brother in Rutherglen and other family members and friends across the city. But primarily he walks for pleasure, whether it is his regular turn around Queen's Park before breakfast on Sunday mornings in the summer, his frequent trips through Pollok Estate or over Cathkin Braes, or his solitary rambles to East Kilbride or Barrhead.

Many of his walks were in public parks. Glasgow may have had horrendous overcrowding problems in some inner-city areas (see 'Housing and Factors', pp. 207-209), but the 'Dear Green Place' was well-served with parks and green spaces. It has often been said, but never quite proved, that Glasgow has more green space per capita than any city in Europe. In Thomas' day, the city had 31 parks, several outside the city boundaries. The outlying recreational areas included Ardgoil, a 'Highland ridge of a wild and picturesque nature' between Loch Long and Loch Goil, according to one guidebook of the period; Balloch Castle and its estate on the shores of Loch Lomond; Cathkin Braes Park; Rouken Glen; and the Linn Park. Thomas mentions walking over Cathkin Braes and having tea in Rouken Glen, but he would be aware of the other parks and estates, even those beyond the reach of the tram network.

Queen's Park was opened in September 1862, on the 143 acres of Pathhead Farm that the Glasgow Corporation (the city council) purchased five years earlier. English architect and garden designer Sir Joseph Paxton advised on the layout, and much of the work to turn the farm into a park was carried out by the unemployed. The queen of the title is not Victoria but Mary Queen of Scots, whose forces were defeated in 1568 at the Battle of Langside, on the southern boundary of the park.

Rouken Glen was gifted to the city by Archibald Cameron Corbett, later Lord Rowallen, in 1906. Its celebrated features include a 'Highland Glen' complete with falls, cliffs and crags. The picturesque waterfall, which is surrounded by steep woodland, was formed from a smaller natural waterfall, which was doubled in height in the early part of the nineteenth century to feed a reservoir that supplied a print works on the Auldhouse Burn at Thornliebank.

Cathkin Braes, a large expanse of natural hillside, is sited five miles south of the city centre. It includes one of the highest points on the south side of the city and affords spectacular views over greater Glasgow and as far north as Ben Lomond and Ben Ledi. The natural environment of the park includes ancient woodland, grassland, heath and scrub, with many long-established paths through the park giving a constantly changing environment and view. What is now the eastern portion of Cathkin Braes Country Park was gifted to the city in 1887 by James Dick, who had made his fortune in rubber soles, with the condition that it should be kept in a natural state and open for public enjoyment. The western portion was added in 1940.

Pollok Estate, although not gifted to the city by the Maxwell family until 1967, was a popular haunt of the citizens of Glasgow's south side in Thomas' day. Sir John Stirling Maxwell, whose family had owned the estate since the middle of the thirteenth century, gave the people of Glasgow access to the enclosed parkland around Pollok House from 1911. Ramblers such as Thomas would have been attracted by the natural woodlands, farmlands and the activity along the White Cart Water, which flows through the estate and was used to power a sawmill in Thomas' time. Pollok

Postcard of Queen's Park Gates and Victoria Road.

Postcard of Rouken Glen Park bandstand.

House, the stately former family home, is now in the care of the National Trust for Scotland. This is singularly appropriate, since the informal meeting that set up the trust was hosted by Sir John Stirling Maxwell here in 1931. The district of Cowglen, through which Thomas walked on his way to Barrhead, was part of the Pollok estate.

Barrhead, in Thomas' day a thriving industrial town, sits eight miles south-west of Glasgow on the slopes of the Gleniffer Braes. In the nineteenth and early twentieth centuries its industries included iron founding, tanning, making porcelainware and carpet weaving. The road between the outer suburbs of Glasgow and the town travelled through farms and open countryside, with fresh winds blowing from the west and south-west, free from industrial pollution.

Thomas talks of sitting in the parks and listening to music. The Glasgow Corporation had Parliamentary powers to spend £4,000 each year on providing music in its city parks, although the annual bill often amounted to more than £10,000, with the difference coming from the sale of reserved seats. The city fathers no doubt thought this was money well spent on 'civilising' the population, just as the city libraries offered 'improving literature'. Thomas seems to derive as much pleasure from walking as from music and reading, all of which he enjoys several times a week.

Tuesday, 21 April
Men up today to sort our 'lum'. They took it away.

Wednesday, 22 April
Tommy cracked his skull in the back green today, fell off the kitchen table and again cracked his skull on the door. We were glad to get his remains safely to bed. Got Tommy a jar of 'Virol' as he is not as well as might be.[28]

Thursday, 23 April
Got our lum put up today.

Monday, 27 April
Went out to Ruglen at night to consult my tailor for a new suit. Bought four clay pipes and broke three of them on the way home.

Monday, 4 May
Got the doctor's little bill today.[29] *£2 14s 0d.*

Wednesday, 6 May
Factor here and got his blood money.

Saturday, 9 May
In the afternoon Agnes and I went out to the green fields and beat the room carpet.[30] Great fun. And then I laid it well and truly.

[28] Virol was a health food made from bone marrow.
[29] Presumably for the tonsillectomy.
[30] In the days before vacuum cleaners, spring cleaning involved taking the carpets outdoors, laying them on grass or hanging them on washing lines, and beating them to remove dust and dirt.

Sunday, 10 May

This is the day the Aquitania leaves the Clyde, so I met Andrew at 9 a.m., walked into the town and managed to get on to a Renfrew car and walked from there to Langbank and watched the boat passing.[31] *And then we walked back to Renfrew. Rained all the time. About half a million folk helped us to watch.*

Monday, 11 May

Agnes at Ruglen in afternoon. Josephine and Small Lily here at tea time and after that Lily and John and Pa arrived.[32] We played whist.

Saturday, 16 May

Agnes up nearly all last night with toothache, jaw-ache, earache etc., and has it all day today.

Sunday, 17 May

Agnes still got neuralgia, and I took a very sore throat and sore head. Wonder what's going to happen.

Monday, 25 May

Agnes got a very sore head. Says it will be the bile. 'Ora pro nobis.'

Thursday, 28 May

This is the day we all flit but I didn't.[33]

The liner *Aquitania* was built by John Brown of Clydebank for the Cunard Line, for its fast weekly service between Liverpool and New York. Langbank is on the south side of the river, opposite Clydebank, giving a good view of the ship leaving the yard and heading to sea.

Small Lily was Josephine's daughter and thus Thomas' niece.

May 25 is Whitsun, one of the four Scottish quarter days. Most annual rentals began and ended on this day, so many of Thomas' neighbours would be moving home that day.

Friday, 29 May

Pubs don't open now till 10 a.m., which does not affect me.[34]

Saturday, 30 May

Empress of Ireland CPR rammed yesterday. 1,024 lives lost.[35]

Wednesday, 3 June

Thought we were in need of a little amusement so off we went to the Cinerama.[36]

Thursday, 4 June

At 10 India Street, Rutherglen, on this date 1882 T. C. Livingstone was born.

Sunday, 7 June

We noticed burglars had been at work opposite us. A policeman came up and interviewed us on the matter but we had no clue.

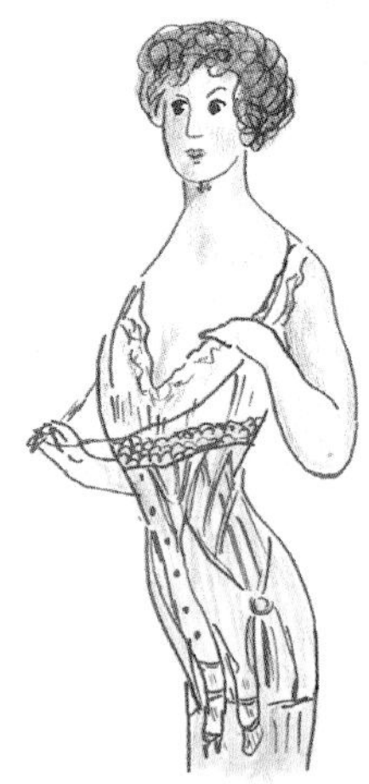

Friday, 12 June

Very busy tonight packing up, as we go our holidays to Rothesay tomorrow. Hallelujah. Agnes got a new pair of corsets today.

---

[34] This change was introduced by the government to preserve the efficiency of workers. See 'Food and Drink', pp. 188-190.

[35] *The Empress of Ireland* was a steamship owned by the Canadian Pacific Steamship Company which collided with the Norwegian ship *Storstad* in the St Lawrence Seaway.

[36] The Cinerama stood at the corner of Victoria Road and Cuthbertson Street, near the Livingstone family home. It opened in 1912 in a former skating rink and closed in 1922.

1914

Saturday, 13 June

Beautiful day.
Very warm, sunshine.
Agnes and Nannie Gordon sailed by Lord of the Isles at 11.30, which was too crowded for comfort.[37] Mrs Gordon and Ella helped them on with the luggage. I followed in ease and comfort by 4.3 GSW and arrived Rothesay 5.55.[38] Agnes and the boy and Nannie met me. After tea we all had a look round.

Sunday, 14 June

Took a walk in the morning to the pier. After dinner we went by Ardbeg and met John and Lily Duncan and the two Jones girls.[39] We took them all up for their tea. Beautiful day.

Monday, 15 June

After breakfast went myself to Bogany and back by Skippers Wood.[40] We hired a pram for 4/- and after dinner we all went to Bogany Point. After tea I paid my twopence and listened to the band. Tommy got a pair of sandshoes (1/11). Weather perfect.

Tuesday, 16 June

We are all getting tanned. Weather perfect.

---

[37] *The Lord of the Isles* was a large paddle steamer, built by Hendersons of Partick, on the Clyde, and operated by Turbine Steamers.

[38] Because Thomas worked on Saturday mornings, he travelled later in the day by the Glasgow and South Western Railway (GSW).

[39] Ardbeg is to the north of Rothesay. The Jones girls were sisters and probably residents of the island.

[40] Bogany Point and Skippers Wood are both to the south of Rothesay.

7.45 **Thursday 25** 12

(176-189)

Took Tommy in the forenoon to the skeoch wood. After dinner I ~~climed~~ climbed the Barone Hill & then we met Isa & Lily. They came up & had tea with us & we saw them nearly home. Got back a little after ten.

Very nice day.

BARONE HILL

JUNE, 1914.

Friday 26

(177-188)

~~4.45~~ 8.20 12.15

Very hot sunny day In the forenoon I walked to St. Ninians Bay & on to Scalpsie Bay & back by Loch Fad. After dinner we all went to the "meadows". no where special at night.

At Scalpsie Bay

Monday, 29 June

Started my work today.

Saturday, 4 July

Their Royal Holinesses the King and Queen are coming to Glasgow next week, so Tommy got a flag.[41]

Sunday, 5 July

I was at church in the forenoon.[42]

Tuesday, 7 July

Lovely day. Got away from my work at 10 a.m. as we have a royal visit today. Agnes met me with the boy so we hied us to Parliamentary Road and saw the King and Queen and the Princess Mary. We took off our hat and went on our way duly elevated. After tea I went myself to Cathkin Braes and saw a glorious sunset. Met an old school mate (Tom Davidson) there and we came down to Ruglen together. Home 10.30.

Thursday, 9 July

'There is many a married-looking man who is only worried.'

Monday, 13 July

Agnes and Tommy away to Lamlash today, so I met them at Central Station and put them on the 12.40 train to Ardrossan.[43]

Thursday, 16 July

Got a P. C. from my spouse letting me know when she would be home. The 'Society' man here at night. He took some of my hard-earned money with him.[44]

[41] King George V and Queen Mary. Thomas is being facetious by saying 'Holinesses'.
[42] Tommy puts wavy lines under both 'I' and 'church', emphasising the rarity of the event. This is the only time in 1914 he records attending church.
[43] Lamlash is on the island of Arran, reached by boat from Ardrossan in Ayrshire.
[44] A collector for an assurance society.

In late July 1914, a severe diplomatic dispute between Serbia and Austro-Hungary was threatening to boil over into war. Austro-Hungary was demanding that Serbia hand over the leaders of the Black Hand Gang, who had killed Archduke Franz Ferdinand in June 1914. On 28 July the two countries went to war. The conflict rapidly escalated, with Russia agreeing to defend Serbia if it was attacked by Austria, and Germany in turn threatening to attack Russia if it intervened in Austria.

Sunday, 26 July

Gun running in Dublin today. Mob knocked up against the military (KOSB). Three killed, about 80 injured.[45]

Very stormy night

Monday, 27 July

War clouds in Europe.

Tuesday, 28 July

Austria and Servia at war now.[46] Things looking bad.

Wednesday, 29 July

Belgrade, capital of Servia, bombarded by the Austrians. Things getting worse and worse.

Thursday, 30 July

Agnes made jam and put it in jars. Russia mobilising. Things very grave indeed in Europe.

Friday, 31 July

Tommy got a bath tonight. All the stock exchanges closed now. Bank rate up to 8%. Germany in a state of war. All Europe mobilising. Things are very bad.

---

45 Guns and ammunition were smuggled ashore near Howth, a village to the north-east of Dublin, on Sunday 26 July, and distributed to members of the Irish Volunteer Force. During a clash with the Dublin Metropolitan Police and the King's Own Scottish Borderers (KOSB) three people were killed.

46 Servia is an archaic term for Serbia. Thomas spells it both ways at different points in the diary.

Saturday, 1 August

Fine day. We went to Queen's Park in the afternoon and at night we went round by the boating pond, Aitken Head Collieries, and Mount Florida and took the car home.

Bank rate up to 10% today. Germany has sent an ultimatum to Russia and France.

Sunday, 2 August

Very wet forenoon. Very heavy rain. Took a walk into town in the afternoon to see the latest war news.[47] *Germany has declared war on Russia. Russia has crossed into Austria. Germany has crossed the French frontier. Our government considering today whether to fight or not. Royal Naval Reserves mobilised. The war of the world. We wonder what tomorrow will bring forth.*

Monday, 3 August

I went to Sam's shop at night and brought home half a stone of flour at 1/-. We are doing a bit of speculation in the provision way owing to the war. Agnes got a stone of sugar at two and a half pence per pound. Sugar selling today at 4d. Unprecedented scenes. Bank holiday extended three days extra. Germany, France, Austria, Russia, Servia all at war. British army and fleet mobilised. Germany warned by Britain. The climax is approaching.

[47] The latest war news may have been posted on the Tolbooth Steeple or Mercat Cross.

Tuesday, 4 August

Provisions getting dearer every day. Serious times ahead. Germany declares war on Belgium. Official declaration of war with France and Germany. Britain sends ultimatum to Germany. The King has called out the Territorials. Government has taken over the railways. Germany has appealed to Italy. Every paper is now a 'war speshull'.[48]

Wednesday, 5 August

Town full of Territorials. Getting ready for our country's defence. Britain declared war on Germany last night at 11 p.m. Now fighting: Britain, Germany, France, Austria, Belgium, Servia and Russia. The biggest war in the world's history.

Thursday, 6 August

Took a run into Sam's shop at night to talk over the 'war news'. All sorts of rumours are going about. The soldiers are lifting horses all over the town.[49]

Friday, 7 August

Germans have lost 25,000 men at Liège and have asked for a 24 hours armistice. Wild rumours going about. Seems to be a great naval battle in the North Sea. Austria and Russia formally at war now. We indeed live in stirring times. A month ago I would have said impossible.

[48] Thomas is mimicking the cries of the newspaper vendor, shouting 'war special!'
[49] The army requisitioned horses from Glasgow businesses for use at the front.

Saturday, 8 August

Went to the Stirling's Library in the afternoon for a book. Liège still holds out against Germans. Armistice refused. French have invaded Alsace-Lorraine. Britain has taken two German colonies. No fight yet in the North Sea. Portugal and Montenegro are reported at war with Germany. Italy still neutral. A nightmare of a war.

Sunday, 9 August

Tommy three years old today. Went into town in forenoon and got a war paper. After dinner we all went to Queen's Park and heard the band playing where the Territorials are quartered in Coplaw Street.[50] *After tea we all went into town and got another paper. Wild fighting in Alsace-Lorraine. Germans routed.*

Tuesday, 11 August

Greenlodge mobilised their forces and invaded us tonight. They went away about 10.15. Germans still getting killed in Belgium. I'm beginning to forget all who are fighting.

The United Kingdom parliament passed the Defence of the Realm Act on 8 August 1914, days after declaring war. This gave the government powers it believed it needed on the home front, such as the right to censor all communications and to requisition buildings or land. The Act also banned the public from flying kites or lighting bonfires (which might attract Zeppelins), buying binoculars (which could be used for spying), feeding bread to wild animals (which wasted food), discussing naval and military matters (which could benefit spies) or buying alcohol on public transport (which wasted resources). The Act also gave us British Summer Time, which was intended to boost wartime production. Pub opening hours in Scotland were restricted to from 12 noon to 2.30 p.m. and from 5 p.m. to 10 p.m. Monday to Saturday, and all alcoholic drinks were produced at a lower strength, both to conserve food stocks and to reduce alcohol consumption.

[50] The 3rd Lanark Rifle Volunteers' drill hall was in Coplaw Street, just west of Govanhill.

Thursday, 13 August

Beautiful day. Very warm. We all went to Queen's Park at night and heard the band. Britain declares war on Austria. Germans getting slaughtered in Belgium. Brilliant Belgian victory. Britannia still ruling the waves.

Friday, 14 August

All sorts of rumours about British soldiers killed and wounded. Food prices getting easier. The scare is over in that respect.

Sunday, 16 August

Brilliant summer day. Took a walk into town before dinner to get a 'war special'. After, we all went to Queen's Park and admired the scenery from the flag pole. After tea we all went to town and got another special. Some French and Belgian successes reported. The Big Battle is coming on. A few million men to fight extending 250 miles.[51]

Tuesday, 18 August

Beautiful day. Agnes staying in the wash-house in the forenoon. I helped her to fold some articles at night, then she washed the marble staircase.[52] The British army has landed in France. Magnificent welcome.

Thursday, 20 August

Nice day. Very warm. Agnes and Tommy out at Ruglen in the afternoon. Lily not well. Getting no news from Belgium. War Office very reticent. Russian successes in Russia and Germany. We all went to the pictures at night.

---

51 The Western Front was now the French and Belgians fighting along a broad front against the Germans. The British Expeditionary Force was preparing to land in France to join battle against the Germans.

52 The common staircase of the house, which residents took turns to wash, was not made of marble.

Friday, 21 August

I did some joiner work to the kitchen table at night. I am putting an extra leaf on it. Brussels is taken by the heathen Germans.[53] The Allies have some little game on, I think. Looks like a trap for Germany.

Thursday, 27 August

Nice day. Agnes bought a fancy pair of (the last part of this message is censored).[54] Bloody fighting in Belgium.[55] Enormous German losses.

Friday, 28 August

Dirty wet day. Germany seems top dog this week, but at a fearful cost. It is reported that they have 200,000 killed.

Sunday, 30 August

Up early this morning (7.20 a.m.), walked into the town in pouring rain to see the latest sad reading. British army badly cut up bearing the brunt of the fighting. Took a walk to Ruglen to see Lily. Disagreed with John's socialistic views of the war. Father here at night. Agnes not well at all.

Thursday, 3 September

The new recruiting office in Cathcart Road seems to be doing business. About 10,000 men have enlisted in Glasgow for the war.

---

53 Brussels was evacuated by the Belgians and occupied by the Germans on 20 August.

54 Thomas is making fun of the official censor, who took a thick blue pencil to news reports from the continent.

55 The Battle of Mons began on 23 August.

Friday, 4 September

Went out to the shop at night to see Sam and then we went to a recruiting office. Sam taking down figures and I watched the recruits having their eyes tested. Germans about 20 miles from Paris. Glasgow has enlisted 15,000 for 'Kitchener's Army'.[56]

Monday, 7 September

A naval action in the North Sea last week. We sunk nine destroyers and damaged seven. This is private information. It has never been published yet, and very few, in fact, nobody, about here knows.[57]

Wednesday, 9 September

Brilliant successes all along the Allied Line, about 180 miles in extent.[58] Things are looking more hopeful.

Friday, 11 September

Nice bright day. Wholesale arrests of Germans in Scotland.

Saturday, 12 September

Hetty here in the afternoon. We all went out and saw Fancy Dress Parade in aid of War Fund.[59]

People were quick to volunteer for Army service. By late September 1914, some 2.25 million men had enlisted and 1.5 million were classified as being in reserved occupations. However, almost 40 per cent of all volunteers were found to be unfit for military service because of poor health.

[56] Lord Kitchener, the Secretary of State for War, set a target of recruiting 100,000 volunteers for what he called the New Army, although it was popularly known as Kitchener's Army.
[57] Thomas worked in the shipping industry, and he may have heard about this naval action through his contacts at sea or in the ports.
[58] The First Battle of Marne and the First Battle of Aisne had begun.
[59] The War Fund was a public subscription to help pay the cost of the war.

Sunday, 13 September

Very cold, showery, windy day. Took my usual walk into town before breakfast.[60]

Monday, 14 September

Not feeling well at night. Bathed my feet and took something 'hot' and so to bed.

Tuesday, 15 September

Stayed in bed all day. Dead to the world. Not worth even half a German.

Tuesday, 22 September

Agnes doing some baking at night. Tommy still got a bad cough. Disaster in North Sea. Three British cruisers sunk by German submarines: HMS *Aboukir*, HMS *Hogue*, HMS *Cressy*.[61]

Wednesday, 23 September

Agnes out seeing Lily at night. I stayed in and watched the child. About 200 wounded British soldiers arrived at Stobhill Hospital last Monday.[62] Some British aviators flew over Cologne and fried a Zeppelin shed.

Thursday, 24 September

Nice day. All the Cormacks (and the lodger) up at night. We had a musical evening.

Saturday, 26 September

Wee Lily here in the evening and went away about nine. Agnes not well at all. She fainted at night. Tommy got new shoes (4/6). Some more German colonies going under.

[60] To buy a newspaper with the latest war news.

[61] All three ships, which were sailing in convoy in the North Sea, were sunk by the German submarine U9.

[62] Stobhill Hospital was commandeered by the army and was known as Stobhill Military Hospital between 1914 and 1918. A railway station was built in its grounds to allow the injured to be transported there.

Sunday, 27 September

Very windy day. I was not out except for war specials. Typhus broken out among the Germans at Brussels.

Tuesday, 29 September

Beautiful day. Agnes and Tommy over at Greenlodge seeing Lily (who is staying there to be nursed) in the afternoon. Cholera has broken out among the Austrians at Vienna.

Wednesday, 30 September

Allies pressing the Germans strongly in the Big Battle.[63]

Saturday, 3 October

Big Battle still raging. German attacks shattered the London Scottish at the front. The first Territorial regiment to be in action. Antwerp besieged. Vienna preparing for a siege. All of us in town in afternoon. This is Belgian Flag Day, so we donned our flags.[64]

The two great battles of 1914, the First Battle of the Marne and the First Battle of Ypres, were both successes for the Allies. At the beginning of the war a German force advanced through Belgium on its way to France, with the intention of capturing Paris. It was halted after crossing the River Marne, and in September the battle named for that river forced its retreat to the River Aisne. This joint French-British victory, one of the most decisive of the entire war, saved Paris and showed the Germans that they were not an unstoppable force. The Battle of Ypres followed in October and November as the Germans moved towards the French ports in the north of the country. Fierce fighting by the British forces around Ypres saved Calais and other ports from being occupied by the Germans.

[63] On the Western Front, where the Battles of Marne and Aisne were continuing.

[64] Flag days, where local charities would take to the streets and give out flags in exchange for a donation, were a regular feature of Scotland in the first half of the twentieth century. The flags were printed pieces of paper, wrapped around a pin, which people would fasten to their clothing.

Thursday, 8 October

Another 100 wounded arrive at Stobhill. 1,500 Glasgow tramwaymen with the colours.[65]

Monday, 12 October

Agnes went to Greenlodge at night to see Lily. Andrew came up to keep me company.

Wednesday, 14 October

Agnes says Tommy is growing too quick, so we got him another bottle of emulsion.[66]

Thursday, 15 October

Agnes and Tommy over at Greenlodge in the afternoon to see Lily, whose condition is very grave. Hopeless, I think, but can only hope for the best. Fleet of liners arrives in England from Canada. Hunt for German submarines on Scottish coast. We sunk one. 3,000 Belgian refugees are coming to Glasgow.

Friday, 16 October

Fine day but nippy, foggy morning. Saw crowds of the Belgian refugees today, a moving sight. I take my hat off to them.[67]

Sunday, 18 October

Beautiful day. Agnes at communion today. After dinner we all went to the Sighthill graveyard.[68]

---

[65] Many people volunteered along with their workmates, in what were known as 'pals' battalions'. The 15th (Service) Battalion (1st Glasgow) Glasgow Tramways of the Highland Light Infantry was formed in Glasgow on 2 September 1914 by the Lord Provost.

[66] Probably an emulsion of cod liver oil. One branded product was Scott's Emulsion, which was advertised as 'the World's Standard Body-Builder and Nerve-Food-Tonic'.

[67] The refugees were lodged in the city and the surrounding towns.

Thursday, 22 October

Wholesale arrests of Germans all over Britain.

Saturday, 24 October

Most bloody fighting on the Belgian coast, by earth, air, water and under the water.

Wednesday, 28 October

Got a telephone message from John today that Lily was sinking rapidly and that the end was expected any moment. I went out before dinner to see her. She was breathing and no more. Agnes went out in the afternoon and I went at 6 p.m. but the end had already come. My father had been telegraphed to come home and Agnes and Nellie met him at the station.[69]

Friday, 30 October

Took the day off my work. Nannie Gordon came here in the forenoon and took Wee Tommy away to Ibrox, and then we went to Greenlodge. The funeral left after 3 p.m. and in Rutherglen Cemetery we finally laid poor Lily to rest. It was a cold, wet day, a fit end to this tragedy, for the more I think of it, the more I realise the bitter tragedy of it all. Agnes went down to Ibrox at night for Tommy, and I went home with father. I was more than pleased to see my wee man again. I missed the little rascal more than I could have thought. He seems more precious than ever now.

Sunday, 1 November

Very dull day. None of us out at all. I'm afraid our thoughts were gloomy, and the day lasted a hundred years. Agnes not feeling well at all. Everything is wrong.

---

[68] This seems an odd destination, given current events, but cemeteries were seen as places for Sunday strolls in landscaped grounds.

[69] Thomas' father was presumably visiting relatives in the north of Ireland.

Monday, 2 November

Wee Isa here in afternoon and evening.[70] Sam, Nellie and John came at night. Poor John. A sad, weary figure. He has got to plough his lonely furrow now. Great bayonet charge by the London Scottish, the first Territorial regiment in action.[71] Bavarians routed.

Wednesday, 4 November

Father off to Edinburgh today for a little before he settles down in Greenlodge. The Elder's wife, Mrs McCracken, here today, to see if we needed any charity owing to the war.[72] So far, we don't. The factor called today and robbed us of some money.

Sunday, 8 November

Tommy very sick today. We find at night that he has got the chicken pox.

Friday, 13 November

British casualties to 31 October: 57,000.

Saturday, 14 November

Hard frost today. After dinner, I went part of the 'complete' walk, a memory of my courting days, but I was alone, the pleasure was gone. When I came in, Lily was in. No need now, alas, to say wee Lily. It's hard yet to realise that Lily is gone for ever. British army to be raised to over two million men.

Monday, 16 November

The war is costing us £1 million a day. My salary won't pay it.

[70] Isabella Ferguson, the daughter of Thomas' sister Josephine.
[71] At the Battle of Messines.
[72] Elders are senior lay members of a church who take part in its organisation and administration.

Tuesday, 17 November

We are now the proud possessors of a new hall clock, a sewing machine which Agnes does not know how to work, and a bed we don't know what to do with.[73] We spent the night stowing them away, and I put up the clock. I will need to increase my insurance policy.

Wednesday, 18 November

Tommy's chicken pox seems to be on the wane (this is not a pun).[74]

Thursday, 19 November

Working late. This is stocktaking day.

Friday, 27 November

Dirty wet day. An old girl of mine, Mrs Robertson, dropped in at night.[75] British army in Belgium 'covered with honour and glory'. Outlook for Allies 'very good and full of promise'. Russia's great triumph 'colossal and decisive'.[76]

Members of the Black Watch in the trenches.

Wednesday, 2 December

Tommy got a bad cough. Made him a wee bridge at night and bought him a new slate.[77] Glasgow Territorials now in the trenches in France.

[73] From Lily's house.
[74] 'The wean' is a Scottish and North of England term for 'the child'.
[75] A former junior work colleague, rather than a former girlfriend.
[76] The quotes are presumably from the two Glasgow newspapers Thomas read, *The Glasgow Herald* and *The Bulletin*.
[77] The wooden bridge was probably for playing with alongside other toys. The slate was used for writing on with chalk or a slate pencil.

Thursday, 3 December

Wild, stormy, wet day. Tommy still got a bad cough and Agnes greatly worried thereby. I put up a shelf in the pantry for the household boots. Belgrade taken by the Austrians.

Friday, 4 December

Stormy day. Some rain. Tommy's cold much worse. Agnes in the depths of despair. All German attacks repulsed in Flanders.

Saturday, 5 December

Bitter cold day. Tommy a little better and Agnes is thusly in a better frame of mind. German trenches captured.

Sunday, 6 December

The 'lum' went on fire while breakfast was being made, which delayed the breakfast somewhat. We took it in the dining room, and then I cleaned all the flues, which seemed badly needing it.

Wednesday, 9 December

Hetty here tonight, which pleased us greatly. We are always glad to see her. Nellie arrived about 9 p.m. with some pictures from John for us.[78] Allies progressing in Flanders.

[78] Probably framed prints.

Monday, 14 December

Agnes and Tommy went in the afternoon to Tollcross to see an old girl of mine (Mrs Robertson) and I went straight from my work.

Wednesday, 16 December

My father and Isa here at tea time. German raid on east coast of England – Hartlepool, Scarborough, Redcar and Whitby shelled by the devils, and then they ran back to their kennel. 130 people killed and 300 wounded.

Thursday, 17 December

We arranged the pictures in the room at night.[79] I wrote to the factor about our lum, as it has struck work.

Sunday, 20 December

The ground white with frost today. Took a big walk before dinner. Through Queen's Park to Shawlands Cross, then car to Pollokshaws West and walked along Cowglen Road and down past Crookston Castle and on to Half Way House and car home. Agnes very ill at night, and I had to apply hot flannels to her.

[79] The pictures from John.

Thursday, 24 December

Tommy got his first Xmas present of the season, a book of boats from Hetty and we got cards. Nannie and Ella here at night, and they gave Tommy a motor car. I sent off a few hundred Xmas cards tonight.[80] *German airplane drops a bomb on Dover. No damage done.*

Friday, 25 December

Got away today at 12.30. We got a few more cards and Tommy got a teddy bear from his uncle John, and a wee card like a horse from Jenny Roxburgh. Agnes not in good form. She has a sore head, so we did not go out at all. Big Russian victory.[81]

Saturday, 26 December

Took a walk to Paisley and car back. German aeroplane off Sheerness but it got chased. Rumours of great naval activity by Germans getting ready for 'Der Tag'.[82]

[80] Thomas may be exaggerating here.

[81] The Russians defeated the Austrians at Tarnow and ended the Austro-German offensive in Galicia.

[82] German for 'the day', which was presumably the momentous battle that would conclude the conflict.

Monday, 28 December
Mr Crozier sent Tommy a big wooden horse today. Cuxhaven, the German naval base, bombarded by seven British waterplanes, assisted by the cruisers *Dauntless* and *Arethusa*, and submarines and destroyers. These were attacked by two German Zeppelins and some aeroplanes, but were easily driven off. The first fight of its kind in the world's history.

Wednesday, 30 December
My niece Lily here at night. Bought a new hat for my Ne'erday.

Thursday, 31 December
After dinner we went into the town and bought Tommy a new coat (15/-) and cap (1/6). Not out again. We will now sit up and watch the New Year come in.

1915

In 1915, the first full year of the war, Thomas records the battleships and merchantmen sunk by U-boats and mines, and notes the captured guns put on display in London 'to decorate our parks with'. In January, he notes 'a great French victory in Alsace Lorraine'. This territory was hugely important to the French, for cultural if not military reasons. The area, known by the Germans as the Imperial Province of Elsass-Lothringen, was created in 1871 by the German Empire after it captured most of Alsace and parts of Lorraine in the Franco-Prussian War.

February was dominated by the imposition of a German submarine blockade on Britain, as retaliation for the Allied blockade of the Central Powers. Germany threatened to sink

British Red Cross nurses close to the front line in Flanders.

enemy ships of all kinds in British waters. In May, Germany torpedoed the Atlantic liner *Lusitania*, which sank with 1,300 passengers and crew, including many American citizens. While the Americans did not react publicly, this was one of the incidents that drew them into the war.

The first significant use of poison gas during the war occurred in 1915, when in April the contents of 5,730 gas cylinders was released by the German army north of Ypres. The 168 tons of chlorine gas formed a cloud that drifted across the French trenches, causing the French to flee. The Allies claimed that this was a clear breach of international law, but the Germans argued that the Hague Conventions on the laws of war forbade only shells filled with poison gas. The Allies, who also used chlorine on the Western Front (where it was known as 'Red Star' after the markings on the cylinders), soon developed effective countermeasures against chlorine, and both they and the Central Powers continued to research more deadly chemical weapons.

The most important military action of 1915 was the Gallipoli Expedition. This was a campaign to open up the Dardanelles, which had been closed by Turkey when it entered the war on the German side in October 1914. In April 1915 a British Expeditionary Force that included the Australian and New Zealand Army Corps (known as the Anzacs) landed in the Gallipoli Peninsula aiming to open the Dardanelles straits, conquer the Ottoman capital of Constantinople and make available a sea route to connect the Allies in the west with the forces of the Russian Empire, which were fighting the Austro-Hungarians and the Germans from the east. The British, Anzac and French forces that landed on the peninsula fought the Ottoman army for eight months before admitting defeat and retreating at the end of the year. The battles were long and hard, and the losses of men on both sides were unprecedented – more than 100,000 lives were lost, and another quarter of a million men were wounded.

Mustafa Kemal Atatürk, who fought on the Ottoman side in 1915, became the first president of the Turkish state in 1923. In 1934, he erected a monument at Anzac Cove to all those who died at Gallipoli. The inscription reads:

> Those heroes that shed their blood and lost their lives ... you are now lying in the soil of a friendly country. Therefore rest in peace. There is no difference between the Johnnies and the Mehmets where they lie side by side here in this country of ours ... You, the mothers who sent their sons from far away countries, wipe away your tears. Your sons are now lying in our bosom and are in peace. Having lost their lives on this land they have become our sons as well.
>
> Mustafa Kemal

The reported horrors of the Dardanelles campaign did nothing to improve voluntary enlistment. In response, the government passed the National Registration Act in 1915, which set up a register of the remaining men, who were then targeted in a number of ways. Posters, public meetings, tales of German atrocities and the threat of public opprobrium were all used to put pressure on men to volunteer. The Derby Scheme – named after Lord Derby, who was appointed Director-General of Recruiting in October 1915 – used door-to-door visits to invite men to 'attest' that they would serve if needed. Thomas mentions filling in his registration form in August 1915 and fielding a visit from the Derby campaign.

A variety of groups in society rallied to the cause, encouraging men to volunteer and women to urge them on. The Women's Social and Political Union, better known as the Suffragettes, decided that its members should give white feathers, a symbol of cowardice, to men who had not signed up. Theatre and music hall artistes, too, joined the campaign, and Thomas must have heard some of their routines and songs on his frequent visits to the theatre. Harry Lauder, for example, toured music halls recruiting men during the evening's performance, while Marie Lloyd sang 'I didn't like you much before you joined the army' and Vesta Tilley chorused 'The army of today's alright'.

None of these inducements would prove convincing enough to lure Thomas to the front, however, and he began 1915 in the bosom of his family.

Friday, 1 January

Had arranged to go to Coatbridge today, but we got word yesterday that Jean had diphtheria and Mr Crozier wasn't well, so we couldn't get. We would not have gone in any case, as Tommy was very ill nearly all day, sick etc. Castor oil put him right. It was a wet, stormy day. The battleship *Formidable* sunk in the English Channel by German submarine. About 600 lives lost. A bad start to the New Year.

Saturday, 2 January

Dirty, wet day. Agnes very ill. She bathed her feet, and I put hot flannels on her back as she was sore all over. I went out the messages at night. Agnes very ill indeed, so I am in the dumps. Tommy all right again.

Sunday, 3 January

Agnes seems worse today and still in her bed. I'm thinking of sending for the doctor. All Ibrox here at night to celebrate the New Year. They arrived 6 p.m., away at 10.15. Weather good.

Monday, 4 January

Agnes still very weak and can eat nothing, and can't get up. Got her a bottle of port wine.[1] Ella Gordon here all day and Mrs Gordon later on. Nice day. Bought a pair of clay pipes.

Tuesday, 5 January

Had to rub Agnes' back and chest as she had such a cough during the night. Ella and Nannie Gordon and Isa Ferguson here today to help us. I was glad when they all went away. It was like a boiler maker's yard. Agnes up a little today. Tommy has got a bad cough. Very wet, dirty day.

---

[1] Port wine, which is red wine fortified with spirits, was thought to be a tonic for the afflicted.

[2] French forces captured Burnhaupt-le-Haut in Alsace. On 6 January the French had occupied the area north of Altkirch in the same province.

Wednesday, 6 January

My niece Isa here all day. Agnes up a little more today, and keeping a little better. Rubbed her at night.

Thursday, 7 January

Dirty, wet day. Agnes up now. Nellie here at night. Great French victory in Alsace-Lorraine.[2]

Friday, 8 January

Dirty, wet day. Agnes not so bad now, but still got a cough. Britain has a vast army now at the front.[3]

Saturday, 9 January

Very nice day. Father here in the forenoon, May Crozier here for a little, also. I took a constitutional to Queen's Park in the afternoon. Agnes went out the messages, being her first appearance out since her illness. German plans for smashing up Britain are made. They will do it with Zeppelins and submarines, end of this month, so they say. 150 captured German guns landed in London to decorate our parks with.[4]

Sunday, 10 January

Thought I would take my wife and family out a walk today, so we got ready, and then the rain came on. We stayed in. Important successes by the Allies in France: Perthes captured.[5]

Monday, 11 January

Wet day today. Bought a new gas mantle, for which Agnes owes me four and a half pence.[6] Josephine here at tea time. I did a little joiner work at night in connection with the 'eight day'.[7] Dunkirk bombarded by German aeroplanes.

By January 1915, one million men had enlisted. The vast majority of the British army was fighting on the Western Front.

The government offered these guns to local authorities, who were required to pay the cost of transport from London.

Perthes-les-Hurles, in the Champagne region, was captured by the French Fourth Army.

Agnes was obviously in charge of the domestic finances.

An 'eight day' is a clock that will run for eight days after being wound.

Wednesday, 13 January

Very stormy, wet day. I have got a touch of cold now in the head. Turkey is going to invade Egypt and chuck Britain out, bless its innocent heart. Roumania is going to join in the war in spring.[8]

Thursday, 14 January

I saw the Glasgow Territorials 5th SR and Glasgow Highlanders leaving for the front in a soaking downpour.[9] The Elder came here tonight and left about 11 p.m. Frightful earthquake in Italy. Thousands killed (24,200).[10]

A sergeant and bugler of the 1st Argyll and Sutherland Highlanders.

Friday, 15 January

Agnes and Tommy went to Moore, Taggart and Co. in the afternoon.[11] She got an ornament for her hat and a pair of socks for me and a new jersey for the boy.

---

[8] Romania in fact declared war on Germany and Austria on 19 August 1916.

[9] The Glasgow Territorials were volunteer battalions. Thomas saw the 5th Battalion of the Cameronians (Scottish Rifles) and the 9th (Glasgow Highlanders) Battalion of the Highland Light Infantry.

[10] The earthquake, on 13 January, shook southern Italy and completely destroyed the town of Avezzano. The final death toll was at least 30,000.

[11] This draper's had its premises on the north side of Trongate, close to Glasgow Cross.

Saturday, 16 January

Very nice day. Took a walk to Ruglen after dinner and back by Dalmarnock and Glasgow Cross. When I got home my father was in. I walked him home about 10 p.m. Have got a very sore nose with the cold.

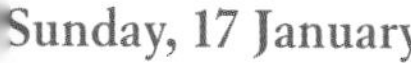

Sunday, 17 January

Very nice day, but cold and frosty. After dinner we took Burnside car and went to Rutherglen Cemetery to see poor Lily's last resting place. We called in at 200 Main Street and had our tea there.

Tuesday, 19 January

Wet, showery day. Agnes met me at 5.30 and we went out to Sam's. Donald and Josephine had to be there also, but they did not come as Donald is not keeping well.[12] The rest of the Fergusons were there, with my father. John White was working late. We all met last year at Greenlodge Terrace, but Lily was there, and now it seems harder to realise that she is gone for ever.[13]

Wednesday, 20 January

Isa has got a situation.[14] I went into the Stirling's Library at night to get some devout literature. Another German 'murder' raid on the east coast of England, this time by Zeppelins. About six killed, and of course the airship got away.[15]

Donald was epileptic.
This family gathering seems to be an annual event.
Isa has found a job.
The censor was careful not to give the Germans precise feedback about their raids so newspaper reports were always vague about locations. This incident was the first Zeppelin raid on a British town, and involved two aircraft, L-2 and L-3, which bombed Yarmouth and King's Lynn in Norfolk, killing two people and injuring 16.

Thursday **21**

(21-344)

Extremely Cold day
wet morning
Got my boots soled &
heeled 4/- and a
pair of slippers at 9½d
Agnes not well last
night.

Still
fighting
in this
Cursed
war.

"It is Creditable to keep up
one's spirits."

JANUARY, 1915.

Friday 22

(22-343)

Your name must be registered before any claim can be recognised under the Insurance Coupon.

Nice day but very cold.

Everybody is seeing a "Zeppelin" in the sky now. A Leith boat sunk by a German submarine crew saved.

Essen reported bombarded by air-men.

A Dreadnought

Monday, 25 January

Brilliant naval victory in the North Sea on Sunday, the first fight in history with Dreadnought cruisers. British cruisers the *Lion*, *Princess Royal*, *Tiger*, *Indomitable* and *New Zealand* met a German 'baby killing' fleet on their way to the English coast and attack them. The German 'blighters' turn tail and run. One German cruiser, the *Blücher*, is sunk with about 700 on board, and two get seriously damaged.[16]

Tuesday, 26 January

I put up new ropes on the pulleys and am making the boy a wee stool.[17] Got a note from the factor putting up our rent by a pound in a year. The bleeding 'Hun', the flaming 'blighter'.

Thursday, 28 January

This is the Kaiser's birthday, so 20,000 Germans are sacrificed in honour of it in an endeavour to smash the Allies at La Bassée.[18]

Friday, 29 January

Very nice day. Not out at night. Agnes washed the marble staircase and I loafed about. Bought two new clay pipes and put a new string on the hatchet.

[16] This was the Battle of Dogger Bank, which involved squadrons of the British Grand Fleet and the German High Seas Fleet. The total of deaths on the Blücher was 792.

[17] The kitchen pulley.

[18] La Bassée, a small mining town north of the Vimy Ridge on the Western Front was the site of fierce fighting in early 1915.

Sunday, 31 January

Wet forenoon. Took a walk to town before dinner. Mr Armstrong (upstairs man) was with me with his boy. We went into his shop as he had to wind up all the chronometers. German raid by submarine on west coast of England: three boats sunk.[19] They say they are going to sink all our shipping. Ora pro nobis.

Monday, 1 February

Read the gas meter and duly appalled thereby. We are in for a hard time of it. Dear provisions, rent raised, future uncertain. Oh, help!

Wednesday, 3 February

The factor here today for his rent. As he had the law on his side it was duly paid.

Friday, 5 February

Very nice day, but very cold. Bread is up to 4d a loaf now, but butter is a penny cheaper, making it 1/5. Germany saying fierce things against Britain. We are in for it, so help me bob.

Saturday, 6 February

Rained all day. After tea we all went to the Art Galleries.[20] We got home at 9.30.

Tuesday, 9 February

We got a postcard from Greenlodge asking us to entertain mon père for the evening. This was awkward as we got no time to reply, and we were going out to see Sam and family, so we took him with us. John White had bought a new air gun so we did some shooting to get us in readiness for 'Der Tag'.[21] We managed home at 11.45 p.m. John saw my father home.

Four British merchant vessels off the Lancashire coast, rather close to home for Thomas.
The Glasgow Art Galleries and Museum at Kelvingrove, in the west end of the city.
'The day' when John and Thomas would see active service.

Wednesday, 10 February

Very cold, dirty, wet day. Not out at night. Agnes amusing herself in the wash-house all afternoon. Most bloody bayonet fighting in the eastern part of the war with the Germans and Russians.[22]

Thursday, 11 February

Admiralty warn us that as from tomorrow aeroplanes will be flying over Glasgow for a time and we must not molest them in any way. I won't.

Friday, 12 February

Cold day. Rain and sleet from morn to night. Got a phone message in the forenoon from Ibrox that Agnes' uncle James Henderson, Montrose Street, died last night.[23] Did not see any aeroplanes today.

Saturday, 13 February

Bitter cold day. After dinner we went up Montrose Street and saw Agnes' uncle's funeral leaving. It was a great turnout. We were glad to get home again in order to be thawed. Great British raid by aeroplanes (34) on Belgian coast.[24] German fortified places all bombarded. Our men all got back.

Tuesday, 16 February

I went to Sam's at night and licked him at shooting, just by the way. It's getting near the 18th.[25] I wonder what will really happen

[22] On the Eastern Front that day, the Germans captured Eydtkuhnen (now Chernyshevskoye, Russia) and Wirballen (Lithuania), but were repulsed at Kosziowa (Kozowa, Ukraine).
[23] The phone message was presumably received at Thomas' workplace, and passed on to him.
[24] Some 34 British aeroplanes raided Ostend, Zeebrugge and other Belgian towns on 12 Februar
[25] On 4 February, Kaiser Wilhelm II had declared that Germany would, from 18 February, treat the seas around the British Isles as a war zone, and threatened that all Allied vessels in the area would be sunk without warning.

Wednesday, 17 February

Tommy got his hair cut and got his customary balloon. Great British air raid by 40 machines, assisted by eight French aeroplanes, on German fortifications in Belgium.[26] On and after tomorrow we are as good as dead men; so says the Kaiser.

Thursday, 18 February

This is the day. From now onward, Germany is going to sink every boat that sails in British waters by submarine and mine. Nothing has happened yet, but they torpedoed a British boat yesterday before their time).

Friday, 19 February

This is pay day. Coals are now 1/6 per hundredweight. We are getting alarmed at the high cost of living. Second day of blockade. A French vessel torpedoed but not sunk. Another Zeppelin wrecked.[27] We are going to give Germany a real blockade.

[26] On 16 February, a Franco-British force renewed the aerial attacks on Ostend, Zeebrugge and other towns in Belgium.

[27] The Zeppelin L-4 crash-landed in the North Sea after becoming damaged by a severe snow storm.

FEBRUARY, 1915

Saturday 20

(51-314)

Some heavy rain today
Freezing at night.
We went to Coatbridge
by ~~3.15~~ 3.12 from the Cross.
Daisy Tommy & I out
for a walk. We got
10 56 train back from
Langloan we got home
at 11.55 pm Hard frost.

A Norwegian boat torpedoed
by the German Pirates.
This is the "blockade"
A Cardiff Steamer torpedoed
in Irish channel 4 drowned.

FEBRUARY, 1915.

1st in Lent.
Quadragesima.

Sunday **21**
(52-313)

Some heavy rain today after dinner I took a walk to Town to see how many more boats were sunk. no more

Allied Fleet bombards the "Dardenelles"

Monday, 22 February
Took Agnes and Tommy to the Cinerama at night. Another boat sunk by German submarine. American boat blown up by German mine. Norwegian boat torpedoed by German submarine.

Tuesday, 23 February
Coal up to 1/8 a bag today. Bread 3¾ pence.

Thursday, 25 February
Very nice day. Germans sink a few more of our boats with their submarines.[28] *We make an air raid on Ostend and kill a few German sojers.*

Friday, 26 February
Engineers' strike getting serious.[29] *It should please the Germans. Still raining.*

Saturday, 27 February
Heavy snow night and morning. Ground white at night. Went to the library in the afternoon for some religious literature. Agnes and Tommy did not venture out. Government interferes in the engineers' strike: they must work.

[28] Seven British merchant ships were sunk by submarines in first week of the blockade.
[29] In the west of Scotland, around 10,000 engineering workers took unofficial strike action to demand higher wages to match the increase in prices in which the war had resulted. The dispute lasted three weeks, and did not result in an increase in wages.

Tuesday, 2 March

Agnes having a day in the wash-house and is knocked-up by night time. Britain has declared a real blockade on Germany.[30] No supplies of any kind are to be permitted.

Wednesday, 3 March

Went to Gas Works in the morning and carried home half a hundredweight of 'coke' (cost 4d). It really weighed about 10 hundredweight. Never again. I'll have 2d worth next time. The engineers strike is over now. They are going to be patriots.

Thursday, 4 March

My leg is strained with carrying the half ton of coke for 100 miles.[31]

Friday, 5 March

Dirty wet wild stormy day. Coals are 1/7 per hundredweight. I'll need to get more coke.[32] German submarine sunk off Dover by British destroyer.[33]

Saturday, 6 March

Very nice spring-like day. Went out in the morning for two pennyworth of coke. A big march-out of all the soldiers in Glasgow in the afternoon, so I took Agnes and Tommy to see them.

---

[30] On 1 March, Britain and France imposed a blockade on all shipping heading to enemy ports.
[31] The local gas works were in Pollokshields, about half a mile away.
[32] While coke was less than half the price of coal, it gave only a small fraction of the heat.
[33] The German submarine U8 was sunk by British destroyers in the English Channel on 4 March, and its crew taken prisoner.

Tuesday, 9 March

Cold day. Out for 2d of coke in the morning.[34] Carried it home on my head so I have now a stiff neck. The German pirates sink a boat near Ilfracombe.

Wednesday, 10 March

Out for 2d of coke in the morning. The boss intimated a small rise in my salary today. Bought a small saw.

Thursday, 11 March

Feeling strong now so got 3d of coke this morning (42 pounds). Tommy got a new pair of boots (4/6). I bought three collars and Agnes squared off the doctor. Every second gas lamppost is lit at night in Glasgow, scarce of coal in gasworks.

Friday, 12 March

Took my usual early morning walk to the place where they make coke and carried home three stone. French progress in Champagne. 10,000 Germans killed.

Opposite page Fingal, *owned by the London and Edinburgh Shipping Company, was torpedoed by submarine U23 off the Northumbrian coast, on 15 March.*

[34] Thomas has been collecting coke before work, which he starts at 8 a.m.

Coke 3

MARCH, 1915.

Tuesday 16

(75-290)

Nice summery sort of day. Tommy still got the cold & Agnes got a sore head. Agnes washed the stairs at night.

Glasgow Boat "Fingal" torpedoed by German submarine on East Coast.

The anchor liner "Cameronia" chased by submarine.

MARCH, 1915. Coke 3

St. Patrick's Day.

Wednesday 17

(76-289)

Cold dull day

Agnes amusing herself in the washing house in the afternoon and night.

This is St. Pat's Day. German submarine reported as beeing seen near Lamlash, Arran

Sunday, 21 March
Took a walk through Queen's Park and on to Pollok Estate. The German pirates' bag for the week is 11 ships (eight sunk and three reached port).

Monday, 22 March
Italy on the verge of war. The place with the fancy name (Przemysl) at last falls to the Russians.[35]

Wednesday, 24 March
Allied troops landed at Gallipoli (Dardanelles). Russians get chased out of Memel (Prussia). Austrian army of 119,000 taken prisoners at the fall of Przemysl.

Troops landing at Anzac Cove in the Dardanelles.

Thursday, 25 March
Very cold day. Agnes very ill at night. She had a sore back, neuralgia and a cold in the head. I had a bad headache all day and night. Altogether we spent a very pleasant evening. The Allied fleet has resumed shooting practice in the Dardanelles.

Tuesday, 30 March
Two female conductors started as an experiment on the Glasgow tramways.[36] Lloyd George is thinking of shutting all the pubs.[37]

---

35 The Siege of Przemysl, which ended on 22 March 1915, was a crushing defeat for the Austro-Hungarian Empire. The town is now in Poland.
36 The manpower shortage led to women working in munitions factories and on the trams.
37 David Lloyd George, the Chancellor of the Exchequer, was greatly concerned about the effects of alcohol on the war effort. In January 1915, he stated that Britain was 'fighting Germans, Austrians and drink, and as far as I can see the greatest of these foes is drink'.

Wednesday, 31 March

Two liners sunk by the German pirates. One of them, the *Flaminian*, bound for South Africa, contained £200 of cotton duck, shipped by my firm.[38] Curse the pirates.

Thursday, 1 April

To encourage his loyal subjects, King George has sworn off the bottle.[39] To encourage King George I will do the same. 'God save the King.'

Friday, 2 April

Sorted the blind so that it wouldn't fall down again on this earth. Tommy took a sleep in the afternoon, so Agnes says he will be after taking the measles.[40]

Saturday, 3 April

I went out to my tailor in the afternoon and got my new 'breeks' and renovated jacket (19/-).[41] Came back in the car with Nellie Shearer, an old Ruglen friend of mine. We went (the wife, wean and I) to the 9 p.m. house of the Majestic and were duly entertained for the sum of 18 pence. We got a postcard from Hetty giving us permission to visit them on Monday.

Opposite page *The seaside location and the 'Kilmu' sign suggests Kilmun, a coastal village on the north side of Holy Loch, near Dunoon, easily reachable by steamer from Glasgow.*

[38] The *Flaminian*, owned by the Ellerman and Papayanni Line, was shelled and sunk by submarine U28 about 50 miles off the Scilly Isles.

[39] Lloyd George's campaign against alcohol included persuading national figures to pledge that they would not drink alcohol until the war was over. King George V supported the campaign by promising that no alcohol would drunk in the Royal household while Britain was at war.

[40] A folk belief.

[41] Breeks is a lowland Scots term for trousers, derived from Scots Gaelic.

APRIL, 1915.

Easter Monday. **Monday 5**
(95-270)

Very heavy rain in the forenoon. this is a holiday so we took 2.22 train from the Cross for Coatbridge & came back by 10.20. Caledonian. Twas 10 years ago we met, ah me, ah us.

1905.

APRIL, 1915.

Tuesday 6

(96-269)

Wet sort of day.
Nothing to report.
Tommy seems all right again.

Russians sweeping all before them in the Carpathian mountains

Turkish Warship sunk by a mine

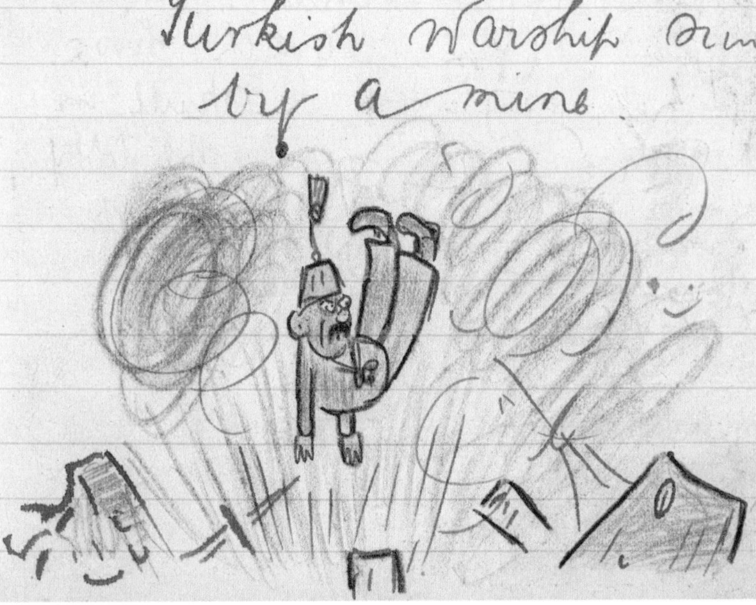

1915

Thursday, 8 April

Germans chucked over the Yser by the Belgians.[42] German armed liner interned in Newport (USA).

Friday, 9 April

Got a phone message today from Hamilton from James Bell, an old office boy of mine, to say he was back from the war. Had been a prisoner in Germany and had been exchanged and was minus a leg. He is a sergeant in the Gordons. His day of the war is over.[43]

Sunday, 11 April

Stayed in all day except in the morning, when Tommy and I went out for a paper and at night I went out for another.

Monday, 12 April

Colder sort of day. Tommy out for a message today for the first time 'all by hissel'.[44] Rumour going about of a naval battle in the North Sea. British casualties to date 139,347.

Tuesday, 13 April

Great explosion at Lerwick, a street destroyed and several persons killed.[45] No particulars can be got. Very mysterious.

---

[42] This setback for the Germans occurred during the Second Battle of the Yser, part of the fight to extend the Western Front to the North Sea. [43] An operator likely took all phone calls to Thomas' place of work and passed on the messages to various people, rather than allowing individual phone conversations. There may have been just one phone. [44] 'All by himself'.

[45] On 12 April there was an explosion in a former fishing net store in Lerwick, which was being used to store naval munitions. Five people were killed, and 22 injured. The store was destroyed, and the quay beneath it was greatly damaged.

Wednesday, 14 April

A big fire at Eglinton Toll in some grain place or brewery, so we all went along and admired it. Agnes did some whitewashing today. Five persons killed in Lerwick explosion, Government stores on fire, gun cotton etc.

Thursday, 15 April

Zeppelin raid on east coast of England last night (Tyneside). One man slightly hurt. Scottish steamer torpedoed by the pirates.[46] 11 drowned.

Friday, 16 April

Ruglen's MP has been killed at the front.[47]

Saturday, 17 April

I went to the library in the afternoon. We went to the Majestic first house at night.

Sunday, 18 April

I went to church today. Communion.[48]

[46] The 'pirates' are the German U-boats and other vessels that target civilian ships.

[47] William Glynne Charles Gladstone, the grandson of the Liberal Prime Minister, was Liberal MP for the Kilmarnock Burghs (which included Rutherglen) from 1911 until he was killed in action on 12 April 1915. He was a lieutenant in the Royal Welch Fusiliers.

[48] This is Thomas' first visit to church in 1915. The Lord's Supper or Communion (Eucharist) is usually celebrated four times a year in Scottish churches.

₹eligion and belief

'homas was a Presbyterian from a religious ackground in the north of Ireland. Whichever hurch his father belonged to in Ireland had no xact equivalent in Scotland and various nembers of his family joined different eformed' groups. Thomas himself joined the Inited Free Church of Scotland, but all the rganisations patronised by members of his amily have one thing in common: they derived om the reformed Church of Scotland stablished by John Knox after the Scottish eformation in 1650.

At the Scottish Reformation, Knox and his ipporters declared that the new reformed nurch should not celebrate the religious stivals of the Catholic Church, such as hristmas, Easter and Whitsun (or Pentecost). 'homas sounds lukewarm about all of these ays, and has little time for the elders and other nurch representatives who came to his door eking donations. Thomas and his family also sit other churches, perhaps because the style of orship is closer to what they would have kperienced if the family had remained in the orth of Ireland. Thomas was the only one of his blings to have been born in Scotland, and erhaps the kirk did not provide the family with ie Presbyterian punch they may have enjoyed Lurgan.

The spirit of the Scottish Reformation was ill strong in some communities. The author J. J. ell, who was brought up in the west end of lasgow in the closing years of the nineteenth ntury, recalled:

> Christmas meant nothing to the working people, unless as a reminder of the approach of the New Year. To many middle-class people it was still a matter almost for resentment, since they regarded it as just one more Anglified innovation. There were middle-class homes like my own, in which, as Christmas drew near, the house became - amiably withal - divided against itself. My father's people, with their old-fashioned ideas and prejudices, did not 'hold with' Christmas; my mother's people, with their new notions and prepossessions, were all for it.
>
> J. J. Bell, *I Remember*
> (Edinburgh: Porpoise Press, 1932).

Thomas found a spiritual home in the United Free Church of Scotland, and he was a member of its branch in the centre of Glasgow, the United Free Tron Church, at 76 Dundas Street, north of Cathedral Street (the site now vanished beneath the Buchanan Galleries shopping centre). The U.F. Church was a Scottish Presbyterian organisation formed in 1900 from the union of the United Presbyterian Church of Scotland (founded in 1847) and the majority of ministers and parishioners of the Free Church of Scotland (founded in 1843). The U.F. Church, which was the second-largest Presbyterian denomination in Scotland, united with the larger Church of Scotland in 1929. The religious orientation of the U.F. Church was Presbyterian, Evangelical and Calvinist, although it accepted the findings of modern science and so-called 'higher criticism' of the Bible.

Thomas was careful to attend church on the four Sundays a year that communion is celebrated. These dates varied across the country, but Thomas went on the second Sunday of January, April, July and October of each year. On other days, however, he found a walk through Queen's Park to be a suitable substitute for collective worship. His celebration of Easter, surely the most important festival in the Christian calendar, was limited to eating a hot cross bun on Easter Friday and having two eggs for breakfast on Easter Sunday. Like most Scots Presbyterians, he barely acknowledged Christmas and, like most of his contemporaries, was at work from 8 a.m. to about 1 p.m. on the day itself. He had two days off for New Year, reflecting the greater cultural importance that was attached to that festival in Scotland.

Politically, Thomas was against Socialism and Communism, and attended a Labour meeting just before the general election in 1918. He was willing to listen to the anti-government and anti-war speeches made in Jail Square, even though he disagreed strongly with them. He was also a voracious reader, and surely was open-minded enough to read books that did not accord closely with his own beliefs. He was a strong supporter of the war and of punishing Germany for its 'piracy' on the North Sea and elsewhere, but he has some doubts about serving his country. Perhaps for the sake of his wife and child, he was reluctant to join up, though when he did volunteer he was proud to wear the armband that showed he had done so. As the war progressed, and he was again found unfit by the army medical examiners, the diaries betray no sign that Thomas faced any hostility in his family, at work or on the street as a seemingly able-bodied man who was not yet in uniform. Some conscientious objectors were sent white feathers or bullets in the post, and faced obloquy in public.

Thomas' social religious background would suggest that he was a supporter of the temperance movement, which campaigned to reduce the amount of alcohol consumed by society, and whose followers were either total abstainers (who pledged to drink no alcohol, except as medicine) or believers in temperance who drank beer and wine but not spirits. Thomas rarely mentions alcohol, except when he visits a hotel and has 'a glass of milk'. Like Thomas' mention of the 'religious literature' that he habitually borrows from the library, the reference is likely tongue in cheek, and he was probably drinking something stronger. He also occasionally buys a bottle of whisky to treat colds that have resisted olive oil and other folk remedies, an indulgence that could perhaps be justified as a medicine. Thomas was godly, but not, one suspects, as godly as he makes out in his diary.

It seems that Paterson and Baxter were going through hard times in early 1933 and Thomas' salary decreased to £1 a week. This affected where he sat in church. In his entry for 22 April 1933, Thomas quotes 'Agnes went to the kirk at night and booked three sittings for the next six months. We have changed over to cheaper seat as we are no longer wealthy'.

1915

'hursday, 22 April

rang up Eddie Campbell in the forenoon and arranged a ıeeting with him and Agnes for the afternoon. She saw him all ight and met me at 5.30 and we all went home together.[49]

aturday, 24 April

ierman success in Flanders. They use bombs with poisonous ımes, and Allies are forced back.[50] British lose four big guns.

unday, 25 April

iermans driven back again in Flanders. The Canadians save ıe day, and recapture our lost guns.

londay, 26 April

'ine day, but a little colder. We have put Tommy on Scott's ,mulsion.

'uesday, 27 April

Ve had the man who sweeps lums in, and he did his duty for 1/6. ierce fighting in Flanders. British hold back German onslaught.

Vednesday, 28 April

'ommy got a very bad cough. Will likely be the whooping cough. Ve are also looking at the mumps. British take the offensive in elgium. Land fighting has started in the Dardanelles.

'hursday, 29 April

Ve got word from the 'busy' one that we would be 'hitewashed at 6.30 a.m. [tomorrow].[51] We removed our all to ıe room and lit a fire there, and slept there. We got to bed ımorrow morning.

Eddie Campbell was highly likely to have been Agnes' cousin Edward.

This was the first time that the German army used chlorine gas. It was deployed against the French army at Ypres.

The 'busy' one was presumably Daniel McCort, who had previously whitewashed the house.

Friday, 30 April

The 'busy' man came at 7.45 a.m. and was away at 8.15 a.m. Prodigious. We got off for 24 pennies. Agnes spent the rest of the day flitting back to the kitchen and washing up. I cleaned the clock at night, and hung it up.

Saturday, 1 May

Was out at Ruglen in afternoon and got a bath.[52]

Monday, 3 May

Agnes washing blankets etc. in the washing house today. Agnes ironing all night. German aeroplane over Dover. It gets chased.

Wednesday, 5 May

Agnes put up the curtains over the bed in the morning. We went to the painters in the afternoon to see about our new wallpaper. German submarine sinks nine British trawlers. The pirates are very busy now. They have threatened to sink the *Lusitania*. She is on her way over from America. We shall see.

Thursday, 6 May

Germans by the aid of poisonous bombs gain a foothold on 'Hill 60'.[53]

[52] Thomas' Rutherglen relatives appear to have had a bathroom with a fixed bath, rather than the tin bath that the Livingstones had at home.

[53] Hill 60 was a ridge near Ypres that was keenly fought for at various points.

Friday, 7 May

*Very warm, dull day.
We dismantled the room at night, getting ready for the men who stick wallpaper up. Bills stuck up all over the town telling us what to do when the 'Huns' drop bombs on us.*

aturday, 8 May

Germany's most accursed act committed yesterday. The *Lusitania*, he world's finest steamer, torpedoed and sunk without warning off the south coast of Ireland. 751 saved. 1,208 lives lost.[54]

unday, 9 May

Very bright, sunny day, but cold, windy and dusty. went to Queen's Park before breakfast and took a walk into town after dinner. Came home in the car nd a female conductor punched my ticket. Agnes very ill all day. The cursed spring leaning has done her no good and I'm etting worried about her health. Great joy n Germany about the *Lusitania*. America rying to feel angry, as there were American itizens on board.

uesday, 11 May

Pouring wet day. We dismantled the room entirely tonight. Agnes a little better. A friend of Agnes from Edinburgh, Sarah Miller, here today. Riots in Canada over the *Lusitania* murder. Germans shoot British prisoners.

The *Lusitania*, the largest passenger vessel on transatlantic service, left New York Harbor for Liverpool on 1 May 1915. On 7 May, the submarine U20 the torpedoed the liner, which rolled over and sank in 18 minutes. A total of 785 passengers and 413 crew died, including 128 American citizens.

Wednesday, 12 May

Bitter cold day. Poor Wee Tommy sick and vomiting all day. The room ceiling whitewashed today. Bread 4d, butter 1/6 now. Great anti-German riots all over the country. The Germans have now threatened to sink the Cunard liner *Transylvania*, which left New York last Saturday.

Thursday, 13 May

Very cold day. Painters in today and varnished the room. Tommy very ill today, so got the doctor at night. His temperature is 101°. Doctor does not know yet what ails him and leaves us with gloomy forebodings.

Friday, 14 May

Tommy still very ill. Doctor up again. His temperature the same. Doctor can't tell us anything yet. Poor wee man. The house is so quiet now. Got rid of the painters. They stuck on the wallpaper and went away. Government throws out some hints about 'conscription'.

Saturday, 15 May

Very nice day. Doctor up again. Tommy's heat down to 99°. Doctor thinks there is nothing wrong with him. I went to Govanhill Library in afternoon. Allies doing well in the west.

Sunday, 16 May

The medical man up again. Says Tommy is all right now. Just to keep him in bed for a day or two and feed him on milk. Tommy at the very cross stage. I was at Queen's Park and Pollok Estate in afternoon admiring all the girls. Revolution in Portugal. Murder! Police!! Au succours [sic]!!![55]

[55] 'Au secours!' is French for 'Help!'

Ionday, 17 May

'ommy keeping better now. He got a little bread to eat today. cut up rhubarb at night. We are going to make a little jam. ;reat British victory north of La Bassée.[56] German lines broken. 'he *Transylvania* arrived safely in port. The King in Glasgow ›day (incognito) speeding the workers.

'uesday, 18 May

.itchener wants another Army of 300,000.[57] King reviews ›ldiers in Glasgow Green today.

aturday, 22 May

'errible train smash at Gretna. Three trains smashed up, one of ıem a troop train. The most awful disaster that has ever appened in Britain. 169 lives lost, mostly soldiers.

unday, 23 May

aly declares war on Austria and thus on Germany. We have ow at war: Britain, France, Russia, Belgium, Italy, Serbia and Iontenegro against Germany, Austria and Turkey. When was ıere such a war?

The Quintinshill rail crash near Gretna on 22 May killed at least 227 people and injured 246, most of them soldiers. The tragedy occurred when a signalman allowed a local train onto the main southbound line, where it was struck by a troop train carrying 500 soldiers of the 7th Battalion of the Royal Scots to the Western Front. This led to a four-train collision also involving two coal trains sitting in sidings on either side of the main tracks. An express train to Glasgow ploughed into the wreckage shortly after. The disaster was compounded when the gas lighting in the trains set the wooden carriages and the coal wagons on fire. It was impossible to record the precise number of fatalities because the roll of the regiment was destroyed in the fire. The disaster remains the worst loss of life in any railway accident in the United Kingdom.

The great victory was part of the Battle of Festubert, on the Western Front.
.ord Kitchener, almost alone among his Cabinet colleagues, saw the war lasting years rather :han months, and was determined to enlist a large army.

Monday, 24 May

Heat wave continues. Agnes took Tommy to see the doctor today. He is to be put on malt.[58] Daisy and Hetty here. I took Daisy out at night the length of Burnside. We spoke to Ian Lamont and we saw a monoplane up above us. It was a fine spectacle. We saw them away by 10.10 from the Cross.[59]

Wednesday, 26 May

Much cooler. Hetty here in the afternoon, so Agnes, Hetty and boy out at the auction sale in West Nile Street to see the 'picture'.[60] The pirates have sunk an American steamer.

Thursday, 27 May

Agnes got toothache all day, and threatens suicide. Tommy gurgling with the cold. King of Italy takes command of his army

Friday, 28 May

Fine day. We went out at night and beat the carpet.

Tuesday, 1 June

Very wet forenoon. Took the office boy over Cathkin at night.[61] *We looked for aeroplanes and saw none. Zeppelin raid on London, six killed.*

Wednesday, 2 June

The price of bread is being reduced in Berlin and is going up in Glasgow. How's this?

[58] Malt extract was regarded as a nutritious food supplement.
[59] Daisy was one of the Crozier girls, possibly Margaret Crozier, the daughter of Robert and Agne
[60] Evidently there was a painting worth seeing on auction that week.
[61] This is possibly Andrew Hamilton, whom Thomas keeps in touch with after he leaves his position as office boy.

Friday, 4 June

Nice warm day. My birthday so I bought a straw hat. Cut up rhubarb at night.

Tuesday, 8 June

Fine day. Father here. I saw him home at night. Prime Minister says there is to be no conscription. Total British casualties to end of May: quarter of a million.

Wednesday, 9 June

Nice day. Went to the library at night and listened for a little while to band in the wee park. Austrian air raid in Venice. Great progress in the Dardanelles. America and Germany getting pretty near war.

Thursday, 10 June

On this date five years ago I got spliced. Agnes washed her head tonight. Indeed she did. Another Zeppelin destroyed by British airmen. More French successes.

Sunday, 13 June

Very windy day. Took a walk to the docks and was pleased to see that the Germans had left us a few boats.

Thursday, 17 June

My holidays begin now. Cold, dull morning. Went out in the morning and engaged a cab to take us to the Broomielaw.[62] We met Hetty at the corner of Jamaica Street then we boarded the Eagle 111. Sailed at 11 a.m. We had tea on board and arrived at Rothesay 2.15 p.m. Very nice weather at evening.

Friday, 18 June

Fine weather today. Took Tommy out in forenoon. We dig sand and sail his wee boat. After dinner we go by Ardbeg and at night through the Meadows.[63] British submarine sinks three transports and three gunboats in the Dardanelles.

Monday, 21 June

Another perfect day. Tommy got a new pail from Hetty. We all went to Ettrick Bay today.[64]

Friday, 25 June

Shetland fishing fleet of 17 boats sunk by German submarines.[65] We want shells and machine guns.

Monday, 28 June

After tea I went to the band performance and Agnes and Tommy went to Port Bannatyne. I met them afterwards on the Esplanade. We had 'chips' at night. Very nice weather today. British navy to be increased to 300,000 men.

---

[62] The Broomielaw is a street in central Glasgow running along the north bank of the Clyde.
[63] The Meadows, a large public park, is to the landward side of the town.
[64] Ettrick Bay, a popular tourist spot, is on the other side of Bute from Rothesay.
[65] Two German submarines destroyed practically all the Lerwick fishing fleet.

Tuesday, 29 June
Lovely day, so we hied us to Ettrick Bay and basked in the sunshine. Tommy got a ride on a 'cuddy'. We went to the 'pictures' at night.[66]

Wednesday, 30 June
After dinner we boarded the good ship *Isle of Arran*, 2.30 p.m. bound for Glasgow. Cold, wet voyage. We arrived [in] Broomielaw, but couldn't get a cab, so we left a bag in the left luggage and took car home like ordinary people. Got home 7.15 p.m. I went out at night for the bag. And so ends our holiday. Amen.

Thursday, 1 July
Very nice day. Started my work today just as usual. Andrew gets married tomorrow so we had a little 'affair' at 6 p.m.

Friday, 2 July
Very warm day and showery. Took Tommy to Queen's Park at night. British destroyer Lightning damaged on east coast by mine or torpedo.[67] One man killed and 14 missing. Pirates very busy just now sinking ships.

Saturday, 3 July
Warm day. We all went to Pollok Estate in the afternoon, and let on we were at Rothesay.[68] Sea fighting in the Baltic. German mine layer sunk.

---

66 A 'cuddy' is a Scots term for a horse or donkey. The 'pictures' was the cinema.
67 The *Lightning* struck a mine in the southern North Sea, off the Thames Estuary. The minefield had been laid by a German U-boat.
68 'Let on' means pretended.

Sunday 4 July

Brilliant day. I went to church in the forenoon.[69] We went to Queen's Park in the afternoon. Maxwell here at night. He is a 'sojer' now. I saw him off. German battleship sunk by British submarine in the Baltic.

Wednesday, 7 July

Agnes got a letter from Girvan inviting her and Tommy down for a week.[70]

TO PARIS.
Germans going to make another try for Paris

Thursday, 8 July

Pa here. Saw him home and went up as Donald was ill. Mrs Cormack and family here in the afternoon. Showery day.

Friday, 9 July

Dull and much colder. Agnes busy getting ready for Girvan. I made jam at night.

Saturday, 10 July

Saw Agnes and Tommy away by the 12.30 train to Girvan. Went out to Ruglen, and had tea at 200 Main Street. Took a walk out to Sam's shop afterwards. Surrender of entire German forces in German South West Africa to General Botha.[71]

Sunday, 11 July

Very stormy day and cold and some showers. I went out to Ruglen by Cathcart and 100 Acre Dyke, dined with Sam, then Sam, Nellie and I went to Cathkin and then we had tea. Sam and I went up to see Donald. I got back to Morgan Street at 10.30 p.m.

[69] Presumably for the second quarterly communion service.
[70] Possible relatives of Agnes who lived in Girvan, Ayrshire.
[72] Louis Botha, Prime Minister of the Union of South Africa, took the side of the British during the First World War, which was not universally welcomed by his countrymen.

Monday, 12 July

'm missing Agnes and the wee man. Got no word from them et, so I'll write tonight. Kitchener and the Prime Minister visit our army in France and Belgium.

Tuesday, 13 July

got a postcard from Agnes and was relieved in mind thereby. Went up to Andrew's for my tea and spent the evening there.

Wednesday, 14 July

Got a postcard from Agnes. She comes home tomorrow.

Thursday, 15 July

I rose at 5 a.m., washed the floors, cleaned the range and lusted up generally. Went to St Enoch's Station and met my well-beloved at 7.33 p.m. from Girvan. She looked well, likewise the boy, although he had a cold. Spent the rest of the evening looking at them. Cara Sposa.[72]

Friday, 16 July

This is Fair Friday, so I left my work at 2 p.m.[73] Mr Gordon dropped up for a little in the afternoon. He is working in Polmadie this weekend.[74] We all went to the pictures at night.

Saturday, 17 July

went over to Greenlodge before dinner to see how Donald was keeping. He is still in bed, but improving. After dinner, I went over to the British Oxygen Company, where Mr Gordon is working and had a look around it. Mr Gordon says they are making poison gas for the front.[75] Tommy still snuffling. Agnes got a sore head. TCL quite well.

Italian phrase meaning 'dear wife' is also the title of a choral work by George Frideric Handel.
The annual Glasgow Fair holidays.
Polmadie is a district of Glasgow south of the River Clyde, adjacent to the Gorbals.
The British first used poison gas at the Battle of Loos on 25 September 1915.

By 1915, both the Central Powers and the Allies were producing deadly chemical weapons, regardless of their legality. From that year, they both used phosgene (known to Allied troops as 'White Star'), which was deadlier than chlorine, and from 1917 mustard gas (known as 'H.S.', short for 'Hun Stuff'). Mustard gas produces large, painful blisters on the skin and internal bleeding. Those affected take four to six weeks to die, often in great pain. By the end of the war, public opinion was against chemical weapons and most of the countries involved in the Great War signed the Geneva Protocol, which banned the use of lethal gas and bacteriological weapons, in 1925.

Sunday, 18 July

Great coal strike in Wales.[76]

Monday, 19 July

Our lady car conductors have now got tartan skirts.

Tuesday, 20 July

The war is costing Britain £3,000,000 a day now.

[76] The miners demanded better wages. The government made striking a criminal offence, but the strike went ahead, from 15 July. Lloyd George visited the coalfields on 19 July and, after concessions were made by the government, the strikers returned to work on 21 July.

Vednesday, 21 July

ermans closing in on Warsaw. Allies steadily advancing in the)ardanelles. Russia sinks about 70 sailing boats of Turkey in the 3lack Sea. Welsh coal strike settled.

Thursday, 22 July

Ve went to Greenlodge at night. Donald keeping better, but ook a bad fit at the tea table. We got home at 11.30 p.m. It is stimated that 5,000,000 men have been killed in this war so far, nd 7,000,000 wounded. O tempora! O mores![77]

Thursday, 29 July

Our lady conductors have now got green straw hats.

British regain trench they lost.

aturday, 31 July

'ery nice day. We went out to Ruglen in the fternoon. Watched them playing at bowls nd then had a seat in the Overtoun Park. gnes not keeping well, at all.

Vednesday, 4 August

This is the anniversary of the war, the devil's irthday, so to speak.[78]

riday, 6 August

aid my house insurance today.) let it burn.

The "Allies."

What times! What customs!' Coined by the orator Cicero.
The flags represent - from left to right - the British Empire, France, Belgium, Russia, Italy, Montenegro, Serbia and Japan.

Sunday, 8 August

After dinner, just as we were going out, Nannie Gordon came in so we all went out. We went to Queen's Park and by the River Cart to Cathcart and home by car. After tea we sat in and sang the 'Hymns of Sankey' and others.[79] Agnes saw Nannie away about 9 p.m.

Monday, 9 August

This is Tommy's birthday (he is four years old now) so we went to the pictures at night. We got our National Registration Papers today, one for Agnes and one for myself.[80]

Thursday, 12 August

Glasgow now has over 700 lady car conductors.

Sunday, 15 August

Agnes very ill all day. We went to Queen's Park in the afternoon and on our return she collapsed, all out, dead beat, up the pole. In accordance with the law, we filled in our National Registration Papers. After that, my name will go on the 'pink form', after that the military will commandeer me, after that I'll go to the front, and after that I'll be killed I suppose. We are living in great times.

Monday, 16 August

Took the boy out for a walk at night. Fitted up a swing for Tommy. Allied fleet bombard the Smyrna Coast.

[79] Ira David Sankey (1840-1908) was an American Evangelical hymn writer and Gospel singer.
[80] The National Registration system centrally recorded all civilians and issued them with Certificates of Registration, their 'papers'.

Tuesday, 17 August

Agnes in the wash-house afternoon and night. Train smash at Pollokshaws: one killed and 20 injured. German submarine bombards towns on Solway Firth. Nobody hurt.

Wednesday, 18 August

Agnes finished her washing in the forenoon, and ironed for the rest of the day, and does not feel well at night.

British gain about about 500 yards in Gallipoli

Thursday, 19 August

This is pay day and my wages are advanced £15 per annum. Agnes paid Dr Gardiner's bill (9/-) today.

Monday, 23 August

The pubs start on short time today, by order of the government.[81]

Wednesday, 25 August

At night we went round by the Hangingshaws and home by Mount Florida. We saw a chip shop there. The woman tempted me and I fell. They were very nice to our supper at night.

Saturday, 28 August

Daisy here about 3 p.m., and we all went out for a walk. Soaking rain came on, so we took car back from Mount Florida. We sat in and had music. I bought Tommy a mouth organ (made in Germany).

---

[81] The Defence of the Realm Act 1914 restricted pub opening times in Scotland to 11 a.m. to 2.30 p.m. and 5 p.m. to 10 p.m., Monday to Saturday only. These hours were not repealed until 1976.

Sunday, 29 August
Agnes thinks she will consult her doctor as she is not up to the mark. We went out to Sam's. Got there at 5 p.m. and then we all went to the cemetery, where poor Lily lies sleeping, and back by the Blairbeth Road. Six German airmen attempt an air raid on Paris. Five German airmen got home again.

Monday, 30 August
Agnes made rhubarb jam today. I sorted out the pantry and put the pram past.[82] Its day is evidently over (nous verrons).[83]

Tuesday, 31 August
Agnes and I got our Certificate of Registration to certify that we have been registered under the National Registration Act 1915. Our King and Country need us. God save the King.

Thursday, 2 September
Germany promises America to warn liners before sinking them.

Friday 3, September
Very nice day. Agnes and Tommy out at night to see opening of a new school.[84] They got home at 10 p.m.

Sunday, 5 September
Allan Liner Hesperian sunk without warning in south of Ireland by German submarine.[85] *Crew and passengers saved.*

Monday, 6 September
The Czar says 'we will fight to a finish'.

[82] To put something past is, in Scottish idiom, to put it to one side.
[83] The French phrase 'nous verrons' means 'we will see'. Thomas is not prepared to entirely discount the possibility of another child.
[84] Presumably Victoria Primary School in Batson Street, Govanhill, which Tommy attended.
[85] The *Hesperian*, which was built on the Clyde in 1907 for the Allan Line, was torpedoed off Fastnet by the German submarine U20, which sank the *Lusitania*. There were 32 deaths.

Tuesday, 7 September

Very wet day, and close. Called in at McGavigan's today to see if I could get Duncan a job.[86]

Wednesday, 8 September

Very hot day. Went into McGavigan's today but it was NBG.[87] We all took a walk to Mount Florida at night and car home again. Ellerman liner sunk by the pirates.

Thursday, 9 September

Zeppelins bombard London: 20 deaths.

Friday, 10 September

The heatwave continues. Donned my straw hat again. Agnes and Tommy in at Coopers in the afternoon.[88] They were speaking to the female Hendersons of Montrose Street. A spy executed today in London.

Monday, 13 September

Agnes and Tommy at Sighthill Cemetery in afternoon. Made Tommy a wooden sword. Another Zeppelin raid on east coast. No damage.

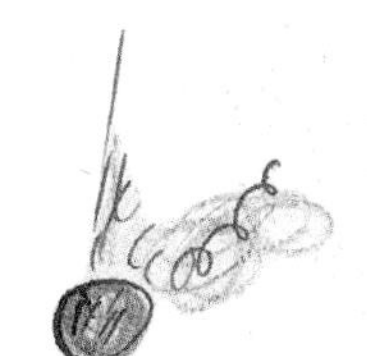

Tuesday, 14 September

I ate mackerel today for dinner. Quoth the raven: 'Never more.'[89] British casualties for a year of war: 75,957 killed, 251,059 wounded, 54,966 missing. Total 381,982.

---

86 McGavigan's was a firm of printers and stationers. Duncan, Thomas' brother, was a signwriter/printer.
87 No bloody good.
88 This may have been one of the Cooper and Co. grocery stores, established by Thomas Bishop (1845-1923) in 1871 and named for his mother-in-law.
89 The choice of fish is obviously being curtailed by German naval activity. The literary reference is to Edgar Allan Poe's poem 'The Raven', published in 1845.

"YOUR COUNTRY NEEDS
YOU"
Nº 0206
DAVID ALLEN & SONS Lᵀᴰ
HARROW
LONDON

Thursday, 16 September

Kitchener wants more men. Seems as if conscription is coming now. War is now costing £3,500,000 a day. Our army and navy is 3,000,000 men. We have an army of 600,000 making munitions of war.

Friday, 17 September

Another German spy executed in London.

Saturday, 18 September

Dirty wet day. Took a walk out to Ruglen and gave my tailor his war bonus. Called in at 200 Main Street and had a crack[90] with Uncle Willie. This is Belgian flag day.

Wednesday, 22 September

Agnes went and consulted her doctor, and got a very bad report as to her general health. She got a bottle and has to go back when it is finished.

Friday, 24 September

We sorted the bed in the room, as Hetty is coming for a few days.

[90] A crack (or 'craic') is a conversation. This is one of the few times that Thomas uses an Irish rather than a Scottish colloquialism.

Saturday, 16 October

Very foggy all day. Got a new rope and attached it to the kitchen ceiling. We all took a walk through Queen's Park in the afternoon. British losses in the Dardanelles up to 9 October: 126,020.

Sunday, 17 October

Very nice day. Nannie Gordon here at 10.30 a.m. to let Agnes and I go to church (communion). After dinner we all took a walk by the Hangingshaws. Agnes saw Nannie away at 7.30 p.m. Allies declare a blockade on Bulgarian coast.

Wednesday, 20 October

It looks as if I'll need to be a 'sojer'.

Thursday, 21 October

Fine day. Agnes went over to see the doctor at night. His report gives me a little more hope. We got a note from the factor increasing the rent 2/- in the quarter. 'Strafe' the factor. I went over to Greenlodge myself at night. Duncan has got a job in Glasgow.

Thursday, 7 October

Agnes at doctor again tonight for medical advice. She required a lot more rest.

Friday, 8 October

Pouring wet day. Agnes bought a new teapot today. Serbia invaded by Austro-German army. Greece to remain neutral.

Sunday, 10 October

Agnes very ill during night. Nerves up the pole and very hysterical. British advance about 1,000 yards in France.

Tuesday, 12 October

Put on my Sunday best and went to see Andrew and his wife at night. Bulgaria attacks Serbia. Great Britain declares war on Bulgaria.

Wednesday, 13 October

Bulgaria declares war on Serbia.

Thursday, 14 October

Smoothed the legs of the table with a file. Zeppelin raid on London last night. 56 killed and 114 injured.

Friday, 15 October

Nice summer day. The rope of the kitchen pulley broke today and nearly knocked Agnes' head off. British Army using 'gas' in France. British submarine sinks two German torpedo boats in the Baltic.

Saturday, 16 October

Very foggy all day. Got a new rope and attached it to the kitchen ceiling. We all took a walk through Queen's Park in the afternoon. British losses in the Dardanelles up to 9 October: 126,020.

Sunday, 17 October

Very nice day. Nannie Gordon here at 10.30 a.m. to let Agnes and I go to church (communion). After dinner we all took a walk by the Hangingshaws. Agnes saw Nannie away at 7.30 p.m. Allies declare a blockade on Bulgarian coast.

Wednesday, 20 October

It looks as if I'll need to be a 'sojer'.

Thursday, 21 October

Fine day. Agnes went over to see the doctor at night. His report gives me a little more hope. We got a note from the factor increasing the rent 2/- in the quarter. 'Strafe' the factor. I went over to Greenlodge myself at night. Duncan has got a job in Glasgow.

Thursday, 16 September

Kitchener wants more men. Seems as if conscription is coming now. War is now costing £3,500,000 a day. Our army and navy is 3,000,000 men. We have an army of 600,000 making munitions of war.

Friday, 17 September

Another German spy executed in London.

Saturday, 18 September

Dirty wet day. Took a walk out to Ruglen and gave my tailor his war bonus. Called in at 200 Main Street and had a crack[90] with Uncle Willie. This is Belgian flag day.

Wednesday, 22 September

Agnes went and consulted her doctor, and got a very bad report as to her general health. She got a bottle and has to go back when it is finished.

Friday, 24 September

We sorted the bed in the room, as Hetty is coming for a few days.

A crack (or 'craic') is a conversation. This is one of the few times that Thomas uses an Irish rather than a Scottish colloquialism.

Saturday, 25 September
Hetty arrived. After tea we all took the car to St George's Cross and 'did' the Great Western Road.[91] Agnes not looking well at all.

Sunday, 26 September
Hetty and I went out a walk before dinner out the Carmunnock Road and back by old Cathcart. After dinner we all took car to Burnside and walked up the East Kilbride Road and down the Calderwood Road, and Blue car home. Agnes seems a little better today. Great British victory in Flanders.[92]

Monday, 27 September
Lovely day. This is the Autumn Holiday, so I have a holiday. Went myself in the forenoon and studied the finer arts in the Art Galleries. After dinner we all took car to Killermont and home by Anniesland.[93] Great Brito-French victory. 21 miles of trenches gained for a depth of about 2.5 miles. 23,000 Germans captured.[94]

Saturday, 2 October
Great march-out today in Glasgow of 10,000 men to encourage recruiting.

Monday, 4 October
Agnes and Mrs Carmichael at some church concert tonight. I stayed at home with Tommy. I like the wee man's company, although I let on I don't.

Wednesday, 6 October
Am expecting a visit from the recruiting sergeant to see why I am not serving my King and country.

---

[91] St George's Cross is to the north-east of the town centre, Great Western Road is the grand boulevard of the wealthy West End of the city.
[92] At the beginning of the Battle of Loos, the British attacked to the south of La Bassée Canal and captured 5 miles of enemy trenches.
[93] Killermont is on the River Kelvin, at the north-west of the city. Anniesland lies to the south of Killermont.
[94] The Allies were fighting both at Loos and in Champagne on the Western Front.

Saturday, 23 October

The King has appealed for more men.

Monday, 25 October

Tommy got new slippers today and *blew his nose*!!!!!!!![95]

Thursday, 28 October

Not at my work today. Not very well. Very wet night. Exactly a year ago Lily died. Position very serious in Serbia. I'm afraid Greece and Roumania will join Germany.

Friday, 29 October

Total British losses to 9 October in all fields of operations: 493,294.

Saturday, 30 October

Not well at all so left my work early and crawled home to bed, and spent the rest of the day non compos mentis.

Monday, 1 November

Got a love letter from Lord Derby egging me on to enlist before they make me.[96]

Tuesday, 2 November

Tommy fell and knocked a hole in the back of his head today.

Wednesday, 3 November

To tone up my system and get more work out of me, Mr Baxter gave me six bottles of Vibrona.[97]

---

95 Another landmark in Tommy's development, evidently.

96 Lord Derby, formerly Edward George Villiers Stanley, was Director-General of Recruitment. His 'Derby Scheme' was a recruitment policy under which men could volunteer to be called up if necessary.

97 Vibrona was a tonic wine. It was 20 per cent alcohol and contained 'alkaloids' that promised to boost the drinker's constitution.

Sunday, 7 November

Agnes in bed nearly all day. Not well at all. Hysterical and fainting at night. Cheerful day.

Monday, 8 November

Wet day. Agnes not much better and not speaking much.

Tuesday, 9 November

Italians capture an Austrian mountain.

Friday, 12 November

Prime Minister says: 'Single men first.'[98]

Monday, 15 November

Sore complaints from Tommy. Is it fever????

Tuesday, 16 November

Tommy in bed all day. Is it the measles???

Wednesday, 17 November

Tommy still in bed. Think it is the cold.

Thursday, 18 November

Hospital ship sunk in the Channel, also boat that went to the rescue. About 80 lives lost. A German mine did the trick.[99] Serbia in grave peril. Greece going to play the dirty game.[100] Strafe Greece!!

[98] The government promised that married men who volunteered under the Derby Scheme would be the last to be called up.

[99] The British hospital ship *Anglia* was sunk by a German mine in the English Channel. Eighty-five lives were lost.

[100] Greece refused to enter the war on the side of the Allies, probably because of the German sympathies of King Constantine, who was married to the Kaiser's sister.

NOVEMBER, 1915.

Friday 19

(323-42)

Fog & frost. Late night.

Monastir (Serbia) in danger.

Some trenches in Gallipoli captured by Scottish Territorials

German Dreadnought blown up by mine, but only a few lives lost.

NOVEMBER, 1915.

Saturday 20

(324-41)

Fog worse than ever today. When I got home took off my boots and dont intend to go out till monday.

I sorted the easy chair with two large screw nails.

Situation in Serbia very serious. Kitchener is off to athens to talk to King of Greece

Thursday, 25 November

Recruiting sergeant up at night to assist me in making up my mind. I did not go away with him.

Saturday, 27 November

Went to Ruglen for a bath. Four German guns arrived at the Square today. Captured from the Huns.[101]

The British Army show off captured German field guns.

Wednesday, 1 December

Serbia practically wiped off the map now. Allies too late again.

Thursday, 2 December

Men took our whirlygig away today. Allies get shoved back in the Balkans.

Sunday, 5 December

About 5 p.m. a nice little girl came up to see us. Hetty Cook by name, a cousin of Agnes. About 6.30 Donald, Josephine and Duncan came in and about 9 p.m. James Crichton came in. He is from France, direct from the trenches.

Tuesday, 7 December

Saw a lady car driver today.

---

101 Captured guns were often displayed in the main squares or parks of British cities.

Thursday, 9 December

Heavy snow at night. Could resist no longer. Joined the army today. Group 39 under Lord Derby's scheme. Tremendous rush of recruits. Was kept waiting three hours. Was sworn in and got my day's pay - 2/9. God save the King.

Friday, 10 December

Rained all day. Went up to Bath Street to see if I could get my khaki armlet, but they were sold out, so to speak. How are the folk to know I've answered my country's call?

Saturday, 11 December

Great rush to enlist.

Monday, 13 December

Went out and saw Sam at the shop to see if he had 'attested'. He had. Rule Britannia. Spring cleaning in our wigwam. Helped Agnes to wash the dinner set at night. Agnes washed the paintwork.

Wednesday, 15 December

Duncan has also 'attested'.

Saturday, 18 December

Bright clear day, but cold. We went to town in afternoon and admired the shops. I have now got my khaki armlet to let folk know I have attested and await the call. First four groups called up for 20 January 1916. I'm in group 39.

Monday, 20 December

Rained all day. Wore my armlet today. Suvla Bay and Anzac (Gallipoli) evacuated by the British. German attack on British at Ypres by poison gas etc. beaten back.

Wednesday, 22 December

Agnes went to town at night and did some Christmas shopping, nd then did a big ironing and then collapsed.

Friday, 24 December

British losses in all theatres of war to 9 December: 528,227. Killed 119,923, wounded 338,758, missing 69,546.

aturday, 25 December

Pouring wet morning, wet dirty day and wishing you Merry Xmas. Tommy got a motor car and a big book and an orange in his stocking, and a wee basket. At 8 p.m. Mr and Mrs Gordon gave us a visit, with Nannie and Ella. They gave Tommy a box of oldiers.

Sunday, 26 December

Dirty day and some rain. We all went to town in the afternoon. Walked up as far as Sauchiehall Street through the Arcade and car home from the Cowcaddens. No war news today. No papers published.

Monday, 27 December

Stormy wet day. Duncan here at night with his girl's autograph album. He wants me to put some masterpieces in it.

THE POWER OF PE

THE TRUCE IN THE TRENCH

British and German soldiers fraternising during the Christmas and New Year tru
photograph, " a crowd of some 100 Tommies of each nationality

Thursday, 30 December

Went over by myself to Greenlodge at night with the album belonging to the girl belonging to Duncan. Got home at 11.45 p.m. with a bottle of 'ginger'.[102]

Friday, 31 December

Extra special wet day. Got away at 4 p.m. Bought myself a new hat. We went out for a little at night. British cruiser *Natal* blown up by internal explosion in harbour.[103]

THE TIME OF WAR
BROUGHT IN THE NEW YEAR

as welcomed on both sides. "At this point," writes the officer who sent us the
ing between the trenches. We found our enemies to be Saxons."

[102] While 'ginger' is a general Glaswegian term for any soft drink, this is probably a bottle of ginger wine, a wine fortified with spirits and ginger, with advertised health-giving qualities.

[103] A fire on board the armoured cruiser HMS *Natal*, which was lying in the Cromarty Firth in the north west of Scotland, led to the explosion of the ship's magazine. The ship sank quickly, killing more than 400 of her 815 officers and men.

1916

Despite the best efforts of the state, the voluntary system used to sign up recruits in 1914 and 1915 was not producing the results the government needed, so it passed a Military Service Act in January 1916 conscripting all unmarried men between the ages of 18 and 41. A second Act, passed in May, called up married men. The acts also set up a system of hearings to allow people to make claims for exemption, for example on grounds of religion or conscience. Poor health was still a great problem, though, and only 36% of the men examined in 1917 were suitable for full military duties, while 40 per cent were classified as incapable of physical exertion.

At the beginning of 1916, the German blockade of supplies for Britain was reducing not only the amount of food available. On 9 February *The Glasgow Herald*, one of the two newspapers that Thomas read to follow the progress of the war, told its readers: 'As the imports of paper and papermaking materials will be much restricted by the government, we shall not be able to place *The Glasgow Herald* so freely on sale as has been the custom in the past. Newsagents' supplies will be restricted to those copies actually ordered by customers, so that readers should in all cases place orders for a regular daily service.'

The Germans began an escalating series of air-raids on the east coast of Britain, especially targeting London, which was first hit by a Zeppelin on 31 May 1915. In 1916, the government responded with a total black-out in areas thought to be at risk of air-raids. This extinguished all but the most essential outside lighting, and ordered householders and businesses to place heavy curtains on all windows and doors so that no light escaped. Thomas notes that all of Glasgow was darkened by the end of February 1916.

1916

aturday, 1 January

ew year opens with wind and rain. We went to the Cinerama fter dinner. P&O liner *Persia* sunk near Crete by U-boat.[1] bout 335 lives lost.

Monday, 3 January

rothers, who have the harder fate –
he men who fall or the women who wait?

uesday, 4 January

lbania joins the Allies. War declared against Austria.

Vednesday, 5 January

ill introduced to compel nmarried men to enlist. Derby groups 6, 7, 8 and 9 alled up for 8 February.

riday, 7 January

gnes baking at night. Getting ready for omorrow.

aturday, 8 January

ine day. Mr and Mrs Gordon and family here bout 5.15 p.m. We had a ight of song and dance. Carriages at 11 p.m.

A school is used as an army recruitment office.

The P&O liner SS *Persia* was travelling from London to India when it was torpedoed without warning by submarine U38 on 30 December 1915, about 70 miles off the coast of Crete. Of he 501 people on board, 167 survived. Among the passengers was Lord Montagu of Beaulieu.

Sunday, 9 January

Showery day and very stormy. As we were expecting Hetty Cook at night I did not go to church. Hetty arrived about 5.30. She went away about 10.30. The last car had gone, so I walked home with her, which was 'the goods'. The walk back was not 'the goods'.[2] I arrived home at 12.05 a.m. to my anxious wife.

Monday, 10 January

Wild day. More rain. British Naval losses to date. Battleships: *King Edward VII, Bulwark, Triumph, Formidable, Irresistible, Goliath, Ocean, Majestic.* Cruisers: *Natal, Argyll, Good Hope, Monmouth, Aboukir, Hogue, Cressy, Amphion, Pathfinder, Hermes, Hawke, Pegasus*

Tuesday, 11 January

A gathering of the clans at Greenlodge, so Agnes went there about 6 and I straight from my work. Spent a musical evening and played divers foolish games. Agnes, Tommy and I got home at 12.15 a.m. Gallipoli completely evacuated by British and French. The Turks are top dog this time.

Wednesday, 12 January

Sat in at night and listened to the wind. Austrian successes in Montenegro, which means Montenegro will share the fate of Serbia and Belgium.

Thursday, 13 January

British victory at the Tigris.[3] Kaiser very ill.

[2] Thomas evidently has a soft spot for Miss Cook, his wife's young cousin.

[3] The Tigris Corps, under Lieutenant-General Sir Fenton Aylmer, was tasked with the relief of Kut in Mesopotamia, where Major-General Charles Townshend's 6th (Indian) Division was under siege by Turkish troops.

aturday, 15 January

'old, dull day. We went to see Hetty Cook and her ma at 5.30 .m. We played dominoes and arrived home 10.45 p.m. Dykes urst in Holland; great damage.[4]

unday, 16 January

/eather like unto yesterday. This is Communion Sunday so 'ent to church. After dinner Tommy and I went out a walk. hortly after 8 p.m. Sam and Nellie gave us a visit. They went vay at 10.30. Sam had on his armlet. Ex fuma fama.[5] remendous fire in Bergen.[6]

Ionday, 17 January

During 1915, nine hies were shot in he Tower.

uesday, 18 January

'ice mild day. We all went out a walk at night. Montenegro ies for peace. British blockade of Germany to be tightened.

'ednesday, 19 January

'et, stormy day. Austria and Montenegro arranging terms.

hursday, 20 January

hunder, lightning, hurricanes, rain, hail, sleet. Agnes cleaning it the room all night. Negotiations broken off between Austria id Montenegro. Fighting again.

---

he Zuider Zee flood on 14 January 1916 breached a number of dykes and inundated the w-lying lands of North Holland and Friesland. Following this disaster, the government of e Dutch built the barrier dam that turned the Zuider Zee into an inland lake.

his Latin phrase (actually 'Ex fumo fama') is the motto of the Royal Burgh of Rutherglen. It eans 'fame from smoke', and refers to the heavy industry that brought prosperity if not xactly fame to the region.

he conflagration destroyed much of Bergen, the second-largest city in Norway.

Friday, 21 January

Dirty, wet day. Agnes in town in the afternoon. She bought me a new tie. Nannie Gordon here at night. British submarine wrecked off Dutch coast. Crew saved.[7]

Saturday, 22 January

Wind, rain, hail, thunder and lightning. I went to Pollokshield[s] Library at night. Great Russian victory in the Caucasus.[8]

Sunday, 23 January

Stormy sort of day. Donned my uniform and took Tommy out a walk. German aeroplanes raid Kent coast. One man killed.

Monday, 24 January

Dry day, but wild. Stormy night as per usual. Agnes baking at night. We entertain tomorrow night. British relief force held up on the Tigris. Heavy losses.[9]

Tuesday, 25 January

Wet, windy sort of day. Mr and Mrs Ferguson, Lily and Isa an[d] Duncan here at night. We had a night of music and revelry. Nobody killed. They all went away at 11 p.m. German seaplan[e] attacks Dover, but gets chased.

Wednesday, 26 January

Agnes went to Ibrox in the afternoon. I reversed the waxcloth [in] the lobby at night to make folk think we had new stuff. Germ[an] air raid on Dunkirk. Five persons killed.

---

[7] The British submarine HMS *H6* ran aground off Ameland Island, part of the Netherlands with no loss of life on 19 January 1916. The crew were interned at Groningen.

[8] On 20 January Russian troops captured Sultanabad in Persia and made great progress in Armenia.

[9] The Tigris Corps, on its way to relieve the British forces under siege at Kut al-Amara, arriv[ed] at the Tigris River on 22 January, where they were attacked by a large Turkish force.

hursday, 27 January

ry sunny day. Total British casualties (all fields) to 9 January. illed 128,138. Wounded 353,283. Missing 68,006. Total 549,427.

riday, 28 January

ot my hair cut. Agnes indignant.

aturday, 29 January

aid the factor today. Rent reduced to pre-war times, according the law.[10] Dull day. I went to library in Langside at night. ustria has wiped Montenegro off the map.

uesday, 1 February

Vent straight to Sam from my work. Agnes and Tommy there, ien we all went to a church concert. Sam helped the choir to iake a noise. Big Zeppelin raid all over England. 67 killed and bout 100 injured.

Vednesday, 2 February

Iice day. Agnes in the wash-house all day. The missing liner *ppam* turns up at an American port with a German Prize rew on board.[11]

hursday, 3 February

old, wet day. When I came in at night, Hetty was in. Then May ime. After tea Nannie Gordon arrived. This is the age of :males: lady car drivers, lady car conductors, lady lamplighters, dy postmen, lady mail van drivers, lady railway porters, lady cket collectors.

The Rent Restrictions Act, introduced in December 1915, controlled rents during wartime.

The British-owned liner *Appam* had been captured off the African coast by a German raider, which had installed a prize crew to take charge of the liner. She sailed into the harbour at Hampton Roads, Virginia, with 429 captives and a 22-strong German prize crew. Under nternational law, the German crew could ask a Prize Court to award them ownership of the aptured vessel, or prize.

Women at home and at work

The Livingstones of Govanhill were a representative example of an upper-working-class family in Glasgow at the start of the First World War. Thomas was employed as a mercantile clerk, Agnes had resigned her job as a cardboard cutter after her marriage, and they lived in a typically working-class tenement flat. Their house had an inside toilet but no bathroom, so bathing would have taken place in a tin bath in front of the fire, filled with water boiled on the coal-fuelled kitchen stove. Thomas writes of visiting relatives to use their bath, using the bathing (not swimming) facilities at Govanhill Baths, and stopping by the 'religious baths' in the Gorbals, intended for Jewish people to purify themselves before attending synagogue.

When Wee Tommy started school, he attended Victoria Primary School, on the corner of Hollybrook and Batson Streets in Govanhill. This was opened as Victoria Public School in 1905 by the Glasgow School Board, regarded as one of the leading boards in Scotland. It set high standards by employing only qualified teachers, and taking over from a number of charities the responsibility for distributing clothing and footwear to needy children and eliminating half-time education – which allowed children under 13 to spend half their time in school and the other half working – before the law required it in 1918.

Thomas and his wife Agnes had parallel systems of finance, both funded by Thomas' wages. Agnes' share of the budget covered food and cleaning materials, clothing for herself and her son, replaceable household goods, such as gas mantles, and transport costs for her visits to friends and family. Thomas was responsible for rent, household insurance, gas and coal, his own clothing, transport, pipes and tobacco, newspaper family outings to the cinema or music hall, holidays and meals bought outside the home.

Before the outbreak of war, the roles of men and women had remained essentially unchanged for generations. Men were expected to be breadwinners; women were expected to obey their husbands, cook, maintain a clean and tidy house, and raise their children. If they did work outside the home, women were expected to leave their jobs when they married and devote themselves to looking after their families. Some employers had this as an explicit policy and were unwilling to hire married women who might leave at inopportune moments to have children. The First World War changed much of this, however. With the success of the pals' battalions that allowed men to volunteer and serve with friends and colleagues, women were called upon to fill the vacancies left by local men departing for the front. One such unit was Glasgow's 15th Highland Light Infantry, or 'Tramways Battalion'. As a result, in 1918, the number of women employed on Glasgow's tramway system peaked at 2,388, of whom 308 were tram drivers. They also took the place of men in other trades, and in munitions work in factories. Thomas, at first mesmerised by the sight of women working as conductors in 1915 seems hardly bothered when one turns up to whitewash his ceiling in 1917.

'rom left to right: *A woman cabbie; a lift-girl;*
nd serving food to 'tired tommies'.

One of the unintended consequences of vomen working outside the home was the ıcreased family income, which resulted in etter fed and clothed children. Women's ıcreased independence, their experiences in vorking as a group in industry and their emands for voting rights were not accepted vith equal approval across society, however. While women were deemed suitable eplacements for men as clerks, shop assistants nd teachers, male trade unionists in the heavy ıdustries that predominated on Clydeside were xceptionally, even militantly, concerned about lilution' caused by women in the workforce. 'hey feared that women would choose not to oin unions or that they would provide softer ırgets for management pressure, thus reducing ıe unions' power.

Women, meanwhile, were being encouraged y the Suffragist movement to demand the same rights as men to vote and to stand for parliament. The authorities who were happy to take advantage of women's labour were not so keen on this challenge to the traditional social order. Just after Emmeline Pankhurst stood up to speak at a Suffragist meeting in the St Andrew's Halls in Glasgow (the façade of which fronts the Mitchell Library in Granville Street) at 8 p.m. on 9 March 1914, the platform was charged by 120 Glasgow police officers, one of whom had a warrant for her arrest. One eye-witness, Leonard Gow, wrote: 'After Mrs Pankhurst had been speaking for a very few minutes, the platform, which, please mark, was occupied solely by women, old and young, was rushed by detectives and policemen with drawn batons who laid out in all directions, hitting and felling women whose only offence was that they crowded around their leader evidently trying to protect her from violence.'

Friday, 4 February
Cold, dry day. Tommy not well. Zeppelin found wrecked in North Sea by a trawler. Being sensible men, they left Zeppelin and its crew to their fate. Great fire at Ottawa. Canada House of Parliament burned down. Seven lives lost. Germans suspected.[12]

Tuesday, 8 February
Weather appalling. Up to the neck in snow, slush, rain etc. So I've got the cold. I went myself to Sam' at night. Family re-union etc. Derby groups 10, 11, 12 and 13 called up for 29 February.

Wednesday, 9 February
Compulsion for the army is now law.

Thursday, 10 February
Tommy got new trousers today. Air raid on Kent by two German seaplanes. Two women and one child hurt.

Saturday, 12 February
I went to Govanhill Library in the afternoon. Glasgow is going to be in darkness on 1 March, so help me bob. British minesweeper sunk in the North Sea by German torpedo boats. Hoch![13]

[12] Fire raged through the Canadian parliament buildings in Ottawa on 3 February 1916. The entire centre block, with the exception of the Library of Parliament, was destroyed and seve people died. Despite rumours of enemy sabotage, a Royal Commission ruled that the fire w accidental.
[13] Literally 'high' in German, used here as a cheer to mean 'hurrah!'.

1916

Sunday, 13 February

Rose about 7 a.m. this morning, in full possession of my faculties nd went to Queen's Park and did not hear the cuckoo. Hail, snow, wind and rain all day.

Monday, 14 February

Vile day of snow and sleet. I made a book case for the pantry on 17 July 1913. I broke it up on 14 February 1916 for firewood. The amous British cruiser *Arethusa* wrecked by a mine. Ten lives lost.[14]

Tuesday, 15 February

All unmarried men called to the colours. My turn next. Ora pro nobis.

Wednesday, 16 February

Vile, unholy weather. Snow, rain, everything.

Thursday, 17 February

Agnes did some ironing at night. I broke the teapot tonight. Great Russian triumph. Fall of Erzerum.[15] Big blow to the Turks.

Friday, 18 February

Rained and snowed all day. Streets in a high old mess. Cameroons campaign ended.[16] We have only to smash up German East Africa now, and Germany is without a colony. Once again, Roumania is preparing for war.

Saturday, 19 February

Very nice day. We all went to Ibrox at night. They have a new iano there, so I went to bless it, so to speak. We had an evening f song and music. This is pay day.

On 11 February the *Arethusa,* which took part in the first significant naval action in the North Sea in August 1914, was hit a mine off Felixstowe. Six people died.

The Russians captured Erzerum in Turkey on 16 February, taking almost 13,000 prisoners and 323 guns.

The Allies spent 18 months fighting to control the Cameroons, a German protectorate on the coast of western Africa.

Sunday, 20 February
I took a walk to Bellahouston Park before dinner. In my absence Tommy tried the edge of the shovel on his head, and lost.

Tuesday, 22 February
I took Agnes and Tommy to the Cinerama tonight. The French bring down a Zeppelin. Crew all killed. Six German aeroplanes shot down. Good business.

Wednesday, 23 February
Very cold day. Tommy went out a message himself today.
I made a sort of blind for the bathroom in order to escape a £100 fine.[17]

Thursday, 24 February
Very cold day. Rain at night. Jenny Roxburgh here in afternoon to tell us not to come to Clydebank on Saturday as her father fell off a building. It's a hard world. Everybody buying green blinds just now. My patent blind a failure, so I painted the globe of the bathroom gas, which was a great success.

Friday, 25 February
Tonight's the night all Glasgow darkened. Took my life in my hands and went over to Greenlodge myself. Great German offensive at Verdun. Terrific battle raging.

[17] The government introduced blackout regulations in areas where they thought Zeppelins might attack. Street lighting was dimmed or turned off, and householders and business owners were required to make sure that no light escaped from their premises at night.

The Battle of Verdun raged from February to June 1916, as the German forces made three prolonged and determined assaults on the French fortress of that name in north-east France. The Germans planned to burst through the Western Front here and make a fresh attempt to capture Paris, but they were resisted, at an enormous cost in men and munitions. The French sustained 550,000 casualties, while the Germans suffered 434,000.

Saturday, 26 February

Dirty, wet, cold day. Snow at intervals. Took Agnes and Tommy to the town at night in order to see the ... illuminations? We came home duly depressed. Cuss all Zeppelins. This is a view of Morgan Street.

Sunday, 27 February

Dirty day of sleet and snows. I did not go out at all. Made myself comfortable and amused the wife and family. Large P&O liner *Maloja* mined in the English Channel. About 150 lives lost. Steamer that went out to assist her also struck by mine.[18]

Monday, 28 February

Broke some wood wherewith to light the fire. Titanic battle still raging at Verdun. Terrific German losses.

The SS *Maloja*, the largest vessel in the P&O fleet, struck a mine within view of Dover on the morning of 27 February: 155 were drowned. The *Empress of Fort William*, which came to the rescue of the *Maloja*, struck a second mine, with no losses.

Wednesday, 1 March

Our only lamppost in Morgan Street has got a coat of paint on the globe to make it still darker. I'll need to wear a collier's lamp on my hat.

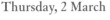

Thursday, 2 March

Military Act in operation today.[19] A seaplane raids south-east coast of England. A baby killed. Verdun battle stopped meantime.

Friday, 3 March

First groups of married men called up for 7 April, groups 25 to 32. I'm in group 39, so I'm in the next lot.

Sunday, 5 March

Dull day. Nannie Gordon here about 4.30 p.m., so we all went out together. We took car to Ruglen and visited the cemetery where poor Lily lies. We went round Grey's Road and got car home from Burnside. I saw Nannie all the way home as everything is so dark. Went up and had a cup of tea with them. Tommy went out for a paper today.

Tuesday, 7 March

Tommy out playing today. Germany going to blockade Britain for ever with submarines and mines.

[19] The Military Act gave some exemptions to conscription, such as people with ill health, those whose jobs were judged to be of national importance or those who were the sole breadwinner in a family.

1916

Wednesday, 8 March

took Agnes and Tommy to the Majestic. Streets most awful dark. Our lamppost at the corner has got another coat of black paint. German fleet reported in the North Sea.

Thursday, 9 March

Duncan has been commanded to report himself for service in a fortnight. Me next. Agnes kind of worried. Russians marching on Trebizond. Germany and Portugal nearly at war.

Friday, 10 March

Very cold weather. Nothing special to report. General Smuts makes a good start against German East Africa. Germany declares war on Portugal. 'Gott Strafe Portugal.' Since the beginning of the war, the Germans have murdered 127 British civilians by bombardment, 276 British civilians by air raids, and 2,750 British civilians by drowning.

Monday, 13 March

Cold, wet sort of day. I went at night and had a wash in the eligious baths, which makes me doubly good.[20] Tis reported my group will be called up on 17 April. So there you are, and where are you? British auxiliary steamer mined in North Sea: 14 lives lost. Russian torpedo boat mined in Black Sea.

Tuesday, 14 March

To 'keep the Home Fires burning' I broke some wood tonight.[21] Agnes made jam at night.

---

0 Govanhill and the Gorbals, the neighbourhood immediately to the north, had a substantial Jewish population. There was a mikvah, or ritual bath-house, in South Portland Street in the Gorbals.

'Keep the Home Fires Burning' was a hugely popular wartime song written by Ivor Novello and Lena Ford in 1914.

Wednesday, 15 March

The government have postponed calling up my group for a little. Austria declares war on Portugal. Verdun battle resumed once more.

Thursday, 16 March

Von Tirpitz (Pirate in chief) resigns.[22] German retreat in East Africa. 'In this world, a man must be either anvil or hammer.'[23]

Saturday, 18 March

Agnes and Tommy away with the Carmichaels to a cake and candy sale. I went to the Langside Library. German losses at Verdun are said to be now 300,000.

Tuesday, 21 March

The powers that be
have put Shades
on the Stair gas
so that
Zeppelins wont
see us.

Wednesday, 22 March

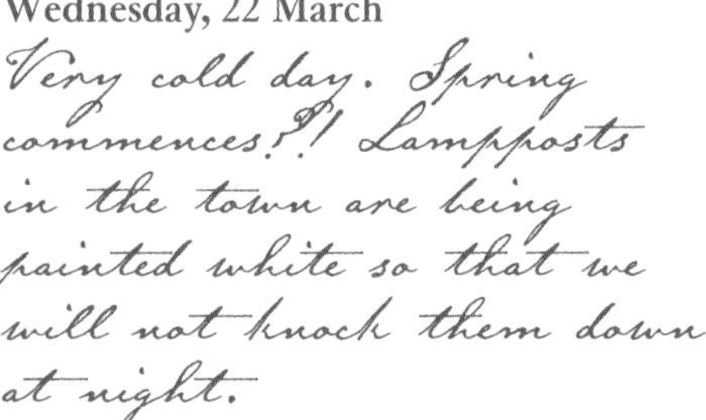
Very cold day. Spring commences?! Lampposts in the town are being painted white so that we will not knock them down at night.

Thursday, 23 March

Heavy fall of snow in the morning. Miss Galloway, our typist, home with me tonight. She is a singist, so we did some warbling. She went away about 10.30 p.m. To guard her life I saw her all the way home. Got home myself 11.45 p.m. Riots and mutiny all over Germany.

---

[22] Alfred von Tirpitz, Commander of the German Navy, firmly believed in a policy of sinking any shipping that could be of aid to the enemy, which angered the neutral Americans. He resigned to appease Washington and prevent the United States stepping into the war.

[23] The quote is from *Hyperion* by Henry Wadsworth Longfellow.

Saturday, 25 March

Wild snow storm all day. Worst we've had for years. After tea we all went into town to the Salon Picture House and saw She and came home duly edified.[24] Word to hand today of a naval duel in the North Sea between British armed liner and German raider, both sunk. The German survivors landed at Leith. German submarine also reported captured.

Monday, 27 March

Agnes and Tommy at a Kirk concert with Mrs Carmichael etc. I stayed at home, broke sticks etc. My beloved got home about 11 p.m. American liner sunk by the German pirates.

Wednesday, 29 March

Serious strikes with Clyde workers. Some of the leaders arrested.[25] German destroyer rammed by British cruiser in North Sea. Not a single German blighter saved.

Thursday, 30 March

Wet day. Having a night of it. My father here at tea time. Hetty Cook and May Crozier here at 6.45 and Duncan about 8 p.m. Duncan brought a photo frame. Duncan rejected by military doctors. The 'Bantams' are now in France.[26]

---

[24] The Salon Picture House stood at 90 Sauchiehall Street. *She*, which was released in 1916, starred Alice Delysia and Henry Victor.

[25] There were a number of strikes in Glasgow in early 1916, over the employment of women in the heavy industries. The authorities were quick to suppress them, and workers' leaders were arrested and tried.

[26] Bantam regiments were made up of volunteers who were fit but below the minimum height requirement of the army. Many of them were miners.

Sunday, 2 April

Lovely day. Warm sunshine. We all went to Queen's Park after dinner, took car from there to Thornliebank and car from Rouken Glen to Paisley. Green car back from Paisley, and came off at Ibrox, and went up and had our tea with the Gordons. Home 10.10 p.m. All the lampposts in Govanhill were out, so I'm afraid the Zeppelins have reached Scotland at last. Another air raid over England last night: 16 killed, 100 injured.

Monday, 3 April

At last, Zeppelins attacked Scotland last night. Great damage in Edinburgh and Leith: 10 killed. An air raid also on England.

Tuesday, 4 April

Agnes in wash-house all night. I put Tommy to bed all by myself. Great German losses at Verdun. Clyde strike ended.

Friday, 7 April

Dull, wet sort of day. Insured my household effects today against air raids. Cuss the Zeppelins. French beating back German attacks at Verdun. Vive la France! Ils ne passeront pas.[27]

Saturday, 8 April

The Gordons stormed our house about 6 p.m. We had an evening of mirth and song. More boats sunk. The submarine menace is getting serious.

[27] 'They shall not pass.' The rallying cry of the French military leader, Henri Pétain, who defended Verdun from the Germans.

Sunday, 9 April

Feeling vigorous, I went to Queen's Park before breakfast. In the afternoon, we all went out by Cathcart and Mount Florida. Duncan here at night. He reports Donald as being very ill.

Tuesday, 11 April

Wind, rain and hail. Agnes over at Greenlodge to see how Donald was keeping. Another spy shot in the Tower.

Thursday, 13 April

Cold, windy day. Broke a few sticks à soir. Agnes went out tonight for a walk. She came back in 10 minutes. Glasgow Socialist gets three years for sedition.[28] British fiercely attacked at Ypres.

Saturday, 15 April

This is the 619th day of the war, the 53rd day of the Battle of Verdun, and the 129th day of the Siege of Kut.

[28] John Maclean, a self-educated Marxist who vehemently opposed the war, had been arrested on charges of sedition. He was found guilty at the High Court in Edinburgh on 11 April 1916, and sentenced to three years penal servitude.

Sunday, 16 April

Pouring wet day. I went to church. Communion. After dinner I went over to Greenlodge to see how Donald was keeping. America doing a war dance just now.

Friday, 21 April

This being Good Friday, I ate a 'Hot Cross Bun'. Germans gain a trench and two craters from British at St Eloi. Russsian army landed in France to help the Allies. French take offensive at Verdun.

Saturday, 22 April

According to arrangement, we all went down to Ibrox in the afternoon. Nobody was there when we arrived, so we all came home again. I cussed and swore. British regain lost ground at St Eloi, and so the game goes on.

Sunday, 23 April

I gave Agnes her usual cup of tea at 7 a.m. and then I went out to Queen's Park. I've got the cold. Agnes got the cold. Tommy got the cold.

Tuesday, 25 April

German steamer tries to land arms in Ireland. Sunk. German battle squadron bombards Yarmouth and Lowestoft. Little damage. Our local fleet engages it and Germans go home. Civil war in Dublin. Post Office in hands of rebels. About 30 killed on both sides.[29]

[29] The German ship *Libau*, which was disguised as a Norwegian fishing trawler, failed to meet its Irish contacts, and was scuttled after being intercepted by the British navy.

Wednesday, 26 April

Mr McCort in at night and did the whitewashing. Agnes cleaned the paint after, and I gave her some assistance. I polished the clock. I got to bed at 1.30 tomorrow morning. Agnes between that and breakfast time. Martial law in Dublin. Sinn Fein declared illegal.

The Easter Rising in Ireland, organised by Irish nationalists opposed to British rule, began on 24 April 1916, when 1,600 members of the Irish Volunteer Force and the Irish Citizen Army personnel took over several key buildings in Dublin, including the General Post Office (GPO), the Four Courts, Bolands Mills, Jacobs Biscuit Factory and the Royal College of Surgeons. Pádraig Pearse and James Connolly, the leaders of the insurrection, declared an Irish republic from the steps of the GPO. The British response was rapid and violent. The 2,000 crown forces in Dublin quickly gave battle, and 20,000 additional troops arrived within two days. A gunboat sailed up the Liffey, destroying much of the centre of the Irish capital. Six days later, the uprising was over, and its leaders were then tried by military courts and executed. While a military failure, the rising was one of the most politically and culturally important milestones on the road to an Irish republic. William Butler Yeats, in his poem 'Easter, 1916', wrote that 'a terrible beauty is born', and the rising is still celebrated in popular song and story.

Thursday, 27 April

Jean and May Crozier here. We had a night of song and music. All Ireland under martial law. Rebellion spreading. British submarine E22 sunk in North Sea by the Germans. This is the eleventh submarine we have lost.

Saturday, 29 April

Warm, bright and sunny day. Took Agnes and Tommy a circular run on the car via Rouken Glen. Notice posted up on the walls signed by the King, saying I've to be a 'sojer'. Derby groups up to 41 called up for 29 May. God save Ireland. Fall of Kut. General Townshend and British Army surrender to the Turks. Another of our failures.[30]

Sunday, 30 April

Lovely summer day. Tommy got a limp today. He has been running about too much. I took a walk to town in the afternoon. Rebels getting rounded up in Ireland. Dublin General Post Office destroyed. Big fires in Dublin. Mob loots the shops. Boat firing from the Liffey. Irish rebel leader shot. God save Ireland again. Erin go bragh.[31]

Soldiers inspect the interior of Dublin's General Post Office.

[30] The British forces under Townshend had been besieged in Kut, Mesopotamia by Ottoman forces since December 1915. Despite sending a British relief expedition under Aylmer, an attempt to buy their way out, and an appeal for help to Russia, Townshend capitulated after 147 days and 13,000 British Empire soldiers were taken prisoner.

[31] 'Ireland for ever' in Irish.

Tuesday, 2 May

Another nice day. Factor called today and got his rent. I was at recruiting office today. Waited an hour and a half to see the doctor and didn't see him. Five million Britons now under arms.

Wednesday, 3 May

Nice sort of day. Compulsion Bill passed first reading today. Three Irish rebel leaders tried by court martial and shot.[32] Ora pro nobis. Big Zepp raid last night all over east coast, including Scotland. Not much damage; about 10 killed.

Sunday, 7 May

German official casualties 2,822,079.

Monday, 8 May

Sent the office boy up to Bath Street recruiting office with a letter asking permission to be examined by a medical man. I got it.

Tuesday, 9 May

Spring cleaning resumed in the room. Agnes does a hard night's work. Turns very ill and it seems to be serious. White Star liner *Cymric* sunk by U-boat.

Wednesday, 10 May

Went for doctor in the morning. Agnes getting worse. I'm getting alarmed. Took a run home in forenoon. Doctor in. Agnes to stay in bed. I spent the afternoon being measured, weighed, examined, sounded etc. by the military doctors. Found wanting, so am passed for sedentary work etc. My King and country don't want me. I made the supper and put Tommy to bed.

RECRUITING

32 In a series of courts martial beginning on 2 May 90 people were sentenced to death. Fifteen were executed by firing squad between 3 and 12 May.

Health and illness

Thomas and his family were frequent users of both doctors and pharmacists, thanks to an almost continuous succession of coughs, colds, neuralgia, Agnes' frequent exhaustion and eruptions of her 'old trouble', Wee Tommy's tonsils and Thomas' own tiredness and headaches. Their relatives' more serious illnesses bring a knowledge of the Glasgow Royal Infirmary.

Before the coming of the National Health Service in 1948, the better-off were treated at home, moving into small private nursing homes if they needed hospitalisation. For the poor, though, treatment was far less comfortable. People who could not afford house calls relied on dispensaries, which offered advice and simple medicines. For serious conditions, there were voluntary, poor law and municipal hospitals. Thomas' income put him somewhere in the middle, in that he could afford to pay for house calls and the advice of the doctor, but if a hospital was needed the family had to rely on the voluntary sector.

Thomas wrote that he was compelled to register with a doctor under the terms of the National Insurance Act of 1911. The National Insurance scheme, which was compulsory for workers earning less than £3 a week, provided workers with sick pay (10/- a week for up to 26 weeks) and unemployment pay (7/- a week for up to 15 weeks). It also guaranteed insured workers free medical treatment. In return, workers paid 4d a week from their wages, to which their employer added 3d and the government 2d. The scheme did not cover the spouses or children of workers.

Doctors varied their charges according to thei patients' ability to pay. The Partick and District Medical Society drew up a scale for its members in 1920, which listed each street in the area according to the type of houses and the likely income of their inhabitants. Fees ranged from 3/- to 10/6 for a consultation, and from 3/6 to 12/6 fo a visit; the charge for delivering a baby varied from three guineas (£3 3s) to 15 guineas (£15 15s) A typical doctor's hours were from 9.30 a.m. to 10.30 a.m. and from 6 p.m. to 7 p.m. Monday to Saturday, with a half-day on Tuesday. Other times were reserved for home visits.

In the early part of the twentieth century, there were few effective drugs. Alkalis, which made the urine less acidic, were used to treat urinary infections; plant-derived salicylates such as aspirin were used to treat rheumatism; quinir was used for malaria; and digitalis for some typ of heart disease. Patients often relied on patent medicines or over-the-counter medications aime at specific ills. These included Scott's Emulsion, Mother Siegel's Syrup and Veno's Seaweed Toni Scott's Emulsion was composed largely of cod liver oil, a natural source of calcium, phosphoru and vitamins A and D. It was given to children with a view to promoting healthy growth and combating colds and coughs. Mother Siegel's Curative Syrup, which contained tincture of capsicum, hydrochloric acid and aloe, was advertised as 'a cure for impurities of the blood'. Veno's Seaweed Tonic, meanwhile, was promoted by Mr Veno as a cure for a wide variety of ailments, including 'indigestion, wind headache, general weakness, kidney trouble, veak and painful back, torpid liver, female roubles, poorness of blood and habitual onstipation'.

Dentists in Thomas' time did little onservation work on their patients, and were enerally only visited when toothache became nbearable and people were happy to pay 1/6 to ave a problem tooth removed. As a result, many eople lost all their teeth by early adulthood, and vore partial or complete dentures. Thomas imself has a partial denture, which he mentions n his diary in May 1913.

Both Thomas' father, Joseph Livingstone, and is friend Jenny Roxburgh are treated in the Royal Infirmary. This institution was founded in 792 in a building designed by the brothers Robert and James Adam, and rehoused in a more nodern replacement designed by James Miller in 907. In between, the hospital had seen Lord ister carry out the first antiseptic surgery, Villiam Macewan introduce the white coat for hysicians, and John Macintyre open one of the rst x-ray departments in the world.

Glasgow's hospitals at the time of Joseph's and enny's illnesses were divided into three classes: ne voluntary hospitals (general hospitals such as ne Royal Infirmary), municipal hospitals nfectious diseases hospitals such as Robroyston) nd the poor law hospitals (such as the Govan oorhouse and Hospital, renamed the Southern General Hospital in 1922). There was also the Glasgow Royal Mental Hospital, which opened 1843 at Gartnavel, and the Princess Louise cottish Hospital for Limbless and Disabled oldiers and Sailors, which opened in 1916 at rskine. There were also a number of private ursing homes, for those who could afford them.

The voluntary hospitals were funded entirely by voluntary contributions, and were managed by boards of governors elected by the contributors, with representatives of certain public bodies 'and representatives of the working class'. Many of the buildings and wards were endowed, and named after their benefactors. Patients did not necessarily enjoy the Spartan regimes of the voluntary hospitals imposed in accordance with Victorian notions of the 'deserving poor' by formidable nursing sisters, who ensured that there was no smoking, drinking or swearing on the wards. However treatment was often at the hands of respected doctors and surgeons, who gave their services free in return for the high medical standing that working in these large teaching hospitals conferred. It also gave a boost to the fees they could command from their students and private patients. The municipal hospitals were under the control of the Glasgow Corporation, and the poor law hospitals under the Parish Councils and the District Boards of Control.

The effects of the war were felt in many Glasgow hospitals. As well as building its own hospital in Bellahouston Park, the army commandeered the Northern General Hospital (later known as Stobhill Hospital) as a receiving hospital for wounded servicemen. The Royal Infirmary and other hospitals set aside a number of beds for the war wounded. In addition, the Red Cross took over the administration building of the North British Locomotive Company to form Springburn Hospital for injured servicemen. All hospitals lost doctors and surgeons to the army and navy, and many were left dependent on the old and the infirm or on medical students not yet called up to minister to the sick. Women medical students and doctors were able to step into some of the gaps this created.

As in other professions, the war created opportunities for female doctors and nurses to work in areas from which they previously had been excluded. Queen Alexandra's Imperial Military Nursing Service recruited women to serve alongside the army medical service in theatres of war. In addition, the Scottish Women's Hospitals for Foreign Service - which was funded privately after the War Office rejected the idea - established field hospitals staffed entirely by women. By 1918, there were 14 Scottish Women's Hospitals in France, Russia, Serbia, Salonica and Macedonia, where more than 1,000 female doctors, nurses, radiologists, orderlies and drivers had given service.

Spanish Influenza swept the world in 1918 and 1919, killing between 20 and 40 million people, more than died in the First World War. It hit Glasgow particularly hard, and was not a pleasant way to die. One contemporary account chronicled the progression of the illness:

> It starts with what appears to be an ordinary attack of la grippe. When brought to the hospital, [patients] very rapidly develop the most vicious type of pneumonia that has ever been seen. Two hours after admission, they have mahogany spots over the cheek bones, and a few hours later you can begin to see the cyanosis [blueness due to lack of oxygen] extending from their ears and spreading all over the face. It is only a

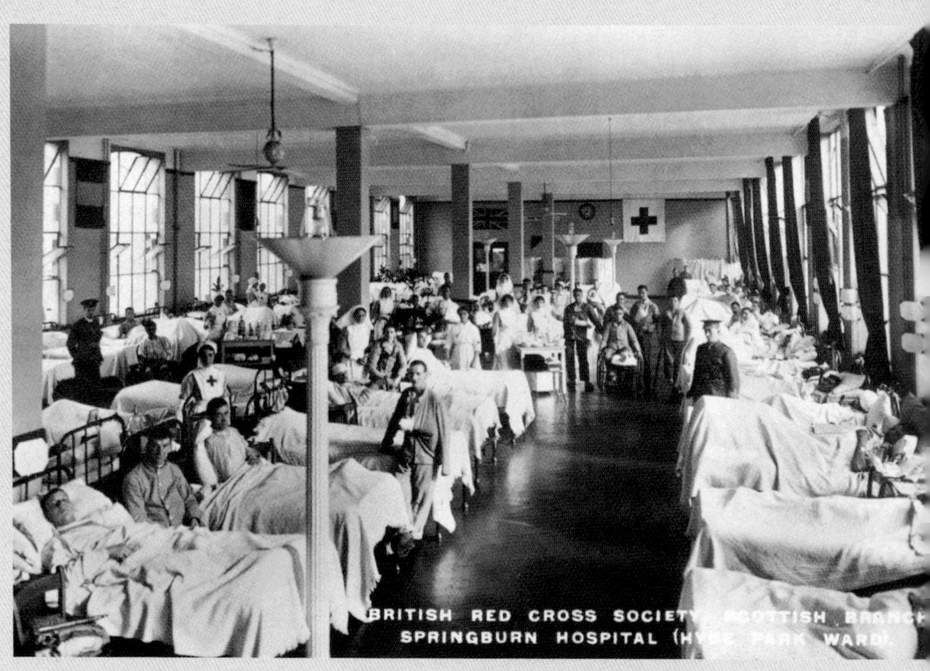

matter of a few hours then until death comes and it is simply a struggle for air until they suffocate. It is horrible.

Letter dated 29 September 1918, discovered in a trunk in 1959, and published in the British Medical Journal *22 December 1979 by Professor R. N. Grist, a Glasgow physician.*

Generally speaking, however, in the early ears of the twentieth century Glasgow's health vas improving, at least as indicated by a steady ecline in the death rate. In 1870 the death rate vas 29.6 per thousand, and by 1920 it was 15 per housand, which was the equivalent at the time f saving 16,000 lives a year. The Glasgow Corporation took a paternalistic interest in all spects of its citizens' lives, and provided a wide ange of services that elsewhere had been left to ne private sector. As scientific and medical dvances made it clear that there was a direct nk between clean environments and good ealth, the corporation began to provide sanitary ervices such as cleaning the streets and disposing f refuse (from 1800), providing a public water upply from Loch Katrine (in 1859) and opening ublic baths and wash-houses (from 1878). All of nese alleviated the worst effects of poor housing nd enhanced the health of those in better rcumstances.

Smoking was already seen as medically roblematic in the early years of the twentieth entury. The 1908 Children Act prohibited the le of tobacco to children aged under 16 based n the belief that smoking stunted their growth. n 1914 the American inventor Thomas Edison rote to Henry Ford, the pioneering car manufacturer, about the health aspects of smoking: 'The injurious agent in cigarettes comes principally from the burning paper wrapper. The substance thereby formed is called acrolein. It has a violent action on the nerve centers, producing degeneration of the cells of the brain, which is quite rapid among boys. Unlike most narcotics, this degeneration is permanent and uncontrollable. I employ no person who smokes cigarettes.'

Despite the growing concerns about the dangers of tobacco, Thomas enjoyed his 'thick black' throughout the war - when supplies were available, of course.

Thursday, 11 May

I telephoned doctor in afternoon to call and see Agnes. He is not so pleased now. I worked late tonight.

Friday, 12 May

Doctor up again. Agnes confined to bed. I'm working late again and washed the kitchen floor when I came home.

Saturday, 13 May

Lily Ferguson here in the afternoon to see the invalid. Connolly and another rebel shot.[33] The last of the leaders.

Sunday, 14 May

Rained all day. Agnes still in bed. Doctor up at 8 p.m. He says Agnes is doing fine.

Monday, 15 May

Josephine here at tea time and Nannie Gordon at night. Agnes up for a little today. Things are looking better.

Tuesday, 16 May

Very nice day. Agnes up a little more today. Mrs and Miss Clark here in the afternoon to see if we wanted to take our holiday house in Rothesay. Maybe we wanted, but we are not taking it.

Thursday, 18 May

The Summer Bill is now law. On Saturday I have to put the clock forward one hour.[34]

---

[33] Easter Uprising leader James Connolly, who was born in Edinburgh, was executed by firing squad while tied to a chair. He was too seriously wounded to stand.

[34] The British government introduced British Summer Time as a wartime measure, to save fuel on the home front. Like the restricted pub opening hours, it was not repealed at the end of the war.

Saturday, 20 May

Nannie Gordon here in the afternoon. I cleaned the room windows and laid the carpet. We sorted up the room generally. Air raid on Kent. One of the aeroplanes shot down.

Monday, 22 May

Agnes very ill early in the morning and got worse during the day. I went for doctor at dinner time and stayed off my work. Doctor calls it lumbago, so Mrs Carmichael and I spent the afternoon boiling Agnes alive with hot fomentations.[35] I went back to my work at 5.30 and worked till 9 p.m.

Tuesday, 23 May

This being the King's birthday, I had a holiday. Spent the morning boiling Agnes. Doctor up again. Agnes worse and very fevered. She can't eat or sleep. Went to doctor for powders. Tommy out all day. I wrote Hetty at night, asking her to nurse Agnes for a season. Fierce fighting at Verdun.

Wednesday, 24 May

This is Empire Day so I doff my hat to the good old flag. Got Agnes some more powders and went round at night for a sleeping draught. Doctor up today. Says her complaint is pyelitis (see dictionary).[36] *Hunted Tommy up at night and put him to bed.*

Lumbago is a general term for lower back pain, usually brought on by lifting heavy weights. Wet washing, presumably, in Agnes' case.

Pyelitis is an inflammation of the renal pelvis, the central part of the kidney. Symptoms include pain and tenderness in the loins, irritability of the bladder, remittent fever, bloody or purulent urine, diarrhoea and vomiting. This is probably what is referred to later in the diary as Agnes' 'old trouble'.

Friday, 26 May

Very nice day. Doctor up today. I went round at dinner time for a bottle. Doctor told me Agnes was very ill indeed. Jean Crozier here at night. We got a letter from Hetty and James Cook intimating the death of their mother, who is an aunt of Agnes. I am asked to funeral. Military Act is now law. Everybody must be in the army except those on war work and medically unfit.

Saturday, 27 May

Doctor up in afternoon. I have to get Agnes citrate of potash.[37] Her temperature down a little, but very worn out at night.

Sunday, 28 May

Doctor up. Agnes slowly improving. She has to get curds and cream for her dinner. Duncan up at night.

Monday, 29 May

Doctor up. Agnes' temperature normal now. She has to get a switched egg. Josephine here at night.

Tuesday, 30 May

Fine day. Doctor up. Agnes to be allowed to sit up in bed.

Got a note from the military calling me up on the 13th June.

Wednesday, 31 May

Doctor up again. Agnes to get potatoes for her dinner. Hetty Cook here at dinner time, and Lily at night. And so ends the merry month of May.

[37] A diuretic.

Thursday, 1 June

Agnes still very weak. May Crozier here at night. I wrote up to Bath Street and returned my calling-up notice. I'm not going to be a soldier yet. Russians held up in Armenia.

Friday, 2 June

Doctor up today, says Agnes is getting on fine. Mrs Gordon and Nannie here at night. Agnes up at night for half an hour, but was in a state of collapse by the end of said half hour. Wae's me. Battle of Verdun something ferocious.

Saturday, 3 June

sa here at night. Agnes a wee bit better today and was up over two hours at night. Hetty went away home at night about 10 p.m. Word today of a terrific sea battle in North Sea [Battle of Jutland]. Entire German fleet engaged, beaten and sent home with great loss. British losses (sunk) *Queen Mary* (battle cruiser), *Indefatigable* (battle cruiser), *Invincible* (battle cruiser), *Defence* (cruiser), *Black Prince* (cruiser), *Warrior* (cruiser), *Tipperary* (destroyer), *Sparrowhawk* (destroyer), *Ardent* (destroyer), *Fortune* (destroyer), *Turbulent* (destroyer), *Nestor* (destroyer), *Nomad* (destroyer), *Shark* (destroyer). Five or six thousand of our men lost.

The greatest naval battle of the war was fought between the British Grand Fleet and the High Seas Fleet of the Imperial German Navy on 31 May and 1 June 1916 in the North Sea off Denmark. The Battle of Jutland, the only full-scale clash of battleships of the war, ended inconclusively, despite the severity of the fighting and the number of ships involved. By the end, the British losses totalled three battle-cruisers, three armoured cruisers and eight destroyers, with 6,094 killed, 510 wounded and 177 captured. The German losses were one battle-cruiser, one pre-dreadnought, four light cruisers and five torpedo boats, with 2,551 killed and 507 wounded. After this conflict, the German navy restricted its operations against the British navy to submarine and mine attacks.

Sunday, 4 June

My birthday. Agnes not so cheery today. Hetty being away, I suppose. I suppose I did my best to keep things going. Jenny and Kate Roxburgh here in the afternoon. To keep things humming Mrs Gordon and Ella arrived about 6 p.m.[38] Agnes up for an hour or so.

Monday, 5 June

Doctor up today. Nellie here at dinner time, and Josephine came tumbling after. Agnes to get eating her usual. I brought my own pet typist up at tea time to see Agnes. Agnes got up about 8 p.m., and did a little sewing to keep her hand in. She'll be better one of these days.

Tuesday, 6 June

Agnes made the dinner today all by herself. We had no visitors today. Disaster near Orkney. British cruiser *Hampshire* mined and sunk, about 12 survivors. Lord Kitchener and staff on board and all drowned.

Wednesday, 7 June

Agnes up for a little today and at night. Mrs Cormack came in at night and wearied the immortal souls out of us for a brace of hours. Day of mourning in the British Empire for Lord Kitchener.

Friday, 9 June

Father here in the afternoon. He told Agnes that Donald has given up his situation. He is no longer fit.[39] Duncan came at night. Agnes feeling so-so. I washed the floor and cleaned the windows.

---

[38] When Agnes is not able to carry out her household work, the women of the family rally round to help. Thomas may polish some brass or cook breakfast, but he is not expected to wash, dry or iron clothes.

[39] Donald's epilepsy had evidently worsened and he had given up his job in a grocer's shop, probably in Bridgeton.

The sudden death of Lord Kitchener in June 1916 was a great blow to the British and other Allied forces. Field Marshal Horatio Herbert Kitchener was a respected Anglo-Irish career soldier turned politician, who was appointed Secretary of State for War shortly after hostilities began in 1914 by Prime Minister Herbert Henry Asquith. Despite Kitchener's poor performance as a politician, he stayed in government because of his popularity with the public. He died on 5 June 1916 when the cruiser HMS *Hampshire*, which was carrying him on a diplomatic mission to Russia, struck an enemy mine west of Orkney and sank. Kitchener, his staff, and 643 of the 655 crew members drowned or died of exposure. His body was never found.

A monument to the military leader was constructed on Mainland, Orkney, near where the *Hampshire* went down. A panel reads: 'This tower was raised by the people of Orkney in memory of Field Marshal Earl Kitchener of Khartoum on that corner of his country which he had served so faithfully nearest to the place where he died on duty. He and his staff perished along with the officers and nearly all the men of HMS *Hampshire* on 5th June, 1916.'

aturday, 10 June

gnes very ill-looking when I got home. Ella Gordon here oing odd jobs.

unday, 11 June

Nice day. Agnes up from dinner time. Tommy has got a bad ough. German official casualties: 2,924,586 total. Killed 734,412; risoners 146,665; missing 191,857; wounded 1,851,652.

Monday, 12 June

gnes up all day. Isa here at night. They did some painting on hat of Agnes', which is a great success. Doctor up for the last me (so he says). Agnes to drink four pints of milk a day and nust get a holiday. In a weak state of mind tonight I bought Tommy a flute.

Wednesday, 14 June

Beautiful summer day. I'll need to be getting a straw hat. Agnes out today for the first time and feeling fine. Great rejoicings.

Thursday, 15 June

Beautiful day. Got my summer straw hat today. Agnes at Queen's Park in afternoon with Daisy and Mrs Carmichael. Mrs Cormack in at night with Tom Howard (the lodger) direct from the trenches.

Friday, 16 June

Agnes went to doctor and got a bottle to put the breath of life in her. I went to Greenlodge Terrace at night. The Elder here in my absence. Got home 11.15 p.m. Agnes very indignant.

Saturday, 17 June

Took Agnes and Tommy in car to Ruglen. We had a word with Mina Henderson and Jessie Keith. We then walked up Stonelaw Road. Saw some soldiers being reviewed. We spoke to Mr and Mrs Clark. After that we had a seat in the woods and then got train from Burnside to Mount Florida and car home. Agnes feeling fine.

Sunday, 18 June

Was at church myself today. Communion. Agnes not so chirpy today. We all went to Queen's Park after dinner. Tommy had on his new suit.

uesday, 20 June

gnes not so well. I'm getting worried again. Made a cricket bat : night for Tommy. At his request.

Vednesday, 21 June

/e went to Greenlodge at night. Donald very ill again. Agnes' ack is very sore again, so I'm afraid she is in for her old trouble gain. Miserable times.

riday, 23 June

gnes in bed till dinner time, then she got up nd went to the doctor and got a new bottle. She ent to bed early. I cleaned all the windows at ight.

aturday, 24 June

'ery warm day. Agnes not well at all. What a life! very fit man between 18 and 41 in Great Britain considered to have enlisted. God save the King.

unday, 25 June

gnes stayed in bed all day. I'm not feeling well ow myself. Think I'll bust up. Tommy broke is bat yesterday. Evidently he uses it as a ammer.

'hursday, 29 June

gnes at doctor today and got another bottle. cleaned the covers and room fire irons. Sir oger Casement sentenced to death today for igh treason.

Casement (above), a former British consul, was an Irish nationalist who had tried to recruit the Germans to that cause after the start of the First World War. He was put ashore in Ireland days before the Easter Rising by a German U-boat, captured by the authorities and tried on charges of treason, sabotage and espionage against the Crown. He was found guilty, sentenced to death, and hanged at Pentonville Prison in London on 3 August 1916.

Saturday, 1 July

At last! The big push!! British and French take the offensive. Great fighting. The Battle of the Somme started at 7.30 a.m. today.

Monday, 3 July

Nice warm day. Tommy getting abused by the young microbe nex door called Alec Gray. So I spoke severely to the aforesaid young microbe surnamed Gray. His ma then abuses Agnes. I'm thinking of taking a run over to Belfast in August. The 'push' continues.

Wednesday, 5 July

Seeing that Agnes is a little better, I thought a little entertainment would do her no harm, so off we went to the Majestic.

Thursday, 6 July

Fine day. We have a woman today to do the washing. Agnes very tired at night. I went over to Greenlodge at night. Donald up but he is a wreck.

Monday, 10 July

Agnes went to doctor at night and got another bottle. He has given her permission to go to Prestwick for a fortnight. A super U-boat arrives in America with a little cargo.

The Battle of the Somme, which lasted from 1 July until November 1916, was one of the largest and bloodiest battles of the war. More than 1.5 million people were killed or injured in six months as the Allies tried to break through German defences in northern France. On the first day alone, Britain sustained 67,470 casualties, including 19,240 dead.

'uesday, 11 July

'ommy very ill, sick nd vomiting. 'onsternation. What will t be? We gave him nedicine and put him to 'ed. I showed Agnes how o iron at night. I did a 'ew dozen hankies.

Vednesday, 12 July

ained all day. Tommy a little better, but Agnes not so well. My air is turning grey. Josephine up for a little at night. Donald is oing to a home for some months to see if it will help him. Vould to heaven it could cure him. U-boat shells Durham coast: ne woman killed.

'hursday, 13 July

Jice warm sunny day, so on goes my hay hat again. Tommy eeping better and out all day. Ella here in afternoon arranging bout Prestwick. Agnes very busy getting ready.

Friday, 14 July

Very nice day. This is Fair Friday so got away at 2 p.m. To celebrate it in a befitting manner, we all went to the Cinerama i the afternoon. The government have cancelled all holidays, so that we can get plenty of shells.[40]

Saturday, 15 July

Not being a munition maker, I have a holiday. Spent the forenoon helping Agnes to pack up. I also cleaned the kitchen windows. We met the Gordons in St Enoch Station. Saw Agnes Tommy and them safely away. I shed a few tears. She is away for a fortnight. I went home and out again. Went to the Barrow and then to People's Palace.[41] Came home for tea. Walked out to Ruglen and called up at 200 Main Street.

Sunday, 16 July

I'm all on my own now. Went to Queen's Park before breakfast Went out for a big walk after dinner. Round by Clarkston and Giffnock.

Monday, 17 July

Got a postcard from my well-beloved. 'All well.' So was duly elevated. The war is costing Britain £6m a day.

Tuesday, 18 July

Very dull day and too cold. Pity the poor orphan. I think I'll make a dinner tomorrow night. Wonder how Agnes and Wee Tommy are doing. British going ahead: 84 guns and 11,000 prisoners since the big push started, and the French have taken 12,000 Germans. Holidays postponed till after the war.

---

[40] Holidays for munition workers were suspended until the end of the war.
[41] The People's Palace is a social history museum on Glasgow Green.

Wednesday, 19 July

Beautifully warm, sunny day. Hope Agnes is getting the same. Laid in a fresh stock of provisions, to wit loaves, cheese and cocoa. Walked out to Ruglen at night. Up Stonelaw round Blairbeth and down Mill Street. Called in at Bowling Green and saw Sam. Went up to house with him and had tea. Home 12 p.m. Saw an aeroplane. Got a letter from my dearly beloved today. I will write her anon.

Thursday, 20 July

Weather perfect. Very warm. Made unto myself at night sausages and potatoes. After that I took a walk to Maxwell Park. Saw another aeroplane tonight. German naval prisoners in Britain – 136 officers, 2,056 men. British naval prisoners in Germany – 45 officers, 364 men.

Saturday, 22 July

After my solitary dinner I went over Cathkin Braes. Had a glass of new-laid milk there. It was fine. Called in at the Gorbals Library on my way home. Got the messages and then had my tea. Got a postcard from Agnes. She is well.

Communications

Thomas' diary mentions only a few communication methods, and these make his world seem almost medieval when compared to today's society. People visited each other's houses, often to make arrangements for a later, longer visit or to invite one family to visit another. There were postcards and letters to keep in touch over greater distances, such as when people were on holiday. Christmas and New Year cards were also posted to distant friends and relatives. There were at least two mail deliveries a day, even on Christmas day, but none on Sundays. Postage was cheap - stamps were 1/2d and 1d - and deliveries were quick and often.

There was, for a few people, also the telephone. Thomas' office was connected to the network, but the diary entries suggest that there was only one receiver and that it was the preserve of a distant department, perhaps the boss's secretary. He writes of getting telephone messages, and only once or twice of taking or making a call himself. Messages and calls were generally restricted to family illness and death.

Perhaps more available, but less frequently used, was the telegram, a message dictated to a phone operator or handed in at a post office, then sent across telephone lines to an office near the recipient, printed out and hand-delivered. Payment was by the word, so messages were kept brief.

For news of the war, Thomas relied on two newspapers, *The Glasgow Herald* and the *Bulletin*. The first, a daily broadsheet published in Glasgow since 1783, provided detailed local, national and international coverage of current affairs, business and politics. The second, also produced daily in the city from 1915, was an illustrated paper that provided a more visual record of the day's events in the United Kingdom and on the war front. Thomas often copied the headlines from these papers into his diary, or summarised the contents of news stories. Press stories concerning the war, both on the Home Front and abroad, were vetted by the official censor.

In the early months of the war, only one journalist was allowed to cover the Western Front and he was a serving army officer. The official censor also received telegraphic reports from the British Army fighting units, and edited these before issuing them to the press. Under pressure from the media, especially in America, the War Office later allowed selected Fleet Street reporters to go to the front, but continued to censor their reports and those of their home-based colleagues to manipulate public perception of the war. This was for two reasons: to ensure that the enemy did not receive accurate feedback from any of their actions and to ensure that the British and Irish people were not exposed to so much horror that they lessened their support for the war.

The censor could not stop criticism, however. The *Daily Mail* consistently lambasted the government for its handling of the war, and on 21 May 1915 published what would prove to be the most important editorial of the whole conflict:

> Lord Kitchener has starved the army in France of high-explosive shells. The admitted fact is that Lord Kitchener ordered the wrong kind of shell - the same kind of shell he used largely against the Boers in 1900. He persisted in sending shrapnel - a useless weapon in trench warfare. He was warned repeatedly that

the kind of shell required was a violently explosive bomb that would dynamite its way through the German trenches and entanglements and enable our brave men to advance in safety. The kind of shell our poor soldiers have had has caused the deaths of thousands of them.

Within a week, the Ministry of Munitions was reated under the control of Lloyd George. After he war was over, General Douglas Haig (above) uggested that there may have been too much of n emphasis in the press on shells: 'During the attles of 1917, ammunition was plentiful, but the un situation was a source of constant anxiety.'

In Glasgow, the *Herald* recorded the eginning of the First World War with five ecks of headline at the top of page seven (the ront page was reserved for advertising) of its Vednesday 5 August issue:

Britain's decisive hour.
War with Germany proclaimed.
All military forces called out.
Government take over railways.
The nation's patriotism.

Beneath this were six crisp paragraphs umming up several feet of grey column inches hat followed. They read:

Great Britain declared war on Germany at eleven o'clock last night. An ultimatum was yesterday sent to Germany demanding a reply within 12 hours. The ultimatum expired at midnight, before which hour an unsatisfactory reply was received. The whole of the military forces in the country, including the Territorials, have been called out, and the Government have taken over the railways. We are authorised by the Foreign Office to publish the following official statement:

Owing to the summary rejection by the German Government of the request made by His Majesty's Government for assurances that the neutrality of Belgium will be respected, His Majesty's Ambassador to Berlin has received his passport, and His Majesty's Government declared to the German Government that a state of war exists between Great Britain and Germany as from 11 p.m. on August 4.

Elsewhere in the newspaper, under the headline 'Glasgow receives the news quietly', the *Herald* reported: 'Despite the gravity of the situation involved in the declaration of war between Germany and Great Britain, the reception of the news in Glasgow was of a milder nature than one would have been led to expect. Owing to the lateness of the hour and the fact that rain was falling heavily there were not a great many people in the streets. Those, however, who had evidently remained late in anticipation of an issue received the intimation quietly, and there was no demonstration of any kind.'

Sunday, 23 July

Very warm day indeed. To cool myself, I took a cold bath. I did indeed. Tried my hand today with fried sliced 'sossijes' and potatoes. The fried article was a trifle hard but managed to get my teeth through. Terrific thunder and lightning late in the afternoon. Best I've seen for six years. Had to mooch milk for my tea from Mrs Carmichael.[42] Went to Queen's Park at night.

Tuesday, 25 July

Good weather continues. Got a letter today from Agnes. She is coming home on Saturday. My word. So I wrote her a love letter in return. Worked late tonight and then took car to Dumbreck and went what we used to call the complete walk. Got home at 11 p.m. British still advancing. Last night's list: dead 686, wounded etc. 3,565.

Friday, 28 July

Cleaned all the windows a night, polished the grate and washed round the room, lobby, scullery etc. At 1 a.m. I took supper. 104th week of the war, 158th day of Verdun battle, 29th day of Battle o the Somme.

[42] To 'mooch' is to scrounge.

Saturday, 29 July

Rose at 5.30 a.m. and washed the floor, scrubbed the table and did the name plate, bell etc. Got my holidays today. Gave the house its final polish. Went to St Enoch Station and met my dearly beloveds at 6.30 p.m., both looking fit and well. Zeppelin raid in east coast of England. No damage.

Sunday, 30 July

None of us out today. Too busy looking at each other. Being troubled much since yesterday afternoon with a certain looseness of the bowels, I went to the chemist in the morning who gave me a bottle which 'strafed' the complaint.

Monday, 31 July

My holidays start today. Went in the forenoon to the Art Galleries and got my mind and soul elevated. After dinner we all went to Pollok Estate. After tea we visited Greenlodge Terrace. Josephine has started work as a grocer in Cochranes' shop at Bridgeton Cross. Weekend casualty list: dead 903, wounded etc. 4,106.

Wednesday, 2 August

In the forenoon I went down to Bellahouston Hospital and after some coaxing managed to get in and saw James, who was wounded in the hand in the 'Big Push'.[43]

Thursday, 3 August

Went into town before dinner and paid the factor and the fire insurance. After dinner Agnes went and saw the doctor and then we all went to town and visited the St Enoch Picture House and saw Charlie.[44] I spent the rest of the night getting ready – I'm going to Belfast for a week. Another Zepp raid on England.

This was a temporary military hospital, built at the west end of Bellahouston Park in the south-west of the city, during the First World War. After the war, the injured soldiers were moved to Erskine Hospital.

The St Enoch Picture Theatre opened in Argyle Street in 1913, in the former Crouch's Theatre of Varieties. That night's programme evidently featured Charlie Chaplin.

Friday, 4 August

After a fond farewell to my wife and child last night, I left at 10.15 and got train from Central at 11 p.m. Boat left Ardrossan at 12.45 p.m. Arrived Belfast after a very reasonable sail about 7 a.m. Went to Northern County Station with my bag and got a wash up. Then hunted up my breakfast. Had a look round for 'digs'. Went to see my aunt, and decided to stay there. After dinner I visited Smithfield, and the museum.[45] After tea my uncle and I had a walk round by the dam and then went down to station and lifted my bag. This is anniversary of the war.

Saturday, 5 August

In forenoon I started to explore Belfast. Had a look at County Down Station and as far as Holywood Arches, and came home. After dinner went down to Falls Park and then took car to Bloomfield.[46] After tea I had a seat in Woodvale Park and went down town. Got home 10.15 p.m. Weather perfect.

Sunday, 6 August

In the forenoon I took my aunt a run in the car and had a seat in the Alexandra Park. After dinner I went to Ormeau Park and admired all the little Colleens. After tea I walked out past Ligoniel and back by Horseshoe Rail, got car home from Cliftonville.[47] Home 10.30 p.m. Weekend list – dead 1,751, wounded etc. 4,377

Opposite page *Newtownards lies 10 miles east of Belfast, at the northern end of Strangford Lough, and Mount Stewart is an eighteeenth-century house and garden, the home of the Londonderry family. The Somme Heritage Centre, which opened in 1994, stands a little to the north of Newtownards.*

[45] Smithfield Market, in central Belfast, was a covered market with dozens of shops.
[46] Holywood Arches and Bloomfield are neighbourhoods in east Belfast.
[47] Ligoniel is a village on the edge of north Belfast, Cliftonville is nearby.

AUGUST, 1916

Bank Holiday. Monday 7

(220-146)

Took 9.20 train to Newtownards & then motored to Mount Stewart Left my stick in the motor. Had a very pleasant welcome from Agnes' friends there. Uncle Robert & I out trout fishing. & then Isa came with us for target shooting After tea Isa & I went out to see Jim & his wife (Mabel) I wheeled Isa's baby we were speaking to Minnie Hamilton & her man.

ME.

PORTAFERRY

How I motored to Mt. Stewart

Had a great day entirely. staying here all night.

16980. 64588
1377 4243
18357 41831

AUGUST, 1916.

Tuesday 8
(221-145)

Weather still keeping brilliant. Uncle Robert & I did some fancy target shooting in forenoon. After dinner I took a walk down to the lodge & brought up the post & some fish. I also got back my stick. Went back then with Jim's wife & had tea with them. Jim & I then went out with a gun & I shot 2 bats.

Slept all night in Jim's Cottage.

Tonight's Casualty list
Killed 639.
Wounded etc 4435.

Last night
Dead 738
Wounded etc 2808.

Vednesday, 9 August

Vee Tommy's birthday. More lovely weather. Sawed and hopped wood for a while. Had a crack and small walk with /linnie and then looked up the kennels. Dined with Jim and hen had a walk round. Mabel then went part of the way with ne to the kennels and I had tea there. Uncle Robert then saw ne on to the 5.30 motor. We all parted with deep regret. Caught .27 train from Newtownards to Belfast. Big Zepp raid on east oast and part of Scotland, eight killed.

'hursday, 10 August

'ery hot day. Took car to Ligoniel and then walked out country, ack to town by Cliftonville. Called in at Northern County tation and got my ticket, then did some shopping for a little resent for Agnes and Tommy. After dinner went to the dam nd read my paper. Said farewell to my aunt and got 6.30 train) Larne and sailed to Stranraer by SS *Princess Maud*. Had a ery nice sail and exactly six hours after leaving Belfast I arrived 1 St Enoch's Station. Walked home and arrived there at 1.30 .m., where my own wee wife was waiting on me, and had a ice tea ready for me. Amen.

'riday, 11 August

Ve all slept in today. Naturally spent the day in looking at my 'ell-beloved and my son and heir.

aturday, 12 August

'his is the last day of my holidays, so after breakfast we all took ar to Paisley.[48] We did the sights and visited the museum, and ten had our tea in a tea room. We then went to a picture house, nd got home about 6.30 p.m.

Paisley lies eight miles west-south-west of Glasgow and is the county town of Renfrewshire.

Tuesday, 15 August
Nice sort of day. Working late. Agnes and Tommy came into the place and got me home. The policeman in the key office gave Tommy a penny.[49] British destroyer *Lasso* mined or torpedoed off Dutch coast.

Friday, 18 August
German official list of casualties admits 3,000,087 losses. Austrian losses during June and July 830,000. Tonight's casualty list – killed 666, wounded etc. 4,166.

Saturday 19 August
We took car to Netherlee in the afternoon. Had a seat in Cathcart Cemetery and admired the view, and then took car home. To get the graveyard taste out of my mouth we went to the Majestic at night.

Tuesday, 22 August
We went to the cathedral at night and listened to an organ recital.[50] The organist is a better player than me. Big explosion i Yorkshire munition factory, 40 killed and 60 injured.

Wednesday, 23 August
Poor Wee Tommy not well today. 35 Zeppelins destroyed since war began.

[49] The key office was presumably where the keys to the various offices, stores and cupboards were kept, supervised by a trusted employee who would record each person who borrowed key. Perhaps, because of the wartime importance of the shipping company, a policeman ha been seconded to the job.

[50] Glasgow Cathedral, also known as the High Church, stands about a mile north of Glasgow Cross. It is the principal Church of Scotland, or national Kirk, place of worship in the city.

hursday, 24 August

ommy not much better, in bed all day. What's it going to be? gnes got him a motor to keep him cheery.

Friday, 25 August

Rained morning, noon and night. Tommy all right again. Big Zeppelin raid over England including London: eight killed.

Saturday, 26 August

Rained nearly all day. At night we all went to the Majestic. We are getting quite frivolous or reckless.

uesday, 29 August

ince 1 July, Britain has taken 15,469 German prisoners and 46 guns.

Vednesday, 30 August

gnes and Tommy met me in town at 6 p.m. and we went to he picture house and saw *The Battle of the Somme*.[51]

The propaganda film *The Battle of the Somme* was made by the British Topical Committee for War Films, and released on 10 August 1916. In using footage of the first days of the battle it exposed the home front for the first time to the horrors of mechanised warfare.

Friday, 1 September

James up tonight, the soldier I was down seeing in Bellahouston Hospital on 2 August.

Saturday, 2 September

After tea we all went to the Majestic.

Sunday, 3 September

Great Zeppelin raid on east coast and London: two killed. One of the Zeppelins with its entire crew destroyed near London by one of our aviators.

Monday, 4 September

Tommy's days of freedom are over. He started today to go to school, one called Victoria School in Batson Street. A momentous event. Poor Tommy. Capital of German East Africa surrenders to British. Great advance by British and French at the Somme battle.

Tuesday, 5 September

The airman who destroyed Zeppelin gets a VC.

SEPTEMBER, 1916.

37583.
593
38176

163738
2544
166282

Wednesday 6

(250-116)

Some rain in the forenoon but nice enough day. We have all got the cold,

British win Leuze Wood
fighting at Combles & Ginchy.

U. Boat blown up by British Aviator.

Last nights list Dead 593
Wounded etc 2544

SEPTEMBER, 1916.

38176. 166282
1211 3764
39,387 170046

Thursday 7

(251-115)

Very nice warm day. Our colds are much the same

British active on Macedonian front
Last nights list Dead 1211
Wounded etc 3764

1916

Friday, 8 September

10th week of the war. 200th day of the Verdun battle. 70th day of the Battle of the Somme.

Monday, 11 September

Got doctor's bill today. Puzzle: when will it be paid?

Wednesday, 13 September

After this my dinner hour is from 12.30 p.m. to suit domestic rrangements.[52] Mrs Carmichael and Mrs Mackenzie in tonight rying our sewing machine. Great French advance: 1,500 prisoners.

Friday, 15 September

Tommy got a flower from his teacher for being a good boy. Agnes not well at all. She went to the doctor and got a bottle. 'm keeping well so I cleaned the kitchen window. Great British dvances in France on six miles of front. Trenches at Thiepval aptured.

Saturday, 16 September

British advance continues. Thousands of German prisoners. British using monster armoured motors for charging the renches.

To tie in with Tommy's school timetable.

Sunday, 17 September

Entertained the household with music at intervals.

Monday, 18 September

Agnes bought a griddle, or as the Scotch call it, a 'girdle', so I have no doubt we'll be able to bake scones etc.[53] British doing brilliant. Our motor monsters knock h... out of the huns.

Tuesday, 19 September

One of Agnes' cousins, Mollison, Broughty Ferry, killed at the front.

[53] The reference to the Scotch betrays Thomas' Irish roots.

Wednesday 20

(264-102)

Nice day. but a little Sharp. Agnes did a little work on the Sewing machine. bright.

Britain wants another million men. = I'm here when wanted. Holland says "Nemo me impune lacessit." or "Noli me tangere" So to speak. Serbian Army into Serbian territory again.

Reported Ultimatum from Greece to Germany.

50196.	209799
766	3929
50962	213728

SEPTEMBER, 1916.

Thursday 21

(265-101)

Nice day. Tommy had to bring a penny to school for a picture of the boy hero.

This is it.

In Aid of the "JACK CORNWELL" WARD at the Star & Garter Home

I Cleaned the brass poker shovel tongs & kerb that lend an air of distinction to our drawing room.

Greece sends a stern??? note to Germany demanding back its kidnapped army.

50962	213.428
982	3275
51944	217.003

Friday, 22 September

Agnes cleaned the spoons so that folk could mistake them for silver.

Sunday, 24 September

After breakfast I donned my best and strolled down to Govan and looked at the boats. In spite of the U-boat menace, I crossed over the Clyde to Partick by the ferry.[54] Great Zeppelin raid over England: 38 killed and 99 injured. Zeppelin brought down in flames and another captured with its crew.

Monday, 25 September

Lovely day. This is the autumn holiday, so Tommy and I had a holiday. Tommy very sick all day, vomited and had a sore head. Went into town after dinner and telegraphed to Coatbridge that we could not come out. Wandered into a picture house in New City Road. Came home for tea and went out for doctor. Tommy's temperature 102°. Doctor thinks it is his stomach. I don't know what to think. A melancholy holiday.

Tuesday, 26 September

Doctor up today. Tommy a little better and his temperature down a bit. Another big Zepp raid over England: 36 deaths. Query: when are they coming here? Great Franco-British victory. Thiepval taken by the British and Combles by the French and British. Hoch!

Opposite page *John 'Jack' Travers Cornwell, who was born in London in January 1900 and was therefore sixteen at the time, was celebrated for his gallantry at the Battle of Jutland. He was posthumously awarded the Victoria Cross, one of the youngest recipients ever. The Boy Cornwell Memorial Fund was established in his memory to provide a wing at a naval hospital. The twenty-first of September 1916 was designated Jack Cornwell Day and every school pupil in the British Empire was asked to give a penny to the fund.*

54 Thomas is being facetious. The ferry crosses an upriver stretch of the River Clyde, far from the open sea.

Wednesday, 27 September

Doctor up again. Tommy a great deal better and his temperature normal. Went myself at night to Greenlodge. Home 11 p.m. To protect my valuable life these dark nights I took my stick la plus grande.[55]

Thursday, 28 September

Tommy up in the evening. He is getting a little food now.[56] School Board officer up for Tommy today. British take more ground. Great damage done to Krupps by the French air raid. Hoch, hoch.

Friday, 29 September

Tommy not so bad now. Doctor up today and I don't think he is coming back. Amen!

Saturday, 30 September

A threatened scarcity of water, so we filled the house with it. 3,000 dead Germans in Combles. Hoch.

Sunday, 1 October

The old time starts today again, so I put back the clocks one hour last night. Tommy sang a little hymn tonight and I accompanied him on the piano. This will be his first to music, I think.

[55] His biggest stick.

[56] School Board inspectors visited houses where children were known to live if they were not attending school. This was designed to deter truants.

Monday, 2 October

I mended Alec Carmichael's 'scooter' tonight. British defeat Bulgarians. Roumania gets walloped. Germany going to renew her submarine campaign against Britain.

Tuesday, 3 October

Very wet day. Spent a quiet evening at home. Put some studs in Tommy's boots and shoes.[57] Put a bit of wood in the bunker to keep the mice in their place.[58]

Thursday, 5 October

Nellie here in the afternoon. Jenny Roxburgh here at night. I saw her away at Queen St Station by 10 p.m. train. Bulgars in retreat before the British

Friday, 6 October

Put a few studs in my boots tonight. British advance further towards Bapaume and we use poison gas at Armentières and Loos. Big Cunard liner *Franconia* torpedoed in Mediterranean Sea: 12 lives lost.

Saturday, 7 October

Agnes, Tommy and I at Coatbridge by 2.40 train from Buchanan Street. I took a walk down myself to the hotel and had a glass of milk with Mr Crozier.[59]

Studs are small metal plates attached to nails, which are hammered into the soles and heels of shoes to lessen wear on the leather.

Thomas evidently suspects that the mice are coming into the kitchen through a hole in the coal bunker.

The milk may have been something stronger.

Sunday, 8 October
Agnes and Tommy at Mrs Carmichael's church in the afternoon with the aforesaid Mrs Carmichael.

Monday, 9 October
Tommy started school again today. German submarines appear off New York. Several British and neutral boats sunk.

Tuesday, 10 October
America very uneasy about U-boats' new move.

Friday, 13 October
British 'tanks' in action in Macedonia.[60] British prisoners in Germany: 30,101. German prisoners in Britain: 39,020.

Saturday, 14 October
Weather today is the absolute, absolute limit. Perfect hurricane all day and rain by the bucketful.

Sunday, 15 October
Agnes went to church today, but did not get in. To cheer her up I took her to Sighthill Cemetery after dinner.[61]
J'y suis, je n'y pas reste.[62]

Monday, 16 October
Father in when I got home. He says Donald is very ill. Saw father home, and went up for a little and had a cup of tea. Got home without meeting any of the Redskins.[63]

---

[60] The first tanks were used during the Battle of the Somme in August 1916. The Royal Tank Regiment was formed from the Heavy Machine Gun Corps earlier that year.
[61] Sighthill Cemetery, opened in 1840 as Glasgow's second garden cemetery, stands about one mile north of the cathedral.
[62] Tommy has adapted the French expression 'J'y suis, j'y reste' ('Here I am and here I stay') to mean 'Here I am, here I don't stay' in reference to his cemetery visit ('J'y suis, je n'y reste pa is the correct usage).

Tuesday, 17 October

Had a musical evening at home. Among those present were Daisy and May Crozier and Hetty Cook. They all sang several songs tastefully accompanied on the piano by Mr Livingstone. I saw Daisy and May off from the Cross about 10.15 p.m. and then took Hetty Cook to Jamaica Street and shoved her on to her car.

Thursday, 19 October

Father here at dinner time. I guessed the worst when I saw him. Donald died this morning. We went over to Greenlodge Terrace at night.

Friday, 20 October

Fine day. Tommy not at school today. I went over to Greenlodge at night to see about funeral. Agnes saw about the wreath today. Another Cunard liner sunk.

Saturday, 21 October

Donald buried today in Riddrie Cemetery.[64] I met Duncan, Jack, John Martin and Jack Cavins at Union Street. Took car to Rouken Glen, met Josephine, Lily and Isa and somebody else there, and then Sam turned up. We got car to Barrhead. Funeral left there about 1.15. We got to Riddrie about 3 p.m. and there laid Donald to rest. We went back to Greenlodge for our tea and got home at 8.30 p.m. 'Naked came I out of my mother's womb, and naked shall I return thither; the Lord gave and the Lord hath taken away; blessed be the name of the Lord.'[65]

Troublemakers. Thomas is casting himself as a frontier scout or cowboy, in danger of attack from hostile Native Americans.

64 Riddrie Cemetery lies in Riddrie, a suburb in the north-east of Glasgow.

65 From the Book of Job.

OCTOBER, 1916.

18th after Trinity. **Sunday 22**
(296-70)

Fine day. Sam & Nellie out to day about 2 o'c. We had dinner then we all went out to the Cemetery. We all went home with Sam & Nellie for tea.

Got home 10.20 pm.

Austrian Premier assasinated.

British torpedo German Cruiser in North Sea of course she does not sink.

OCTOBER, 1916.

Monday 23
(297-69)

Fine day but wet night. Wee peggy here all night playing ~~with~~ Tommy.

Got my hair Cut tonight at 6 p.m.

Before.

after.

Air raid on Sheerness last night. One raider shot down.

Air raid today on Margate.
Very little damage.

Tuesday, 24 October

Helped Tommy
with his lessons
at night
A. says ah.
B. " bi
Y " 'igh.
O " O
U " ugh.
I " fed up
AB CD
H F

Thursday, 26 October

British airmen bombard German blast furnaces at Metz.

Saturday, 28 October

Two years ago Lily died, and I often think of her; too often.

Previous page *Count Karl von Stürgkh, the Austrian Prime Minister, was assassinated by Dr Friedrich Adler in Vienna on 21 October 1916 as a protest against the war and the suspension of the Austrian parliament.*

aturday, 4 November

Jice night. So I went over to Greenlodge for the bed and edding which Josephine is giving us for Tommy. Duncan elped me over. This is Red Cross flag day. Irish shipping isaster: 90 lives lost.[66]

Ionday, 6 November

Iy boss intimates to me today that my salary is increased.

Vednesday, 8 November

'otal German losses now are 3,755,693 men.

riday, 10 November

'his is the birthday of my wife. Long may she reign.

aturday, 11 November

Ve had a sort of party tonight. First came father, then Lily and er boy (Jonny), then Josephine, Isa and Jack, lastly Duncan. 'hey filled our little cabin. We played divers games and had ausic etc.

unday, 12 November

'ommy got a bad cough, so he stayed in bed all day. Agnes not p to the mark. As I said before, my hair is turning grey. I went ut before dinner. Took car to Springburn and wandered round y Maryhill.[67]

'assenger ship the *Connemara* collided with a coal transporter and sank at the mouth of Carlingford Lough, in the north of Ireland, on 3 November 1916. More than 90 people were killed.

Springburn and Maryhill are working-class districts in the north-west of Glasgow.

NOVEMBER, 1916.

Monday 13

(318-48)

Very dull mild day. So I threw off my overcoat. Tommy's cough bad so we kept him in bed all day. Agnes not keeping any better so I'm afraid her old trouble will come back again. I'm a very worried man.

Serbia doing well just now

NOVEMBER, 1916.

Tuesday **14**

(319-47)

Working late tonight

Tommy's school burned early this morning. As it was in the morning Tommy was not burned. As Tommy is still in bed, he would not have been burned in any case.

Dull mild day.

Another Great British advance in France. Over 4000 prisoners.

German naval attack in Gulf of Finland. Russians beat it off. Germany loses several destroyers.

Food and drink

The First World War hugely influenced the availability of food and drink in Glasgow, both in terms of quality and quantity. Quality varied as scarce ingredients were replaced by more readily available alternatives: white bread loaves became brown when processed wheat flour was replaced by wholegrain, diluted with potato flour. Quantity was controlled first by the market and then by the government, as imports were reduced by enemy action on the ships that brought meat, grain and other staples to the UK from the countries of the British Empire and other trading partners. The U-boat blockade of the British and Irish isles threatened to starve their citizens into submission. Times were tough, of that there is no doubt, but adding whole grains to white bread probably did people some good. And if pipe tobacco, cigars and cigarettes were in short supply, there were likely health benefits to that too, not that people of the time would necessari have appreciated this.

A government propaganda poster issued in April 1917 made it plain how Britons would survive the privations. In black type on a plain background, it proclaimed: 'The enemy is going be beaten in the homes of Glasgow: The women are going to do it'. This was an exhortation to those in charge of buying food and cooking it not to stockpile supplies and to avoid any waste. At t time the poster was issued, one in four merchant ships heading for British ports was being sunk by U-boats, and there was great concern in government circles that it was only a matter of time before the country would run out of food. I spring 1917, the food stocks of the nation were reduced to a mere three weeks' worth.

At the start of the war, the government took hands-off attitude to food production and consumption. Prices rose steeply in 1916, and

THE ENEMY
IS GOING TO BE
BEATEN IN
THE HOMES OF
GLASGOW
THE WOMEN
are going to do it

lative food rationing Britain, Germany l Austria.

ocers were accused of making excess profits m the troubled times. In 1917 a propaganda r was launched to encourage thrift, but it was t really until 1918 that the British government roduced food rationing, partly as a reaction to malnutrition being suffered by the poorest in iety. First it was sugar, and then butter, jam, , bacon and fresh meat. Sugar was rationed m 31 December 1917 to 29 November 1920; tter from 14 July 1918 to 30 May 1920; margarine from 14 July 1918 to 16 February 1919; lard from 14 July to 16 December 1918; raw meat from 7 April 1918 to 15 December 1919; bacon and ham from 7 April to 28 July 1918; jam from 2 November 1918 to 15 April 1919; and tea from 14 July to 2 December 1918. Each house had three ration cards: a meat card, a card for butter or margarine, and a sugar card. Each adult was allowed 15 ounces of beef, lamb, mutton or pork, five ounces of bacon, four ounces of butter, margarine or lard, and eight ounces of sugar a week. These amounts remained static until rationing was ended.

The government was quicker to act on drinking, concerned that the efficiency of workers, especially those in munitions and other war-related occupations, could be reduced by alcohol consumption. Brewing and distilling also used valuable supplies of fuel, grain and sugar, which were needed for food. The Defence of the Realm Act restricted pub opening hours, and so-called Munition Ale, brewed at a lower strength to reduce the amount of grain needed, was introduced. In October 1915, the government passed the No Treating Order, which banned people from buying alcoholic drinks for others. Duty was raised, too, and the price of a bottle o whisky rose from 4/- in 1914 to £1 in 1918.

A child is bathed in a Glasgow tenement sink.

For tenement dwellers, the kitchen was the h of family life. The room was dominated by the fireplace, which usually sat opposite the gas- or coal-fuelled cooker. The cooking range was used supply hot water for cooking, cleaning and bathing; as a cooking hob and oven; to heat heav solid metal irons for ironing clothes; and to provi background heat for the room. The kitchen wou also include a sink, various cupboards and shelve where dishes, pans and cooking utensils were ke and a scullery where small amounts of perishabl foods would have been stored.

The scullery included a window open to the elements, which helped keep the temperature lower there than in the rest of house - though i summer, butter, cheese and milk had to be eate on the day of purchase. The coal bunker would also be competing for space, while above head height washing would be drying on a pulley, perhaps dripping on to the linoleum floor belo A curtain usually concealed the bed recess, into which a bed frame with a horsehair mattress a heavy bedding was jammed. The space below bed, and shelves above, were used for storage.

A typical Scottish meal of the period might Scotch broth (a soup of vegetables and mutton) mince and potatoes (minced beef cooked in gra with peas and carrots, and served with either whole or mashed potatoes) and potato scones (f bread made with potato flour) and jam. Agnes was a frequent maker of baked goods and jam, both for her family and for the many visitors who came to the house.

Vednesday, 15 November

gnes went to some school at night, where they are teaching var cookery. Times are hard. Eggs 4d each, loaf 5d each, otatoes about 1/10 a stone.

hursday, 16 November

ndrew's wife up in the forenoon for a 'heart to heart' alk. The paper says I've to be re-examined, so here's ıck. I'll be a 'sojer' yet. Blast the Kaiser. Government is oing to take control of the food.[68] High blinking time.

riday, 24 November

I'm working late again. Fed up.

unday, 26 November

n the afternoon I took Tommy with me and went up to Sam's to ee how he had got on with the military. He has got exemption.

uesday, 28 November

nother Zeppelin raid last night in north of England: two epps destroyed. A German aeroplane drops a few bombs on ondon today. Another naval raid on east coast.

Thursday, 30 November

Government takes over Welsh coal pits.[69]
St Andrews Day.

Sunday, 3 December

Rumours of a change in the government. High time or we lose the war.

The government appointed Lord Devonport as Food Controller, to regulate the supply of food and to encourage food production, and hinted that it would take control of bread production.
The government announced on 29 November 1916 that the Board of Trade would take control of the south Wales coalfield from 1 December 1916, to ensure supplies.

Monday, 4 December

Our one and only porter at my work on the spree, so I go down to jail and bail him out for two guineas.

Tuesday, 5 December

Attended the court in the morning. Our one and only Barnes fined one guinea. In the name of the firm I paid it. I went to Ruglen to get my allowance of godliness. Agnes washed her hair. Asquith and Lloyd George resign.[70]

Wednesday, 6 December

Agnes went to the 'war cookery' class at night. I stayed in and broke some firewood, mended a little box, sawed a ham bone in two, brushed a few dozen pairs of boots and in the middle put Tommy to bed. Bonar Law refuses the Premiership. The King summons the Cabinet.

Thursday, 7 December

Nellie's grandmother dead aged 95. A good old age. Lloyd George – Prime Minister.[71] Explosion in a munition factory in north of England: 26 women killed.

Friday, 8 December

Saw the Redskins today for the front.[72] Some in khaki and four 'braves' with their war paint on. A new War Cabinet made – go on with the flaming war!!! Policemen in the back greens tonight making the loyal subjects pull down their blinds.

Saturday, 9 December

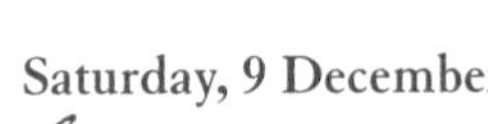

Speculated in a War Loaf today.[73]
Anchor liner Caledonia sunk by U-boat.

[70] On 1 December, Lloyd George, Secretary of State for War, declared that he could no longer be part of the coalition government. On 3 December, Herbert Asquith, who had been Prime Minister since 1908, and who was facing mounting criticism over his handling of the war, announced that he would reconstruct the government. The following day, the King approved the reconstruction, and on 5 December both Lloyd George and Asquith resigned their positions.

[71] Lloyd George was Prime Minister from 1916 until 1922.

Tuesday, 12 December

Sold our one and only pram today. It has done its duty. We were good friends. Our hearts are broken. Farewell.

Wednesday, 13 December

Had a very sore ear-ache yesterday – am sort of deaf of an ear today. Germany desires peace and makes peace proposals, which I don't think will be accepted.

Thursday, 14 December

Germany's peace proposals get the frozen shoulder.

Sunday, 17 December

Rose before the break of day. Made two cups of tea, one for my one and only, and other for myself. Then took a walk to Ruglen by the country and home by Oatlands. Very foggy and frosty.

Wednesday, 20 December

I cleaned a few boots. Lloyd George makes a great speech.[74] *No peace. British nation to be mobilised. Go on with the war.*

Friday, 22 December

Sent off a few hundred Christmas cards.

Saturday, 23 December

Took a walk out to Ruglen in afternoon and made my tailor accept a little present of money.

More than 400 Native Americans from the western plains of Canada fought for the British Empire in the First World War.

The War Loaf was made with whole wheat and other grains as well as potato flour. It had a darker colour that the usual bread, which was made from wheat grain alone.

Lloyd George made his first speech as Prime Minister on 19 December 1916. He laid out his government's plan for conscription, the state control of shipping and other critical issues.

DECEMBER, 1916.

4th in Advent.
Peace Sunday. Sunday **24** •
(359-7)

Not out all day
So don't know
what kind of weather
we are getting

This is the night
we hang up our
stockings

DECEMBER, 1916.

Christmas Day. Monday 25
(360-6)

I wish you all a merry Christmas.

Dirty wet day maxwell in the place today I got away at 1 p.m. maxwell, Andrew Sutherland & I adjourned to the "Rogano" then went and got photographed

Took Agnes & Tommy to Cinerama at night.

Switzerland sends a peace note to the fighters

DECEMBER, 1916.

Boxing Day. Tuesday 26

(361-5)

Nice sort of day
I Cleaned brass pokers
etc at night.

Tommy got a
scarf + a game
of ludo from
Coatbridge.
From us he
got various articles
slippers etc and
a drawing slate.

Tommy wrote a letter
of thanks to uncle
Bob at night.

2 British destroyers sunk
by collision in North
Sea 55 lives lost.

Great British victory in Egypt.

'riday, 29 December

Rose at cock crow and cleaned room windows. Did a ittle joiner work tonight. Sorted up the wooden bed ittings to suit the room. Brilliant success.

aturday, 30 December

leaned the kitchen window and then went to Langside Library or mental refreshment. The house is about ready now for the New Year.

unday, 31 December

Ve are now sitting up to see the New Year come in, trusting nd hoping that the incoming year will bring peace, happiness nd prosperity. Amen.

revious page *Rogano, now best known as Glasgow's oldest and most refined restaurant, was reviously an up-market bar with the ambience of a gentleman's club. The four young entlemen were clearly living beyond their means for an hour or two on Christmas Day.*

1917

With best wishes for a
Happy New Year.

Monday, 1 January

Being New Year day, I am on holiday. So is Tommy. Seeing half the railway stations are closed, and a big lot of trains off, and railway fares put up 50% from today, I went into town in forenoon to see about a train to Coatbridge. We got 2.20 from the Cross, and visited our friends in Coatbridge. Hetty Cook there. We got 9.20 train back, travelling in a manner befitting our noble station in life, viz. first class. The Carmichael clan first-footed us.[1]

Tuesday, 2 January

Wild wet day, and still very mild. Ella Gordon here in forenoon, asking us down to Ibrox at night, which invitation we gratefully accepted. She brought Tommy a scarf for his Ne'erday.[2] Britain stops the export of coal to Norway.

Wednesday, 3 January

Wilder, wetter and stormier than ever. Very mild. Started work today. Met my niece Lily in Buchanan Street. She told me Sam's boy Wee John was away with diphtheria. Josephine and Wee Jack here at 7.30. Tommy got from them a little case containing two pencils, one pen, one rule, one pen wiper and a piece of 'injy' rubber.[3]

Thursday, 4 January

Agnes and Tommy down at Clydebank in afternoon to see Jenny Roxburgh and family. I went straight from my work by car. Train smash near Edinburgh. NB express, 12 killed and about 40 injured.[4]

[1] 'First-footing' is a Scottish custom, ensuring that the first person over the threshold in the New Year arrives with good wishes, and pieces of cake and coal, representing a steady supply of food and warmth.

[2] Until relatively recently, Scots celebrated New Year far more than they did Christmas. Here, Tommy was given a scarf for New Year day (Ne'erday).

[3] The pen would have been a wooden shaft with a metal nib. The pen wiper was for removing excess ink, and the piece of India ('injy') rubber for erasing pencil errors.

riday, 5 January

Vent out to Ruglen at night to inquire as to Wee John, but got o one in. When I got home, Duncan was in. British transport *vernia* (Cunard Line) sunk in Mediterranean by U-boat. About 60 lives lost. During 1917, 582,423 of the enemy taken prisoner n all fronts.

aturday, 6 January

ook Agnes and Tommy to town in afternoon, and admired the hops, and looked at the things we would buy when the war is ver. Allies have a war 'pow wow' in Rome.[5] Lloyd George ttends. TCL does not.

unday, 7 January

ouring wet day. Took a swim out to Ruglen to see how Wee ohn was keeping. Got them in this time. Sam and Nellie came ack with me. Spent an enjoyable evening. I ate an orange onight. It was rotten.

Ionday, 8 January

Tommy's holidays over now. Agnes n wash-house today. Called in at Hugh Paterson's on my way home nd got 12 bed boards for 2/3. Did a little sawing with same.

Tuesday, 9 January

)id some wood splicing at night. Agnes ironed all night. ;reat Russian victory on Riga front. Greece gets 48 hours o behave itself.

Two trains belonging to the North British (NB) Railway Company collided head-on at Queensferry Junction, near Edinburgh. Twelve people were killed and 48 injured.

Representatives of the British, French and Italian governments met in Rome from 5 to 7 January.

Wednesday, 10 January

This is the day the War Loaf is official. Agnes 'plunked' her cookery class tonight. Did some sawing. Roumania still retreats.

Thursday, 11 January

Again, Agnes ironed at night. I did nothing of vital importance. Word to hand from America: death of Buffalo Bill.[6] Great British victory in Egypt. Two British warships sunk by the enemy in the Mediterranean. Ben-my-Chree and Cornwallis; 13 lives lost.

Friday, 12 January

Cleaned all the handles of brass in the house, including the jam pan. The Allies publish the peace conditions to America. The Great British War Loan launched today – another reply to Germany.[7] Think I'll invest a million or so. Greece climbs down

Sunday, 14 January

Before dinner I went out for a walk by myself. Queen's Park, Maxwell Park, and back by Paisley Road. After dinner we all went to Queen's Park.

[6] William F. Cody, better known as Buffalo Bill, brought his Wild West show to Glasgow on two occasions: a long engagement in Denniston during the winter of 1891-2 and a shorter stay in Govanhill in August 1904.

[7] The government asked the public to invest in this scheme, which was used to fund the war, and which promised to return investor'smoney with interest after hostilities were over.

[8] A military expression meaning war until the last weapon.

Monday, 15 January

Tommy not at school.

Tuesday, 16 January

School Board officer up for Tommy.

Thursday, 18 January

Tommy still got a bit of a cough. British troop train smash in Paris, 10 killed. Greece accepts the Allies' demands in full.

Friday, 19 January

Saw searchlights in the sky tonight. The government thinks it will put CIII class (mine) to farm work.

Saturday, 20 January

Took a walk to the Library de Langside in the afternoon. Agnes spent the rest of the day going the messages. Tommy got a new pair of house shoes. Great munition factory disaster near London: 70 killed, 500 injured.[9] Canada has raised about 400,000 men for the war.

Sunday, 21 January

Stood at the Jail Square and listened to the Clincher, Scott Gibson and a few others spouting forth words of lewdness and treason, blasphemy and socialism.[10] As the Clincher said, 'No wonder we cannot win the war!' Great explosion in munition factory in Austria: 40 killed. Explosion in munition factory in Germany: 10 killed.

---

9 Around 50 tons of TNT exploded in a munitions factory in Silvertown in West Ham, then in Essex. A total of 73 people were killed and more than 400 injured.

10 There was a tradition of public speaking on or near Glasgow Green on Sundays. Jail Square, now called Jocelyn Square, stood opposite the main entrance to Glasgow Green, next to the High Court building. Alexander Petrie was known as the Glasgow Clincher from the title of the newspaper he wrote, edited, published and sold. He was an outspoken critic of Glasgow Corporation and other authorities.

Monday, 22 January

Bright day, but cold as ever. Agnes went to the wash-house at night, but Sam and Nellie came up so Agnes did not get much done. Tommy at school today. Germany seems to be in a very bad way for food.

Tuesday, 23 January

Agnes up at 4.40 a.m.!!! and went to the wash-house. All boys of 18 must join the army immediately. Germany's doom is sealed.

Wednesday, 24 January

The military may put me to a coal mine to replace men called up. Fighting in North Sea. German torpedo flotilla smashed up. We lose a destroyer.

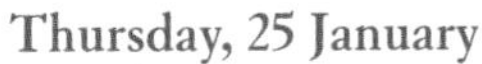

Thursday, 25 January

Agnes nearly cut her finger off today. The output of whisky and beer to be reduced by 30%.[11]

Friday, 26 January

Got a letter from Jenny Roxburgh saying they would all be out on Saturday. Agnes did a big baking at night. German U-boat shells the Suffolk coast for three minutes, then bolts for its life. No damage done.

[11] As well as diverting grain for food use, this was intended to reduce alcohol consumption, which was seen as reducing the efficiency of workers.

Saturday, 27 January

Had a small party on tonight. Jenny Roxburgh and her three sisters arrived at 4.45. Had a great time. Tommy got a fancy affair of flags sent by Miss Fraser.

Monday, 29 January

Tommy got a medical ticket from school for me to fill in. Has he had the measles, scarlet fever, the mumps, whooping cough, corns, warts, bunions, DTs, wooden legs, brain fever, etc., etc., etc.[12] British success at Transloy. British auxiliary cruiser *Laurentic* (White Star Line) mined south coast of Ireland. About 350 lives lost.

Wednesday, 31 January

Plot to murder Lloyd George.

Thursday, 1 February

Not feeling well tonight at all, so sat in and did nothing. Think I've got the cold. Germany declares a blockade on the entire world. Ora pro nobis!

On 1 February 1917 Germany promised a strategy of 'unrestricted' submarine warfare, which meant the sinking without warning of all merchant ships, Allied or neutral, in European waters. The Germans hoped by this policy to starve Britain into submission, and they came close to succeeding. The submarine campaign reached its height in March and April 1917, when about 750 Allied and neutral ships were sunk.

12 Thomas is making fun of the long list of medical complaints, and has inserted a number of spurious categories, including DTs (delirium tremens, an affliction of alcoholics).

Friday, 2 February

Tommy got a card at school. He is to be medically examined next Thursday. Wild wrath in America with Germany. Britain gets ready for the U-boats.

Sunday, 4 February

Agnes and Tommy at church today. My cold seems not so bad, but I did not go out. Got in a bottle of olive oil to drink; see if it will do any good.[13] Diplomatic relations broken between USA and Germany. In a year or so they might be at war.

Monday, 5 February

I'm feeling much worse again. America very war-like now.

Tuesday, 6 February

Left my work at 4 p.m. All out. Bathed my feet and went to bed. Looks as if I wasn't well. Brazil and Spain protest to Germany.

Wednesday, 7 February

In bed today. Had to rise in the forenoon as the daft wife upstairs called Dunn flooded the kitchen by leaving her taps turned on. Went upstairs and cussed, then went back to bed. The factor here in the afternoon for the rent. He got it. He is giving us paint for the kitchen. I got up at night and Agnes went to her cookery class. Hetty Cook in at night.

[13] Olive oil was a popular home remedy for colds.

Housing and factors

In the early days of the twentieth century the majority of Glaswegians lived in rented properties owned by private landlords and administered by factors, or property managers. Houses were rented by the year, beginning on 28 February, so on that day each year the streets were thronged with horses and carts laden high with household goods as people 'flitted' from one rented property to another. This was one of the four Scottish term days, equivalent to the four quarter days observed in England when servants were hired and rents and rates were due.

The traditional term days date back to the medieval period, when everyone's calendar was based on the church's high days and holy days. In Scotland, the traditional term days were Candlemas, or the feast of the Purification (2 February); Whitsunday or Pentecost (15 May); Lammas, Long Mass, or the Feast of First Fruits (1 August); and Martinmas or the Feast of St. Martin (11 November). In order to standardise the days on which servants were hired and houses were let, which had become quite varied across Scotland, the government passed the Removal Terms (Scotland) Act in 1886. This detached the term dates from their religious origins and fixed them as 28 February, 28 May, 28 August and 28 November. Thus, Thomas' diary entry for 28 May 1914 noted: 'This is the day we all flit but I didn't.' The family had just moved into their new accommodation at 14 Morgan Street, so were not part of the great flight on that occasion.

Glasgow is traditionally divided into four geographic areas. There is the city centre, where Thomas worked; the east end, where the factories and their workers were housed; the west end, where the middle classes lived; and the south side, which was mainly residential and included a mix of working-class and middle-class housing. The district of Govanhill, where the Livingstones lived, was firmly in the working-class area of the south side, about a mile south of the Clyde.

William Power, writing in 1922, described 'the pleasaunces of Govanhill, Mount Florida, Shawlands, Strathbungo – in short, that vast borderland of tenements and terraces and cottages known as the "South Side", which at its western end burgeons into the gorgeous villadom of Pollokshields, with lakes, parks, feudal battlements and an outlook over ancient policies to the wooded slopes of Renfrewshire'.[14]

The industrial revolution turned Glasgow into the workshop of the world, and increasing scales of production meant ever-bigger factories, shipyards and railway works, which demanded ever-expanding workforces. These workers came from rural central Scotland, the Highlands and islands, and from Ireland, and took whatever accommodation they could find. Few new houses were built to accommodate the new armies of labour and overcrowding was rife as landlords sought to maximise their rents by squeezing large families into small houses.

One solution to this was the 'ticketed house' scheme, instigated in 1863. Town Council inspectors measured each house and issued a ticket that had to be affixed outside its door, showing the size of the house and the number of adults allowed to live there. A typical ticket read '2200,

[14] William Power, 'Glasgow To-Day', *The Book of Glasgow* (Glasgow: Alex Macdougall, 1922), p.82. 'Pleasaunce' or 'pleasance' is used to mean a pleasure ground or pleasantly laid-out garden with trees and ornaments. Power is referring here to planned suburbs with tree-lined streets and small parks.

5½ adults', which indicated that the volume of the house was 2,200 cubic feet and that a combination of adults and children (those under eight counted as half an adult) adding up to 5 ½ could live there. Inspectors made calls during the night to ensure the rules were being enforced by the landlords.

Nevertheless, by 1921 the Royal Commission on housing in Scotland declared Glasgow the most overcrowded city in Europe, with 40 per cent of households meeting its definition of overcrowded (two people living in one room). The city's population, which had more than doubled since 1821, was 1.1 million people. Conditions in the centre of the city were horrendous, with 700,000 people living on 1,800 acres of land. As the Royal Commission observed, one-seventh of the population of Scotland was living on three square miles of land.

The Glasgow Corporation first took serious action to ameliorate the overcrowded and unsanitary conditions in which many of its inner-city citizens were living in 1866, when it passed the Glasgow Improvements Act giving the Corporation the power to demolish the dilapidated and unsanitary houses that at the time covered about 90 acres in various parts of the city. The City Improvement Trust that was set up to implement the legislation formed 30 new streets and widened 26 existing ones. In the late 1880s, the property market had collapsed and the trust could not find any builders willing to build on the ground it had cleared, so the Corporation intervened and began constructing houses itself. The sandstone tenements of High Street, Saltmarket and Calton were the result. Blocks of houses that shared a common central staircase and back court (or garden), these were solidly built, three to five storeys tall, with two to four houses on each floor. Thus, between them, the Corporation and the trust began the public provision of rented housing in Glasgow.

The tenants who were displaced from the overcrowded slums by the construction of tenements had previously paid £2 a year in rent, and could not afford the minimum £8 a year that the trust was now asking. The tenants of the new houses therefore ended up being the better-off working classes, not the poor whose homes had been demolished. Inspired by the temperance movement of the time, both the trust and the Corporation excluded public houses from their housing, depriving the men in many communities of a social hub.

The back court, where much of the social life of the tenement took place.

As well as the work of the trust, the arrival of the railways into Glasgow, particularly around Glasgow Cross, led to the demolition of many slum areas to allow for the construction of stations, bridges, tracks and ancillary buildings. This allowed light and air into a good number of the wynds and alleys of the city.

Despite these efforts at improvement, during the First World War conditions were still grim in many parts of Glasgow. The Royal Commission on Housing in Scotland reported that in 1921 there were 40,654 one-apartment houses and 112,672 two-apartment houses. A 'one-apartment house' was a house with one room, generally with an outside toilet, and was known locally as a 'single end'. A two-apartment house - i.e. a house with two rooms - was called a 'room and kitchen'. Thomas and his family lived in the latter, in an apartment composed of a kitchen that doubled as a living room and included a bed recess where the adults slept, and a 'front room' or parlour that was only used when guests arrived.

One investigation of Glasgow's housing in 1922 reported:

> The conditions are appalling. As many as eight persons have been found living in a single apartment, with only one bed. In a two-apartment house, two families were discovered, 11 persons altogether. One of the adults had tuberculosis. In the East End, two families, comprising 15 persons, tenanted a room and kitchen suitable for four persons. This is why Glasgow has to spend £800,000 per year on health measures, principally in the treatment of diseases - tuberculosis, fevers, measles and troubles which flourish in the fetid atmosphere of congested areas.[15]

While Thomas, Agnes and Wee Tommy did not live in the worst sort of housing, they did live almost exclusively in one room: the kitchen, where parents and child slept and where cooking, drying of laundry, ironing, bathing and other domestic chores took place and must have made the room pretty damp and noisome. Add coal fires, gas lighting (at a time when the domestic supply was composed of about 10 per cent carbon dioxide, a powerful poison), draughts and vermin, not to mention Thomas' 'thick black' tobacco, and we have a heady mixture of pollutants and toxins swirling around the house.

The factor, who collected rents and arranged for repairs to houses, was not a popular figure. To Thomas, he was a devil in human form, as wicked as the Kaiser and as deserving of being strafed or lynched. The factor's duties included supervising repairs to the commonly-owned parts of tenement buildings, such as the roofs, downspout, main plumbing and any back-court buildings such as wash-houses. There was always a lingering suspicion that too many repairs were carried out at too great a price, probably by cronies of the factor. The factor also dealt with advertising vacant properties, assigning leases to tenants, and evicting those who caused a nuisance or failed to pay their rent.

15 James Willock, 'Glasgow's Municipal Services', *The Book of Glasgow* (Glasgow: Alex Macdougall, 1922, p.165.

Thursday, 8 February

Andrew up to see me at dinner time. Tommy got medically examined at school, and passed with flying colours. Class A. I went out for an hour in the afternoon, which I felt to be quite enough. British capture Grandcourt on the Western Front. Anchor Liner *California* sunk by U-boat: 43 lives lost.

Friday, 9 February

Agnes rubbed my manly CIII chest with anointed oil. Andrew up at dinner time. I was allowed up at tea time. Great number of our merchant boats getting sunk. They are going to starve us.

Saturday, 10 February

I have still a bad cough. Got up about 4.30 p.m. Got my bosom rubbed at night. British destroyer mined: five saved. Big British victory in Egypt. America funking again.

Monday, 12 February

Resumed my work today. Went in at 9.30 and managed to hang on till 5 p.m. Went and saw my doctor at night. He gave me a bottle. Duncan here at night. China protests to Germany. The Scandinavian nations [are] too near Germany, so they say nothing. More British successes in the Ancre. British nearing Kut, in Mesopotamia.

Tuesday, 13 February

Foggy and frosty. Feeling very done up at night. Many boats sunk. Munition factory blown up in Yorkshire. British surround Kut.

Wednesday, 14 February

Agnes went to her cookery class. This is the last night. White Star liner *Afric* sunk by U-boat. America still doing nothing. Evidently waiting till the Germans shell New York.

Thursday, 15 February

Not feeling well at all tonight. Think I'll need a day or so in bed. All the coal mines taken over by the government.[16] American boat torpedoed. Yankeedom once more excited.

Friday, 16 February

I'm not feeling much better. The Great War Loan closes today. I did not invest.

Saturday, 17 February

Great scarcity of potatoes.

Sunday, 18 February

Very dark day. We had the gas lit nearly all day. Kept Tommy in bed as he has a bad sort of cold. Feeling 'no weel' myself. Great British victory on the Tigris: 2,000 captures.

Monday, 19 February

Agnes very bad with her old trouble. Tommy not at school. Being in a weak frame of mind, I paid the gas bill today. Also being 'non compos mentis', I thought I had left the door of the warehouse open when I shut up. Went back and found it all right. 'All out' at night. British success in Egypt.

The government announced that from 1 March the coalfields would be taken over for the duration of the war and run by a Coal Controller in the Coal Mines Department of the Board of Trade.

Tuesday, 20 February

Dirty wet day. Agnes still pretty ill. Tommy very deaf with the cold. I'm not well either. 'So help me bob.' British get repulsed at Kut.

Wednesday, 21 February

Agnes very ill today. She fainted in the forenoon, and nearly did it at night. I went to my doctor at night and got another bottle. Tommy still pretty deaf.

Thursday, 22 February

Nellie Hamilton (Andrew's wife) up in the afternoon. My niece Lily phoned me today to say that Josephine would be out on Sunday.

Friday, 23 February

Agnes' back very sore today. Duncan up tonight. I feel a little better tonight. All neutral shipping still held up with the German U-boat blockade. Still no potatoes.

Monday, 26 February

Fine day. Tommy starts school again today. I don't feel so chirpy today. German destroyers raid the Channel. A few shots fired into Margate. Not much damage. Great Turkish rout. Kut captured by British.

Tuesday, 27 February

The game is up. Had to retire back to bed this morning. Got the doctor in to sound me. Influenza. Milk diet, etc. Andrew up at dinner time to see me. Germans retreating from the Ancre.

Wednesday, 28 February

Slight improvement in my physical condition today. Andrew up at dinner time. Duncan up at night. To save our country from defeat and starvation, he has volunteered for National Service. Cunard Liner *Laconia* sunk by U-boat. Some Americans killed. USA says nothing.

Thursday, 1 March

Doctor up. Looks at my tongue, sounds me and says I'm a lot better. Andrew up at dinner time. British still keeping the Germans on the move on the Ancre. German 'Taube' drops a bomb or two on Broadstairs.[17]

Friday, 2 March

Wet sort of day. Andrew up at dinner time. I'm a lot better today and eating well. Got up for an hour tonight. Agnes went to my society in the afternoon to report.[18] British nearing Bapaume.

Saturday, 3 March

Got up today at 5 p.m. I feel a little shaky. Great potato famine all over the world.

Tauben were German planes with translucent linen wing coverings, which made them very difficult to spot. The wings were curved back, like a bird's, and controlled by warping their shape, giving them the name of dove (Taube in German).

On 9 August 1907 Thomas joined the Scottish Clerks Association. Agnes may have visited the offices of this association, or a friendly society of which Thomas was a member, to claim sickness benefit.

Sunday, 4 March

Woe and woe and lamentations. What a piteous cry was there![19] The wind blew during the night. When Agnes got up, the house was inches deep with soot and the fire wouldn't light. We had to remove to the room.[20] Agnes spent the day cleaning up the kitchen. I got up all day. I had to! Hetty Cook here about 5 p.m., then Duncan came about 7 p.m. Duncan saw Hetty away. I composed a letter to the factor.

Monday, 5 March

I am feeling fine so went round and saw the doctor. Got his permission to start work tomorrow. Andrew looked up at dinner time. Men came up in the afternoon to see the lum. They found that a wee door was off, hence the soot. They put on an old one 'pro tem'.[21] Josephine here at 8 p.m. British destroyer mined in North Sea. All hands lost.

Tuesday, 6 March

Resumed business relations today with my firm. Got our kitchen lum swept today for 2/-. Agnes very busy at night cleaning up in the kitchen. Soot still lying about. I stayed in the room in comfort and ease. Feeling better today than I have for many a long day. Got potatoes to my dinner today.[22]

Wednesday, 7 March

Feeling vigorous now, so I broke up some firewood at night. We flitted back to the kitchen today. Looks as if there is going to be great scarcity of food in the near future.

[19] From the poem 'Edinburgh after Flodden' by William Edmondstoune Aytoun, published in 1864.

[20] The front room or parlour, which would generally only have been used if guests were present.

[21] The Latin phrase 'pro tem' (pro tempore) means 'for the time being' or temporarily.

[22] 'To my dinner' is a Scots idiom meaning 'for my dinner'.

[23] To 'improve the shining hour' is to make the best use of time. The phrase comes from the children's poem 'How Doth the Little Busy Bee' by Isaac Watts, written in 1715.

Thursday, 8 March

Feeling fine now. Improved the shining hour at night by playing cards with my well-beloved.[23] British making for Baghdad. Bad day for British airmen in France. French destroyer sunk by U-boat in the Mediterranean; over 100 lives lost.

British troops marching to Baghdad.

Friday, 9 March

I cleaned the brass-work of the kitchen at night, while Agnes amused herself with a hot iron. Shipping and food question getting a bit serious. Count Zeppelin (the air raid man) dead.[24] RIP.

Saturday, 10 March

Went to Calder Street Library in afternoon. Looks as if there is to be a famine in the land. All American boats to be armed. British transport sunk in the Channel by a U-boat. Over 700 lives lost, mostly South Africans for work in France.[25]

Sunday, 11 March

Very nice day and sunny. My father here in the afternoon to borrow a 'bit'.[26] He got it. I went a walk in the afternoon to Queen's Park and saw the Garden Allotments.[27] I have not got one. Rumoured capture of Baghdad by the British.

Monday, 12 March

Lily, my niece, and her boy John Martin here at night.[28] Government threatens to search houses for hoarded food. Great British triumph in the east. Capture of Baghdad (where the caliphs come from). Turks in full retreat.

Ferdinand Adolf August Heinrich Graf (Count) von Zeppelin died 8 March 1917.
Black South Africans were to fill the jobs left by French men called into the army.
For his drill.
To reduce Britain's reliance on imported food, the government encouraged people who did not have gardens to rent allotments where they could grow vegetables.
In this instance, boy means boyfriend.

British artillery men transporting a gun through the Somme.

Wednesday, 14 March

Tommy's face out in spots. Great alarm. Doctor sent for. He says it is likely his stomach. Gave him some powders. Hetty here when I got home, I saw her away by 10 p.m. train from Queen Street. American boat sunk. British three miles past Baghdad. British army advance on the Somme.

Thursday, 15 March

Nice sunny day, but coldish. Spots seem to be spreading over Tommy. So once more we send out the SOS call to the doctor. His glands are swollen, so we think of the measles. Diplomatic relations broken between China and Germany. China seizes all German shipping lying about.

Friday, 16 March

Doctor up in the forenoon. Tommy has the German measles. Doctor says it is a mild case. Duncan up at night. Revolution in Russia. Czar dethroned. The Duma are in full power. The Czar and Czarina are prisoners. British destroyer mined in Channel.

Saturday, 17 March

Tommy of course is in bed. He has a cough. Went to Sam's shop t night. Brought home some sticks. Zeppelin raid over England. One of the Zepps brought down in France. Great British triumph in France. Bapaume captured.

The Russian crowd in Red Square salutes Joseph Stalin (right) and Leon Trotsky during the Russian Revolution.

unday, 18 March

Very stormy day. I did not go out at all. British and French advance continues. Grand Duke Nicholas in supreme command f Russian Army. German destroyers raid Kentish coast.

Monday, 19 March

Great British advance on 40-mile front to a depth of seven to 0 miles. French advance between 30 and 40 miles. Many towns aptured, including Peronne. Turkish rout continues from Baghdad.

Tuesday, 20 March

I went myself at night to Ruglen. Business – Sam's choir in Town Hall making melodious noises. Got home at a late hour. British and French still following up the Germans. British destroyer torpedoed in the Channel. More American boats being sunk.

Wednesday, 21 March

Nellie here at night to go with Agnes to the Alhambra to see this sort of thing.[29] *British and French still advancing. Turkish force cut off at Aden. Riots in Germany.*

Thursday, 22 March

Bright sunny day, but bitter cold. Agnes got a touch of the bile today. Andrew's last day at his work today. He goes into military life on Monday. Two British minesweepers sunk.

Saturday, 24 March

Dull sort of day. Have got a bad cold in the blinking head. In case of accident, I bathed my feet at night and drunk hot lemonade (imagine). French battleship *Danton* sunk in Mediterranean by U-boat: 300 lives lost and about 800 saved.

Sunday, 25 March

Hot lemonade was a failure. Andrew up to say farewell. His wife came with him. Riots reported all over Germany.

Monday, 26 March

I brought home some real medicine, at 1/6 the gill.[30] Bathed my feet at night and went to bed happy.

---

[29] The Alhambra Theatre, at 41 Waterloo Street in central Glasgow, specialised in variety and music hall acts, particularly Scottish ones.

[30] Whisky. A gill is a quarter of a pint.

'uesday, 27 March

'he 'fire water' did me no good. So I got a sweating powder in the hemist for 2d. Am I in for influenza or the measles? Bathed my :et again tonight, put the powder on my tongue, took a drink of mmon water, went to bed and sweated all night. Bread up again.

Vednesday, 28 March

.m feeling not so bad now. Agnes doing some sewing machine vork: looks like a fancy quilt. Got a form today, asking me to olunteer for National Service. British hospital ship sunk by a U-oat. Two British destroyers sunk, one by mine, other by collision.

'hursday, 29 March

'roop ship mined off Cape of Good Hope. All on board saved. ig British victory in Palestine. About 1,000 prisoners taken, ncluding some Austrians and Germans.

aturday, 31 March

ine sunny day. Wind coming from the North Pole. Sewing achine operations suspended as the needle broke last night.[31] Iore villages captured by the British. Another German raider at rge in Atlantic.

unday, 1 April

'ather here for a little in the afternoon. Put a new needle in the achine today. Hetty Cook here at tea time. I deposited her on a ar at 9.30 p.m. Agnes bathed her feet tonight.

Ionday, 2 April

Iost outrageously cold north-east wind blowing. Snow at night. ritish and French threaten St Quentin.

An example of Thomas using the language of the military for domestic events. He is a great believer in what the Victorians called 'elegant variation', using a rich variety of phrases rather than repeating a common one.

Tuesday, 3 April

Snow about a yard deep in the morning. Got a letter from Andrew today. President Wilson calls on the American senate t declare war on Germany.

Wednesday, 4 April

Tommy out today for the first time. Not much doing tonight. Needing a new pipe, so I boiled an old one. British and French still moving on. Great preparations for war in U.S.A.

Thursday, 5 April

I oiled the [sewing] machine tonight, and broke the driving belt so had to mend it. Germans cross the Stokhod (Volhynia) and Russians suffer heavy losses. Britain wants another half million soldiers for July. American senate votes for war with Germany.

Friday, 6 April

This is the day we eat hot cross buns, but owing to the war we did not. American House of Representatives vote solidly for wa with Germany. So that does the trick. Brazilian steamer sunk b U-boat, with loss of life. Brazil wants war. Air raid over Kent b German Taube. No damage.

When the Germans extended their policy of 'unrestricted' submarine warfare to American ships, the United States was compelled to declare war, according to President Woodrow Wilson, in order that 'the world must be made safe for democracy'. And free trade, he could have added. To Wilson, Germany's policy was in violation of international law and his country's ideas of human rights; to his predecessor, Theodore Roosevelt, Germany's actions were simply 'piracy'. Other factors that may have helped draw the US into the fray were the sabotage by German agents of an ammunition depot and a munitions factory in New Jersey.

1917

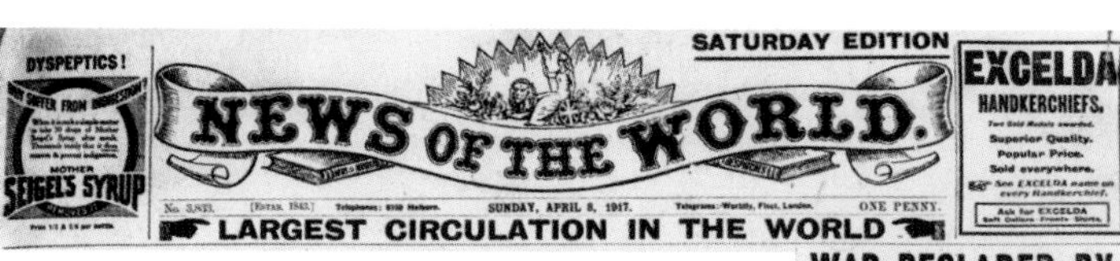
DYSPEPTICS!

MOTHER SEIGEL'S SYRUP

SATURDAY EDITION

NEWS OF THE WORLD.

SUNDAY, APRIL 8, 1917. ONE PENNY.

LARGEST CIRCULATION IN THE WORLD

EXCELDA HANDKERCHIEFS.

Superior Quality. Popular Price. Sold everywhere.

See EXCELDA name on every Handkerchief.

Ask for EXCELDA Soft Collars Fronts Shirts.

aturday, 7 April

Ionday being a oliday, and not eing busy, I got vay at 12.30 m. United States declares war on Germany. All German iipping in America – about half a million tons – is seized, kewise all German wireless installations. Ne plus ultra.[32] ussian and British troops join forces in Mesopotamia.

WAR DECLARED BY UNITED STATES.

RESOLUTION PASSED BY BOTH HOUSES OF LEGISLATURE.

ARMY OF 2,000,000.

I advise that Congress declare that the recent course of the Imperial German Government to be in fact nothing less than war against the Government and people of the United States; that it formally accepts the status of a belligerent which is thus thrust upon it, and that it takes immediate steps not only to put the country in a more thorough state of defence, but also to exert all its power and to employ its resources to bring the Government of the German Empire to terms and end the war.—From Mr. Wilson's address to Congress.

It was carried by an overwhelming majority. The House of Representatives, after 17 hours' debate, also adopted the resolution by an overwhelming majority. The figures were:

	Senate.	Lower House.
For war	82	373
Against	6	50
Majority	76	323

WAR ON MANKIND.

MR. WILSON'S INDICTMENT OF GERMAN RULERS.

ARMY OF 500,000 MEN TO BE ENROLLED.

Sunday, 8 April

This being Easter Sunday, I ate a pair of eggs to breakfast. Could not get a newspaper today, so don't know how the war is getting on.

onday, 9 April

his is the spring holiday. Snow fell overnight. I got up at 6 a.m. id walked through Queen's Park. Everything white with ow, and this is spring. We all went to the Savoy Picture House the afternoon.[33] Cuba declares war on Germany. German inboat blown up by its crew, and Americans take crew of over 0 prisoners. Greatest air battle of the war fought on Western ont. 46 German machines down; British lose 28. New Big ish by British from Arras to Lens.

'his Latin phrase means 'the highest point' or 'the most profound degree'. Thomas seems to nean that there could be no better news than this.

'he Savoy Picture House, in Hope Street at its junction with Renfrew Street, in the city entre of Glasgow, opened in December 1916. The Savoy Centre and Tower, on the same te, retains the name.

Tuesday, 10 April

Bitter cold day. Some heavy snow in the afternoon. After a most terrific cannonade, British launch their spring offensive on a 50-mile front. Battle of Arras has begun. Heavy German losses. We capture about 10,000 prisoners. The fighting is proceeding. Vimy Ridge captured by Canadians. British torpedo two German torpedo boats off Zeebrugge. One sunk, fate of other unknown. United States breaks off with Austria. All interned ships seized.

Wednesday, 11 April

The papers say this is the coldest April for 39 years, and I believe it. Agnes going to the wash-house tomorrow, so went down tonight and lit the fire. I am starting some alterations on the book case, and hope the military will let me finish it. Arras victory. Over 11,000 prisoners now. 100 guns, 60 trench mortars and 163 machine guns captured. The great Hindenburg line smashed. Brazil breaks relations with Germany.

Thursday, 12 April

Agnes got up at 4.30 a.m. I think she must have finished her sleep in the wash-house. She was finished by dinner time. Did some work at the book case tonight. The loaf is costing us sixpence now. Vile weather on Western Front.

6d

Friday, 13 April

The food stocks in this country were never lower, so help me bob. British patrol boat lost in Channel by mine: 18 lives lost. British again advance. Brazil seizes all German shipping.

1917

Saturday, 14 April

Most vile weather today. Very heavy snow, sleet and everything bad. Great explosion in USA munition work: 150 lives lost. Two British hospital ships sunk in Channel. One by mine, other by U-boat. British army fighting fiercely. 13,000 prisoners now captured and 200 guns. Internal conditions in Russia are very grave.

Monday, 16 April

Agnes not keeping well, so went round and saw the doctor at night, and was told to take to her bed at once. Seems to be a form of her old trouble, and threatened with complications. British army still smashing the German line. Our patrols penetrate into Lens. Great German attack on Bapaume-St Quentin Road beaten off. 1,500 Germans left. USA guard-ship interned by Turkey.

Tuesday, 17 April

Agnes in bed all day. Very weak and vomiting all the milk she drank. She is very ill tonight indeed, and I don't know what to do. Feel quite helpless and hopeless. Great French offensive started in 25-mile front. 10,000 Germans captured. So, with the British line, a fierce battle is raging on a 75-mile front.

German prisoners of war.

Wednesday, 18 April

Agnes not suffering any pain now, but is very weak. Went for doctor at night, and then got a bottle of medicine. The greatest battle of the war now raging. Combined length of offensive 125 miles. The French have now taken 14,000 prisoners. British strike again: 227 guns taken so far. American warship attacked by U-boat. Great riots in Berlin. All newspapers are 1d each now, from last Monday.

Thursday, 19 April

Very stormy day. Agnes much the same, and very weak. Nellie Hamilton made the dinner today. I broke a plate tonight. So help me bob. Great French progress on the Aisne. They have captured so far 17,000 Germans and 75 guns. Battle front extends 150 miles.

Friday, 20 April

Dull, cold, windy day. Got myself a new hat. It has evidently affected my brain as I went and paid the gas bill. Doctor up at night. Says it is a haemorrhage. I went down at night with the ash pan and shook the carpets. I broke a butter plate tonight. Am feeling very tired. This is 'America Day' all over the country.

Saturday, 21 April

Beautiful day. Jean and Hetty here in the afternoon. Agnes much the same. So as not to poison Agnes with an overdose of medicine, I speculated in a measuring glass. Bathed Tommy at night. 19,000 Germans now captured by the French.

Sunday, 22 April

Very nice day. I got up at 7.45 a.m. Did the grate and washed all the floors and made all the meals. Agnes feeling not so bad, not having to get up. I am dead tired at night. Naval raid on Dover by six German destroyers. Two British patrol boats engage them, and then there were three. We suffer no loss in boats. 33,000 Germans captured in the last week, and 330 guns.

Monday, 23 April

Very nice day. Went down with ash pan in morning and got a most terrific fall. Took Tommy to school. I had a very sore head all day. Agnes not so well tonight. Two hospital ships sunk by U-boats. 75 lives lost including some Germans on board. Haig getting ready for another blow.

Tuesday, 24 April

Nice sunny day. Bought a new pipe today, with real amber mouthpiece. Agnes much better. Doctor up today: his final visit. Agnes to go on to her usual food and to do herself well etc. Nannie Gordon here tonight. Much trouble having weakened my brain, I went round today and paid a doctor's bill. My head very sore today. Haig resumes the offensive. We take 1,500 prisoners. British airship shot down off Belgian coast.

Wednesday, 25 April

Mrs Gordon here when I got home. Put a new mantle on the gas, better to see my wife's dear countenance. Josephine popped in about 7.30 and popped out about 9.45 p.m. I don't feel well at all. Maybe I've injured some of my inside works when I fell. Took a pill at night. British have now taken 3,000. German making margarine etc. out of the German dead bodies.[34]

[34] This was a rumour that gained global currency from April 1917. Reports, first in the French press and then worldwide, stated that the Germans were distilling glycerine from corpses and using it in both munitions and margarine.

Thursday, 26 April

I felt very ill in the morning and had to go back to bed. Agnes had to get up and do the work then. This won't do her any good, so I got up at dinner time and went to my work. Have lost my appetite. Agnes done up at night.

Friday, 27 April

Agnes had a terrible night of pain last night. A little better this morning and was up all day. Duncan here at night. I'm not so bad now. Explosion at Houston munition works.[35] Some women killed. American armed steamer sinks U-boat. Record number of British boats sunk last week by U-boats. Looks serious. So help me bob.

Saturday, 28 April

Very stormy day. Cold. Agnes out today for the first time. I've got the cold in the head something wicked. Seeing that Agnes had bust my old lamp, Aladdin-like I gave her a new one. Tobacco is going to be very dear.

Sunday, 29 April

Agnes seems to be keeping fine. I cleaned the pan we used to make jam in. Scarpe River battle raging.

My tin hat

Monday, 30 April

Tommy very sick at dinner time so we put him to bed. Agnes went to her medical man ce soir and renewed her bottle. Feeling sort of reckless at night, we played at 'bad man's pictures'.[36] Germans resisting British advance desperately. American senate adopts conscription.

[35] NFF Georgetown (National Filling Factory Number 4), also known as the Scottish Filling Factory, was near the village of Houston, Renfrewshire, to the west of Glasgow. The factory employed around 12,000 employees in April 1917, most of them women.

[36] They played card games. A reference to the Presbyterian antipathy to gaming.

Tuesday, 1 May

Tommy sick in the morning but all night later on. So that her hand would not lose its cunning, Agnes cleaned out the press tonight. Ten years ago today, on 1 May 1907, it was a wet night, so Agnes and I did our courting indoors.[37]

Wednesday, 2 May

Tommy evidently is all right again. Took a walk out myself at night to see how things were growing etc.[38] Came back by Cathcart. 40,000 Germans captured in April in France by the Allies.

Thursday, 3 May

Hot, brilliant weather today. Hetty and Daisy here when I got home. We all saw them off from Queen Street Station 9.15 p.m. Haig starts another offensive. British transport Ballarat torpedoed by U-boat. All saved. Australian troops on board. Tommy starts school again today.

Friday, 4 May

Another warm, sunny day. Cleaned all the windows at night. Paid 7½d for an ounce of 'thick black', and I remember when I got it for 3d.[39] We are at war evidently. We are to have bread tickets in July, so they say. U-boats up the Clyde, so they say. British troopship *Arcadian* sunk by U-boat. 279 lives lost. British break the 'Hindenburg Line'. Terrific fighting.

---

37 Thomas seems to be looking back through earlier diaries which, alas, have not survived.
38 Possibly to view the allotments in Queen's Park.
39 Thomas' 'thick black' was pipe tobacco. Alfred Dunhill, for example, marketed a Best Scotch Thick Black Twist until 1918.

Saturday, 5 May

Put a new cotton pulley rope up in the kitchen. My niece Isa dropped in at tea time. She had to depart shortly afterwards as we were going out. We had a pleasant evening at the Cinerama. British extend their grip on Hindenburg Line. 900 prisoners taken. British destroyer mined in Channel. 62 lives lost.

Sunday, 6 May

Nice warm, sunny day. Went out myself (selfish man) in the afternoon and admired the countryside, 100 Acre Dyke way. Tommy got bathed at night. Big French victory near Soissons. 5,300 prisoners.

Monday, 7 May

Very cold day. Agnes and Tommy out at night looking for a lady to assist at our annual spring cleaning. I have got a cough. Agnes rubbed my bosom with the requisite oil. German aeroplane drops a few bombs over London to remind them that there is a war on. Official report says not much damage done.

British forced back from Fresnoy by the Germans

Wednesday, 9 May

Agnes and Tommy away to Ibrox when I came home. They arrived back at 9.20 p.m.

Thursday, 10 May

Another summer day of most cussed cold east winds and icy cold rain. May Crozier here at tea time. Seeing I have the cold, Agnes saw her away by the 9.15 train ex Queen Street. Just a year ago today the military refused me as cannon fodder. British mine sweeper torpedoed. 22 men missing.

The weather

The climate of Glasgow and its day to day manifestation in the weather are staples of conversation in the city. 'If it's not raining, it's about to rain,' as one unknown wit had it. In the interests of fairness, it is best to leave the description to an outsider. Charles Allen Oakley, who left Devon at the age of 16 to serve an apprenticeship in John Brown's shipyard, settled in the city and wrote one of its best-known books. *The Second City* went through three editions and nine reprintings, evidence of its enduring popularity as a well-written, breezy guide to the history of Glasgow. His description of the city's climate appeared under the heading 'Not such a bad climate, really'.

> Climatic conditions have moulded the character of the Scot of the western Lowlands. Glasgow is thought, not only by the people of other parts but even by the people of Glasgow themselves, to have a severe climate. Certainly it is not kind to the farmer. But Glasgow has one of the best climates in Great Britain for factory work.
>
> Glasgow's closeness to the sea makes snow a comparative rarity. Glasgow is misty, but dense fogs, except occasionally in November, are infrequent. The Midlands of England have more snow and more fog than Glasgow. But Glasgow has, of course, its own disadvantages. In particular, it is wet - not with frequent drizzle in the Manchester sense, but with rainstorms of long duration and severity - although other places in, for instance, South Wales and Lancashire have a heavier rainfall as measured over the year. So, although few realise it, has New York.
>
> It has comparatively little sunshine in summer, and the grey skies of July and August tend to make it depressing. But May, June and September and even October can be splendid months. The people of Glasgow have never had to learn what a hot August day in Birmingham is like, or a snowy January in Nottingham, or an enervating June day in Plymouth, or a biting February day in Newcastle.[40]

Charles Oakley sounds as much a connoisseur of weather as Thomas. But Thomas, as a walker who lived in a draughty house, was acutely aware of the effect of a change in the temperature or precipitation. He was walking in leather boots, and woollen clothes, with perhaps a waterproof coat, hat and umbrella. He had no technical fabrics, no sophisticated waterproof footwear, no socks or underwear of synthetic material that wicked perspiration away from the skin and kept him cool. He was susceptible to downpours, to deep puddles or mud, to clammy weather or blazing sunshine. He kept, as the saying goes, a weather eye on the elements to make the most of his leisure time. His house, also, had none of the technical advances we take for granted. No central heating or double glazing, no fitted carpets or sophisticated insulation, no running hot water. An open fire relied on drawing cold air into the room, and expended a lot of energy heating it on its way up the chimney.

Billy Connolly has remarked that there is no such thing as bad weather, 'just the wrong

40 C. A. Oakley, *The Second City* (Glasgow, Blackie, 1967), pp. 1-2.

clothes'. But for Thomas, Agnes and Wee Tommy, there were few right clothes and the weather figures largely in the diaries for this reason. For Thomas or Agnes there were no summer shorts, no down-filled jackets, no Gore-Tex socks, gloves and weatherproofs. There was no family car to bundle themselves into, snug against the weather, as they drove from door to door to visit their relatives. They had to walk to the tram stop, wait in its inadequate shelter, and walk to their destination at the other end of the journey. They were far closer to the vagaries of the weather than we are, and the types of illnesses they suffered from are perhaps reflections of that. While the Livingstones' various illnesses don't seem to relate directly to the changing seasons, they do seem much more cheerful in the summer months when they are able to take long country rambles away from the sooty atmosphere of the city.

	Average temperature (°C)	*Average rainfall (mm)*
January	3.4	111
February	3.8	74.2
March	5.0	61.2
April	7.3	56.4
May	10.3	64.3
June	13.3	61.1
July	14.6	79
August	14.2	88.9
September	12.0	88.9
October	8.9	110
November	5.6	95.7
December	4.1	98.9

Figures from early twentieth century.

Friday, 11 May

Dull cold day. Working late. I am not feeling so well tonight. Destroyer action in the North Sea. Germans chased back to Zeebrugge. Grave conditions in Russia. Small British success in the Balkans. 500 yards captured on five-mile front.

Saturday, 12 May

Agnes went over to the painter in the afternoon and brought over 10lbs of paint. I'm going to paint the house one of these days. Took a run over to Sam's shop at night. He tells me Duncan is called up for re-examination. I suppose I'll go next.

Sunday, 13 May

Took a walk to Queen's Park in afternoon. Haig strikes the fifth blow. 700 Germans capture. Zeebrugge heavily shelled by British warships.

British army age raised to 50.

Monday, 14 May

Poured solid all day. Had a bath in Govanhill's new Baths.[41] *McCort in tonight and did the whitewashing also the lobby. I started painting tonight. Lily phoned me today that Duncan was passed C2 class. British army age raised to 50. German Zeppelin shot down in North Sea by our navy.*

---

[41] Govanhill Public Baths and Wash-house opened in Calder Street in 1917, designed by Glasgow Corporation's own architect, A. B. McDonald. There were hot baths upstairs and three swimming pools on the ground floor. In addition, there was a wash-house or 'steamie' at the rear of the building. The baths closed in 2001.

Tuesday, 15 May

Cold dull day. A woman in today to do the ceiling.[42] I did some more painting at night. Agnes cleaned the kitchen clock and broke its blinking door!!!!

Wednesday, 16 May

Painted some more tonight. Russia offered peace by Germany. Great Italian offensive launched. Great German efforts to regain Bullecourt from the British.

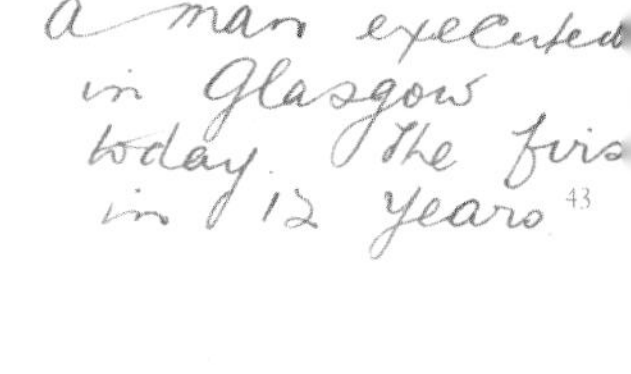

a man executed
in Glasgow
today. The first
in 12 years[43]

Thursday, 17 May

Finished the painting in the kitchen tonight. Nellie here at tea time and away shortly after. Hetty Cook here tonight. I saw her away in car. Not so many merchant boats sunk this week. Italians capture over 3,000 Austrians. American destroyers arrive in British waters.

Friday, 18 May

Dull, cold, wet and windy. Working late tonight. Duncan in when I got home. America's first contingent arrives in Britain. A medical unit. British complete masters of Bullecourt now.

---

[42] Another example of women moving into jobs that had been the preserve of men.

[43] Thomas McGuiness was hanged in Duke Street Prison for the murder of Alexander Imlach The previous execution was on 14 November 1905, when Pasha Liffey was hanged in the same jail for the murder of Mary Jane Welsh.

aturday, 19 May

)id some repainting in the kitchen on some unsatisfactory work. Took a walk over Cathkin at night. British transport *'ameronia* (Anchor Line) sunk by U-boat in Mediterranean. 140 ves lost. Naval fight in the Adriatic. 14 British drifters sunk. HM *Dartmouth* and HM *Bristol* with Italian and French estroyers chase Austrians away.

unday, 20 May

'ook a walk down to the docks to see if we had any ships left. Ve have.

Ionday, 21 May

Ve both got up early. Agnes whitewashed the bathroom and superintended. Dogfight in the Channel. French and German lestroyers. Nobody hurt.

'uesday, 22 May

'his is a holiday. Victoria Day. So I painted the scullery. After linner we all went to the Cinerama. Made a start with painting athroom at night. Japanese destroyers assisting to keep he peace in the Mediterranean.

Vednesday, 23 May

Beautiful summer day, so off goes ny overcoat and on with my Sunday suit. Working late at night. Finished painting bathroom when I ame home. Tommy got new trousers. In order to gain new lease of life Agnes started taking Sanatogen.[44]

Sanatogen was a 'tonic food' sold in powdered form and taken in water. In 1916 it was advertised under the slogan 'There is nothing like Sanatogen for your nerves.' The Sanatogen brand is still healthy, and offers a number of vitamin supplements.

Friday, 25 May

Working late tonight. Agnes finished out the scullery today. Great Italian victory! 10,000 prisoners. 10 batteries of British artillery assist.

Saturday, 26 May

Terrific hot day. Some little showers. We all went to Pollok Estate in the afternoon to get sunburnt. Nellie here re Agnes' costume. I painted inside the press door tonight. Biggest air raid yet on England by German aeroplanes: 95 killed, about 200 injured, three raiders shot down. Another Italian victory, 3,500 prisoners.

Sunday, 27 May

In the forenoon Tommy and I went out by Govan and saw the 'packet of Woodbines', in other words a Russian cruiser *Askold* which has an unusual number of lums, to wit five.[45] It has seen some fighting in the Dardanelles Campaign. We crossed ferry over to Partick and re-crossed at Finnieston, admired all the boats and got car home at the Toll.[46] Tommy tired but happy. Caught three mice in bunker today. Agnes put up the bed hangings at night.

Monday, 28 May

Exceptionally warm. Working late. Thunder and lightning and heavy rain on my way home. Had to see Mrs Dunn and her boy on the car after I got home. Caught another mouse in bunker this morning. Italians have now captured 22,000 Austrians. Ten years ago today I took office boy (Andrew) out in a boat on Burnside. He is now leaving shortly for the front.

[45] The five funnels of the ship reminded people of five cigarettes sticking up from a packet of ten. Woodbines were a popular brand of cigarette.

[46] Partick and Finnieston are two districts on the north bank of the River Clyde. The Toll is probably Paisley Road Toll, a road junction on the south side of the river, near the landing point of the ferry from Finnieston.

Wednesday, 30 May

Another mouse committed suicide this morning. Put green paint on mantelpiece at night, and some plaster in the room grate. I'm a very handy man to have in the house. No getting Tommy in these light nights. Italians captured on Italian front since 14 May: 23,681 men, 36 guns, 148 machine guns and 27 trench mortars. Hospital ship *Dover Castle* sunk by U-boat. Armed liner *Hilary* (Booth Line) sunk in North Sea. British destroyer sunk by collision. Help.

Friday, 1 June

Fine day but very windy. Cleaned kitchen windows tonight. Varnished the mantel and painted the book case. Russian war workers are going to strike.

Saturday, 2 June

Did some artistic work on the kitchen wall, started to put the black line around.[47] After tea I took a walk to Ruglen. Agnes and Tommy went into the town. Lull on the Western Front. British army preparing for another spring.

Monday, 4 June

Rained solid all day long. Have started to come home at dinner time in a motor.[48] It's the goods.[49] Gave my bookcase its final coat of paint. Complained to the factor about our lum, and the man came over and gave it a dose of oil (not castor). This being my birthday, Agnes made a dumpling in celebration thereof. Sir Douglas Haig launches new offensive on Souchez River. Desperate fighting.

47 The kitchen walls were likely painted for the first five feet, and whitewashed above. A painted black line would have been the border between the two finishes.
48 Thomas travels home for his dinner each day. At this time, he was using an early version of a bus, driven by an internal combustion engine, rather than the tram.
49 It is great.

Transport

Transport in Glasgow in the early years of the twentieth century was dominated by the Glasgow Corporation Tramways Department, set up by the local authority in 1872. By 1914 it had 200 miles of track and 500 double-decker carriages, carrying 430 million passengers a year over a network stretching from Dalmuir in the west to Uddingston in the east, and from Bishopbriggs in the north to Rouken Glen in the south. The tracks went beyond the city boundary, to the suburbs where the middle classes lived and to the green places where people of all classes took their leisure. The longest journey, from Paisley to Uddingston, cost 7d for 14 miles.

The first tramway line was a 2.5 mile route from St George's Cross, north-west of the city centre, to Eglinton Toll on the south side of the River Clyde. This route was leased by the Glasgow Corporation to the Glasgow Tramway and Omnibus Company, a private concern, for 22 years. By the end of its lease, the company had extended the network to many parts of the city, on tracks laid down by the corporation. On the north side of the river, the routes reached Maryhill, Kelvinside, Whiteinch and Springburn; on the south, Mount Florida, Pollokshaws and Paisley Road Toll, which marked the boundary with the burgh of Govan. In 1893, when trams were still horse-drawn, the company owned 300 trams and more than 3,000 horses.

In 1894 the corporation became the first British municipality to own and operate its own public transport system and the tramway network was soon extended to the various suburban towns and burghs that became part of the growing city in the years around 1900. By the turn of the century the corporation had electrified the system, putting the horses out to grass and allowing citizens to travel in faster and better-lit cars. By 1910 Glasgow trams were familiar sights as far north as Killermont and

Bishopbriggs and as far east as Uddingston, Baillieston and Cambuslang.

The trams could not stray from the rails embedded in the street or the power lines suspended above, which were carried by cross-wires secured to the walls of buildings with diamond-shaped brackets called rosettes. These can still be seen on some buildings on Glasgow's main roads, more than 40 years after the demise of the trams. The tram took its power from these lines through a spring-loaded trolley pole fixed to its roof. Because there were no turning circles at the termini, trams had a driver's platform at each end. Seats on the lower floor faced inwards, while those on the upper deck faced forward in the direction of travel. At the end of each journey, the conductor flipped the pivoted seat backs so the seats again faced forward. The conductor also, by means of a long rope, disengaged the trolley pole and re-engaged it facing the rear.

The trams were painted in jaunty colours: bright orange, the colour of the Tramways Department, on the lower level, and one of five colours (red, blue, green, yellow or white) on the top. These colours were intended to help passengers identify which cars were approaching. While there were far more than five tram routes, care was taken that no tram routes sharing the same colours ran along the same street. The destination boards at the front and sometimes also along the sides of the tram also proclaimed the service number and route. In 1914, the manager of the tramways was James Dalrymple, whose name was on the side of each car. It was a standing joke that he was better known than the Lord Provost or any other civic dignitary.

The cars offered cheap, clean and reliable transport from home to work, church, sport or leisure. For Thomas or Agnes 'taking a run' into town or to see a relative cost just a few pennies. Fares were calculated by the number of 'fare stages' passed through, but in 1914 the typical fares would have been ½d for 1 mile, 1d for 2½ miles, 1½ d for 3½ miles, 2d for 4½ miles, 2½d for 5¾ miles and 3d for 7 miles.

James Willock, writing in 1922, saw many benefits of the tramway system:

> This far-flung system of municipal transport, to which the Subway has been added this year by purchase from a private company, has a distinct social value. It efficiently and conveniently links up the suburbs and the open country beyond with the city. The facilities it provides for getting about are constant invitations for the citizens to leave the overcrowded centre and live outwith the city. The trams will undoubtedly help to solve the problem of overcrowding in the congested areas of Glasgow.[50]

As well as the tram 'cars', there were also the 'motors', the Subway and the suburban train system. The motors, or motor buses, first made an appearance in 1914, operated by a number of private companies. They all ran services from George Square in the city centre, radiating out to the populous suburbs and sometimes to the countryside beyond: one of the first services went as far as Cumbernauld, 14 miles to the north-west of Glasgow. The motors shared the roads with trams, a handful of private cars and many horse-

[50] James Willock, 'Glasgow's Municipal Services', *The Book of Glasgow* (Glasgow: Alex Macdougall, 1922), pp. 161-2.

Buchanan Street viewed from Argyle Street.

drawn lorries, vans and carts, all easily keeping within the 20mph speed limit. The motors ran on petrol, but a number were converted to use coal gas during the First World War, when imports of fuel were scarce. The gas was carried in a bag slung on the roof of the bus, which caused Thomas to note that they looked like Zeppelins.

The Glasgow District Subway opened to the public on 14 December 1896, under the ownership of the Glasgow District Subway Company. The system, which is the third-oldest subway system in the world after the London Underground and the Budapest Metro, had 15 stations linked by 6.5 miles of twin tunnels, each 11 feet in diameter and ranging in depth from 115 feet (below Glasgow Street in Hillhead) to 7 feet (between Kinning Park and Cessnock stations). Transport buffs are keen to point out that it is the only public transport system that runs on rails 4 feet apart, 8.5 inches narrower than the standard railway gauge. The rather limited route, from the city centre to the west end, Govan, the south side and back to the centre, reflected the spread of the city's population at the time, and changing patterns of work and housing left some stations without a hinterland. By 1918 the system was carrying almost 21 million passengers, but was not making the profits its owners expected. The Glasgow Corporation took over the system in 1922, and the Glasgow District Subway became part of the Glasgow Corporation Tramways Department.

The suburban train system ran from the four main termini in central Glasgow: Queen Street Station (opened in 1842), Buchanan Street Station (1849), St Enoch's Station (1876) and Central Station (1879), each operated by a different railway company and with no connecting services Thomas mentions 'seeing off' his various visitors from Queen Street Station or Glasgow Cross Station. The former, owned by the North British Railway, ran trains to Edinburgh and Aberdeen, while the latter stood on the line owned by the Glasgow Central Railway (part of the Caledonian Railway) that ran from Maryhill Central in the north-west of the city to Newton in Lanarkshire to the east of the city.

Wednesday, 6 June

Blowy, bleak sort of day. Agnes and Tommy in town when I came home, Tommy getting a new pair of shoes at 10/6, which I paid for the last pair of boots for myself. Went to Queen's Park at night. Saw Mr Carmichael in his garden plot and came down the road with him accompanied by Agnes and Mrs Carmichael, who had appeared on the scene. Big aeroplane raid on the Thames. 16 lives lost. Germans lose 10 machines.

Thursday, 7 June

Spring cleaning the room tonight. Another British offensive started in the west on a nine-mile front near Ypres. American warships arrive in France.

British ammunition wagons moving up to the front along the Ypres-Menin road.

Friday, 8 June

Cleaned room windows at night. Duncan arrived at night to cheer me up. Great British victory in the new offensive. Biggest mine exploded in the world's history by us (about 600 tons). 6,000 Huns captured. United States commander arrives in London.

Sunday, 10 June

Very warm, sunny day. Was in Queen's Park before breakfast. Put on my straw hat today. After dinner took Tommy out a walk to Maxwell Park. British have now captured 7,000 Germans in the big victory. On this day in 1910, Agnes and I got married.

Monday, 11 June
Very nice day, chilly at night. After tea Agnes went out to Ruglen to see Nellie re her costume. I took Tommy out later and took her home.

Tuesday, 12 June
Very hot day. A thunder plump at night and a few fireworks. Agnes and Tommy in town in the forenoon. Agnes got ribbon for her hat. British armed fishing boat fights five German seaplanes and destroys two of them.

Wednesday, 13 June
May here at night trimming le chapeau of Agnes. Great air raid on London by German aeroplanes. 110 killed and hundreds injured. Greek king abdicates.

Thursday, 14 June
Cleaned every window in the house tonight. Agnes and Tommy out at Ruglen. Agnes getting a fit-on.[51] They got home 9 p.m. Zeppelin shot down in North Sea by our navy. Big explosion in munition factory at Ashbourne (England). 50 killed.

[51] Agnes was being fitted for her new outfit.

Saturday, 16 June

Weather perfection. Stopped today for my holidays. In the afternoon took Agnes and Tommy to town. Agnes bought a new hat and I a new cap. Nellie here at night with Agnes' new costume. They both went out again to town for more new hats. British armed liner Avenger sunk in the North Sea by U-boat.

Sunday, 17 June

Weather perfect. Very hot. Agnes donned her new blue costume and went to church (communion). She looks a treat. After dinner we all went to Cathcart and had a seat in the cemetery. After tea we went to Queen's Park to see all the knuts.[52] Zepp raid on south-east coast. One Zepp and crew entirely destroyed.

Monday, 18 June

The start of my holidays. We are spending them at home. In forenoon I was in Shawlands by the Cart.[53] In the afternoon we all went to town. Went into the St Enoch Picture House. After tea I went out to Cathcart. Lily here at night. Got new slippers today and Tommy a new pair of canvas shoes. Big German attack. British forced back.

---

52 A knut was, in the slang of the day, a well-dressed young man about town.
53 The River Cart flows through the south side of Glasgow. It features in several district and street names, such as Cathcart and Cartvale Road.

Tuesday, 19 June

Beautiful day. After breakfast I walked across to Ruglen, took car up to Burnside then up East Kilbride Road on to Cathkin. Came back by Mill Wynd. After dinner we all took car to Paisley, had our tea there and went into the pictures. We got home 8 p.m. Agnes did a washing and I cleaned the jam pan. Serious disturbances in Spain. German losses 4,500,000, of which 1,000,000 are dead.

Wednesday, 20 June

Very nice sunny forenoon. After breakfast, rusticated in Rouken Glen.[54] Not out in afternoon. Turned very dull then, and developed into a pouring wet night. So I went to the Palace.[55] British regain lost positions. British transport *Cameronian* sunk by U-boat. About 50 lives lost.

Thursday, 21 June

Pouring wet day, all the day long. I went into town in the afternoon and paid the gas and bought myself a pair of boots at 16/5. We spent the evening in the midst of the Cormack family. Home 11.15 p.m.

Friday, 22 June

Nice sunny day, but a trifle windy. After breakfast I went through Queen's Park, took car from Shawlands to Thornliebank. Walked down by Nitshill and home by Cowglen Road. After dinner we all went to Rouken Glen, and had tea in Bungalow, then walked to Clarkston and from there to Netherlee.[56] Got car home. We all went to the Alhambra at night. Home 11.30 p.m. Portuguese army in France doing some good work.

[54] Rouken Glen, on the southern outskirts of Glasgow, was given to the people of the city by Cameron Corbett, the Liberal MP for the Tradeston district of Glasgow (later Lord Rowallan), in 1904. It opened as a public park in 1906, and in the same year the Glasgow Corporation extended the tram system to its gates.

[55] The Palace, which advertised itself as a 'Theatre of Varieties', was the principal music hall on the south side of Glasgow. It opened in 1904 in Main Street, Gorbals, and by 1917 was also showing films. At the time of Thomas' visit, it offered two shows a night, at 7 and 9.

1917

Sunday, 24 June

Bright sunny day, but wind blowing a hurricane all day. Took a walk out to Sam's in afternoon and walked back. After dinner I met Sam and Nellie at Jamaica Street and we went to Cadder Church by car to Bishopbriggs.[57] After church, Sam and Nellie and William Kirk came home with me for tea. They left about 10.30 p.m. Big munition explosion in Austria. 300 killed.

Monday, 25 June

Bright sunny day, but windy and not warm enough. Took car to Netherlee and walked to East Kilbride, via Busby and Clarkston. Called in and saw Miss Balfour and Miss Hillcoat and had a cup of tea there. Came back by Mains Castle and Burnside. Got home about 3.30 p.m. Went into town after dinner and bought a waterproof coat. After tea I went to Queen's Park. Some very heavy rain. Saw a most beautiful rainbow.

Tuesday, 26 June

Very nice day. Walked out to Rutherglen. Took car to Burnside and from thence walked to Carmunnock and back by Cathcart. Not out after dinner, but after tea we all went down to Ibrox. Got home about 11 p.m. I'm getting sunburnt.

---

[56] The Bungalow was one of a number of tearooms serving visitors to the park.
[57] Cadder is a district five miles north of Glasgow, just north of the town of Bishopbriggs.

Wednesday, 27 June

Very hot sun up till about 2 p.m., then it got very dull ever afterwards. Took car to Netherlee and then started to walk. First Clarkston then Eaglesham, Balligioch, and on to Kingswell, turned there and came back by Newton Mearns and Giffnock. Took car home from there. Home 6.30 p.m. Walked about 20 miles. Not bad for a CIII man.[58] P&O liner *Mongolia* mined near India. 30 lives lost.

Thursday, 28 June

Fine sunny day. Wind a trifle chilly. In the forenoon I took car to Lambhill and walked along canal to Cadder, then on to Bishopbriggs and car home.[59] In the afternoon I went to Bellahouston Park. Spent the night getting ready for Lamlash. Andrew came up to see me at night for a little. He is not long for this country. American troops landed in France.

Friday, 29 June

Rose at an unearthly hour, 5.30 a.m., and then we got train from St Enoch 8.10 a.m. to Ardrossan and *Glen Sannox* to Arran.[60] We met all the Croziers at St Enoch. And we filled a compartment. Scorching hot day. Got there safely, no mines or U-boats encountered. British encircling Lens.

Saturday, 30 June

Another brilliant hot day. Loafed about Arran. Took Daisy out in a small boat. Having a great time.

[58] Thomas had been classified as CIII by the military doctors, and regarded as unfit for service. C was defined as 'free from serious organic diseases, able to stand service in garrisons at home' and the subcategory III indicated 'Only suitable for sedentary work'.

[59] The canal was the Forth and Clyde Canal, which crosses central Scotland.

Sunday, 1 July

Very warm day. Took a walk towards Whiting Bay in forenoon.

Watched some girls bathing

Monday, 2 July

Very hot, sunny day. My holidays are over now. Rose at 5.30 and got 6.40 boat to Ardrossan. Arrived in St Enoch at 9.15 a.m. Agnes and Tommy not coming home for a few days yet. Felt very sad. Had lunch in town. Could not settle down at night. So took a walk to Ruglen. Came home and wrote to Agnes. Great Russian offensive started: 10,000 prisoners.

British held up at Lens.

Tuesday, 3 July

I will be pleased when we are all united once more.

Wednesday, 4 July

German aeroplanes raid Harwich. About 11 killed. Russians capture another 8,000.

Thursday, 5 July

Fine sunny day. Got a letter and postcard from my well-beloved. They are coming home on Friday. Two of the raiding Hun aeroplanes brought down last night.

[30] St Enoch Station, one of four main-line stations in Glasgow at the time, was operated by the Glasgow and South Western Railway. It also owned and operated the paddle steamer *Glen Sannox*, which was built at J. & G. Thomson's Clydebank shipyard in 1892. She was the largest railway-owned pleasure steamer in Britain.

Friday, 6 July

Met Agnes and Tommy at St Enoch 6.15 p.m., both looking well. Tommy with half his nose knocked off with a fall somewhere in Arran. In case I would die of overjoy, Duncan visited us at night. British have captured the past year 70,000 Germans. Old British destroyer mined in North Sea.

Saturday, 7 July

We all went out for a little in the afternoon. We saw an aeroplane on our way home. No bombs dropped. Great German aeroplane raid over London: 57 killed and about 200 injured. Several of the aeroplanes shot down. French submarine sunk by German U-boat.

Sunday, 8 July

Bright sunny day, but very windy and dusty. Took my usual walk to Queen's Park before breakfast. After dinner we all went out the Carmunnock Road and back by Cathcart. After tea we favoured Queen's Park. Great French air raid over German towns, including Essen, where Krupps is.

Monday, 9 July

Working late at night. British destroyer torpedoed in North Sea. Another Russian rush: 7,000 prisoners taken.

Tuesday, 10 July

Feeling vigorous after her holiday, Agnes spent the day in the wash-house. I took a walk around 100 Acre Dyke at night. British armed trawler *Iceland* fights two German seaplanes, knocks them down and captures the four occupants in North Sea.

Vednesday, 11 July

Ve all went to the Palace at night, seeing it's near the Fair.[61] Russians still advance in Galicia. Capture of Halicz. Austrian troops in flight. Germans shove the British back on Belgian oast at River Yser. British naval air raid on Turks. Constantinople bombed.

riday, 13 July

eeing it is Fair Friday, I got away at 1 p.m. and don't get back ill Tuesday morning. We all went to the shows in the Green in he afternoon and admired the sights.[62] I spent about 10d at game and won 2d. We all went to the Palace at night, last house.

aturday, 14 July

Beautiful day of sunshine. Very warm. After dinner we took car to Cowglen Road then went to Crookston Castle.[63] We all climbed to he top and had a good view. Took car home by Paisley Road. Cars ery busy. Got home at 7.45 p.m. British transport *Armadale* orpedoed in Atlantic by U-boat. 11 lives lost. British Battleship *anguard* blown up in harbour. Over 600 lives lost.

unday, 15 July

After dinner we all walked to Ruglen and took car home. After tea we all went to Queen's Park and admired the view from the flag pole. King and Queen visit troops at the front in France.

The annual Glasgow Fair holidays.

There have been entertainments on Glasgow Green during the annual Glasgow Fair holidays for many years.

Crookston Castle overlooks the Levern Water, in the Pollok district of Glasgow, five miles south of the city centre. It dates from the fourteenth century and was owned by the Maxwells of Pollok from 1757 until 1931.

Monday, 16 July

We took a walk to town in the afternoon and I called in at the library. After tea we all went to the Palace, and so my Fair holidays are ended.

Tuesday, 17 July

Josephine, father, Lily and Isa all here at night. Nellie in for a little. The King changes his family name to Windsor.[64] British destroyers capture four German merchant boats.

Wednesday, 18 July

Agnes made gooseberry jam at night.

Thursday, 19 July

Potatoes are now down to 1/4 per stone.

Friday, 20 July

Tobacco (thick black) is now down to 6d per oz.

Saturday, 21 July

This is flag day for the wounded. In the afternoon w all went to town and saw the Procession in Aid of the Wounded.

Selling flags on Soldier's Day, 1917.

[64] George V issued an Order-in-Council on 17 July 1917 that changed the name of the British royal house from the House of Saxe-Coburg and Gotha to the House of Windsor.

unday, 22 July

rilliant day of sunshine and terrific heat. After dinner we took ar to the Dalmarnock Bridge and walked up the Clyde to ambuslang, then took the car home.[65] German aeroplane drops ombs on Harwich. 13 killed.

Ionday, 23 July

Ve all went to Greenlodge Terrace at night. ot home 11.40 p.m. Siam declares war on ermany and Austria. Greece evidently has also ined us.

uesday, 24 July

Ve went to the Palace at night and saw Charlie haplin etc.[66] Russia losing all the ground it on through desertion and mutiny. The Vomen's Battalion fight well and take 100 erman prisoners.[67]

Charlie Chaplin with Edna Purviance in The Fireman.

Vednesday, 25 July

gnes in the wash-house all day. The overnment is going to give us the 4½d loaf. od save the King.

hursday, 26 July

ig guns raging in Flanders, Roumanian offensive started. ussian retreat continued. British armed cruiser *Otway* sunk in Iorth Sea by U-boat, 10 lives lost. British submarine C34 sunk y U-boat. The one survivor taken prisoner.

The walk along the banks of the River Clyde from Dalmarnock, in the east end of Glasgow, to Cambuslang, in Lanarkshire, is about five miles.

By 1917 Charlie Chaplin was working in films in America and was no longer a music hall artiste. Thomas most likely saw Chaplin in the film *The Immigrant*, which was released in June 1917.

The Women's Battalion of the Russian army were all-female combat units formed after the February Revolution in 1917 in a last ditch effort to inspire weary soldiers to continue fighting.

Friday, 27 July

Agnes up all last night with neuralgia, and she got it the night again. Here's luck![68] French heavily attacked north of the Aisne. U-boat grounds off Calais. Crew taken prisoner and U-boat destroyed.

Saturday, 28 July

Lily and her boy, John Martin, who is in the ASC, dropped in to see us late in the evening.[69] John is going soon to France. The British army is now 6½ million men (home 5½, overseas 1 million), navy 500,000 men. It's great!!

Sunday, 29 July

Got up in the early morning for my walk. Saw Mr Carmichael so we went to Queen's Park and went into his estate there and admired the turnips, cabbages, potatoes, onions etc.[70] We visited Sam at night. British and French captures since the Battle of the Somme, July 1916: 3,500 German officers, 165,000 men, 948 heavy and field guns, 780 trench mortars, 2,500 machine guns.

Monday, 30 July

Took a walk at night to Langside Library.[71] British submarine captures German merchant boat in North Sea. Japanese destroyer sinks U-boat in Mediterranean. The terrific cannonade in Flanders continues, the biggest of the war. It is heard in London. Perhaps we are going to do something.

Tuesday, 31 July

At last, great British and French offensive in Flanders on a wide front. Good progress being made. British cruiser *Ariadne* torpedoed by U-boat. 38 lives lost.

---

[68] The phrase may come from the poem of the same name by the Australian comic poet Henry Lawson, published in 1893. One of the verses ends 'We'll laugh an' joke an' sing no more with jolly beery chums, / An' shout "Here's luck!" while waitin' for the luck that never comes.'

[69] The ASC was the Army Service Corps, which was responsible for transporting food, equipment and ammunition from Britain to the various theatres of war. They were nicknamed Ally Sloper's Cavalry after a popular comic-strip character of the time.

Wednesday, 1 August

Hot, blazing day. At evening, Agnes, Tommy and I took car to Ruglen, walked up to the woods and had a seat therein. We spoke to Mina Henderson and Jessie Keith at Burnside. Took 9.12 train from there to Mount Florida and walked home. Big push doing well. We capture over 6,000 risoners and 10 villages. The 'tanks' do great work.

Thursday, 2 August

Cleaned all les fenêtres ce soir.[72] Potatoes are down to 10d a one and as many as you want. Only 21 boats sunk last week.

riday, 3 August

Gas man here today to examine our gas meter (I complained re me). He says its day is done and we are to get a new one (some ay). Got my 'hair that will soon be grey' cut tonight. First hase of the big push finish. We regain lost ground.

aturday, 4 August

fter tea we all went to Shawlands via Queen's Park and walked ack to Mount Florida by the banks of the Cart. Three years ago oday Britain declared war on Germany and so saved the world.

unday, 5 August

fter tea we took car to Sighthill Cemetery but to our sorrow it as shut. My grief was not so great as Agnes'. We came back by arliamentary Road. China decides to fight Germany and Austria.

Mr Carmichael's 'estate' was, in fact, his allotment garden.
Langside Library, in Sinclair Drive, opened in 1915.
The windows.

AUGUST, 1917.

Tuesday 7

(219-146)

The heat wave continues.

Think I'll get a kilt

Had for dinner today cabbage, ham & potatoes the first two articles grown in the Queens Park, I mean the first and last.

Went myself to Queens' Park at night & listened to the band.

British make another little move nearer Lens.

7/8/07 Agnes & I at Jeanie Strain's

Vednesday, 8 August

iberia declares war on Germany.

'hursday, 9 August

'his is Tommy's birthday, some dumpling was made in honour f the occasion. I brought him home the game of 'quoits'. Ten ears ago today I joined the Scottish Clerks Association.[73]

riday, 10 August

Ian up today and left in a new gas meter. Chemical work lown up in London. 13 women killed.

aturday, 11 August

Ian in today from Gas Company and took away the new meter. was left here by mistake.

unday, 12 August

fter dinner I took a walk into Walls Street and spoke love to ie folk who sell us gas.[74] NBG. We all went to Ibrox at night.

Ionday, 13 August

Iave decided to mend the sofa and so laid bare the springs night. I will finish it 'quelque fois'.[75] German aeroplanes raid Iargate and Southend. 32 killed, about 50 injured. Two raiders rought down.

'uesday, 14 August

tarted to the couch at night. With the valuable assistance of gnes I put some new bands under the springs. British estroyer mined in North Sea. Since the war began, 8,748 lives ave been lost in merchant vessels.

Founded in 1886. Some of its records are preserved in Glasgow University archives.
Glasgow Corporation's Gas Workshops and Maintenance Depot was at 24-32 Walls Street, in Glasgow city centre.
French for 'sometimes', though Thomas' meaning here is clearly 'at some point'.

Wednesday, 15 August

Finished the inside work of the couch. Got my calling up notice this morning from the military. I have to join up on 28 August. Woe and woe and lamentations. Mr Baxter has got the lawyer to appeal, as he does not want to lose a good man. China at war now with Germany and Austria. American troops in London.

Cheering on troops of American soldiers as they parade through London, 15 August, 1917.

Thursday, 16 August

The Pope wants peace.

Sunday, 19 August

Big railway strike threatened. Government forbids it.

Monday, 20 August

Started to mend the big easy chair tonight. Tommy got new pair of boots, 12/6. Big French offensive on Verdun front. Success on 11-mile front. British advance slightly at Ypres. Italian offensive on 37-mile front. Tram car smash at Dover.[76] 10 killed. Big munition disaster in Canada.

Tuesday, 21 August

Finished the big chair tonight. Titanic battle raging on Italian front of 40 miles. Austrians captured now number 10,000. 208 Italian aeroplanes assist, and 5,000 big guns, including French and British batteries. French capture 5,000 at Verdun. Italian aeroplane sinks U-boat in the Adriatic. Great fire at Salonica.

---

[76] The driver of Tramcar Number 20 lost control of his vehicle while descending Crabble Hill and the tram smashed into a wall, killing 10 and injuring 59.

1917

A German Zeppelin is caught in spotlights as it hovers menacingly over a British city.

Vednesday, 22 August

Children's party here tonight. Sam's amily, viz. Ina, Jennie and John, here. Played various games etc. Zeppelin raid n Yorkshire. Aeroplane raid in Dover tc. About 11 killed. Eight aeroplanes hot down by us. British naval forces hoot down a Zeppelin off Jutland coast. No survivors. Searchlights blazing over ıs at nights now.

Thursday, 23 August

Ve all went to Greenlodge at night. talians have now captured 17,000 nen. French have captured 7,000. British fighting for Lens. Another oor week for the U-boat pirates.

riday, 24 August

eeing that I'll soon be a 'sojer', we all went to the Palace onight. Terrific battle still raging on Italian front. It appears to e the biggest battle of the war. British pegging away at Lens.

aturday, 25 August

'ery windy day. Some heavy rain. A little chilly at night. We lit he fire. We all took a walk to Mount Florida after tea. Since 9 April to 25 August total number of enemy prisoners taken by Allies is 167,780. Since the war began, the British have captured 31,776. British prisoners in enemy hands number about 56,500. Hoch, hoch.

Sunday, 26 August

Went down to the quay and looked at the boats in the afternoon. We have one or two left yet, I see. The great Italian battle continues. Over 20,000 of the enemy now captured. Rumours that the German High Fleet is coming out. Speed the day.

Monday, 27 August

Started to renovate the 'rocker'at night.[77] Agnes in the wash-house at night.

Tuesday, 28 August

Mrs Gordon here in afternoon to see if I was away in the army. I wasn't. Duncan here at night to see if I had any word about the army. I hadn't. He gave Tommy a shilling for his last birthday. Did a little chair work. Tommy very sick at night. Agnes made plum jam today. Great Italian victory. Monte Santo taken.

Wednesday, 29 August

Did more work with chair. Tommy all right again. Sam up for a little to see if I had any news from the army. I hadn't. A female representative from the Kirk up tonight. We have a new minister. How nice.

Thursday, 30 August

Did some work on rocking chair and cleaned room windows. Our new gas meter arrives at last. Russians still running away. British monitors shell Austrian positions.

[77] The rocking chair.

Saturday, 1 September

Butter is now ¾ per pound. Italy has captured 27,300 prisoners since the offensive began. British bag for the month of August: 7,279 prisoners.

Sunday, 2 September

Maxwell up seeing us tonight. He is in the OTC.[78] Naval scrap off Jutland. British destroyers sink four German minesweepers.

Monday, 3 September

Tommy starts school again today. 'Food Controller' takes charge of beef etc. from tomorrow. Riga district abandoned by the Russians. German aeroplane over Dover, one death. *City of Athens* (City Line) mined near Cape Town.

Tuesday, 4 September

Man up to see if new gas meter was working all right. He said flow of gas to stove was too much, so he remedied that little defect. Terrible air raid on Thames: Chatham and Sheerness bombed. Naval barracks struck. 130 naval men killed, about 100 injured. Pola bombed by Italians. Bruges bombed by British.

Wednesday, 5 September

Warm sunny day. We all went to the Palace at night. When we got home, two females from the church came in. They wanted a donation to give the new minister a new robe. We donated. I'll be needing a new coat this winter. Who'll donate? German aeroplane over London, 19 killed, about 60 injured. Germans enter Riga. Russians in full retreat.

---

[78] The Officers Training Corps was founded in 1906 to train young people in public schools and universities for careers as officers in the Militia, the Volunteer Force, the Yeomanry and the Reserve of Officers.

Thursday, 6 September

Man called today and took old gas meter away. Scarborough shelled by U-boat. Three killed, five injured. German Fleet in Gulf of Riga. The Russians are messing the war.[79]

Friday, 7 September

This is the night Cormacks flitted, so I went to do some work. Got home at midnight. Counted five searchlights in the sky at night. Saw an aeroplane.

Saturday, 8 September

After tea I had a walk to Queen's Park and a look in at the aristocratic library of Pollokshields.[80] Agnes put up the bed hangings, room and kitchen. Went into the shop to buy a 'churchwarden', but found them a thing of the past.[81] Germans start to bombard hospitals with intent.

Sunday, 9 September

Duncan up for me today at 10.30 a.m. We took car to Cathcart and walked from there to Ballagioch.[82] Very hot day, strong sunshine. So we took the motor back from Eaglesham. We thought it was a Zeppelin, as it is driven by gas.[83] Italy's capture are now about 30,000. Sweden getting into trouble with us for giving information about ships to Germany.

Monday, 10 September

After tea we went to the Palace, seeing I'm not in the army yet. Serious news from Russia. Kerensky (prime minister) and Korniloff (commander of army) fall out.[84] We'll get on with the war someday.

---

[79] They are messing up the war, but Thomas is writing in Scots or Ulster Scots.

[80] Compared to Govanhill, a district mainly composed of tenement buildings, Pollokshields, which has many detached and semi-detached villas, was aristocratic.

[81] A churchwarden pipe has a much longer stem than a regular one.

[82] Ballagioch is near Newton Mearns, a town to the south of Glasgow. Eaglesham is a village nine miles south of the city. The route is currently a favourite with racing cyclists.

Tuesday, 11 September

Russia in a state of revolution and civil war. Korniloff marching on Petrograd. Here's luck.

No. G 677501 MINISTRY OF FOOD.
SUGAR
REGISTRATION CARD.

This part to be kept by the Retailer.

I desire to purchase my supplies of Sugar for my household from:—
A. *Retailer's Name* T. Lyons & Co Ld.
Address Cadbury Hall
I hereby declare that no other Sugar Registration Card has been signed on behalf of my household.
B. *Signature* Arthur Griffiths
Address 70 Burbage Road S.E.
Date 22nd Sept. 1917.
5 No. of persons .... Initials AG
TOWN HALL, CAMBERWELL, S.E.
District ....

MINISTRY OF FOOD.
No. G 677501
SUGAR
REGISTRATION CARD.

This part to be kept by the Householder.

C. *Name* Griffiths Arthur
Address 70 Burbage Road S.E. 24
Retailer with whom the Householder has registered:—
D. *Signature of Retailer* T. Lyons & Co Ld.
Address Cadbury Hall
5 No. of persons .... Initials AG
TOWN HALL, CAMBERWELL, S.E.
District ....

Wednesday, 12 September

My niece Lily up at tea time. Got my sugar form to fill in yesterday.

Thursday, 13 September

Did some work on the room bed pieces; shifted the bed supports to a more pleasing position. Sent off my sugar application today. Agnes in the wash-house in the forenoon.

Friday, 14 September

Things settling down in Russia. Kerensky triumphant. Korniloff arrested.

Saturday, 15 September

Took a walk to Sam's shop at night for a crack.

Sunday, 16 September

We all went to church in the afternoon. Train smash in Yorkshire yesterday. Eight soldiers killed.

Because of a shortage of imported petrol, motorbuses were adapted to run on coal-gas, which was stored in large bags on the roof.
Alexander Fyodorovich Kerensky was the second prime minister of the Russian Provisional Government. General Lavr Kornilov, the Commander-in-Chief of the Russian army, was dismissed by Kerensky after a series of misunderstandings.

Monday, 17 September
Winter time starts today. With bared head I solemnly put back the household clocks one hour, late last night. Man up today sorting room gas. The loaf is now 4½d (2lb). Russia declared a republic.

King George V and his entourage watch men at work in Glasgow.

Tuesday, 18 September
The King doing Glasgow this week and round about. I saw him today. Agnes made plum jam at night.

Wednesday, 19 September
Tommy got a half holiday today to see the King, but he did not see His Royal Highness. We all went to pictures at night, seeing I'm still at large. Two U-boats sunk in North Sea.

SEPTEMBER, 1917.

Thursday **20**

(263-102)

Terrific rain and wind today

Cleaned all the windows tonight Agnes put up room curtains.

British attack again at Ypres. Good progress being made

SEPTEMBER, 1917.

Friday 21

(264-101)

Cold windy day

Took a look over at Sam's shop at night to see Sam.

British take 3000 prisoners in latest victory at Ypres

Saturday, 22 September

Hetty coming today to stay for a week or so. We all went to Queen's Park after tea. Agnes got a beautiful blouse from Hetty. Great fire in South Hanover Street tonight. McLaren's premises completely gutted out.[85]

Sunday, 23 September

I took a walk to Govan before dinner. Looked at the boats in the docks to see if we had any left. After dinner we all had a walk by Carmunnock Road and into Rutherglen.

Monday, 24 September

This is the autumn holiday, so I had a day off. We all went to Rouken Glen in afternoon. British destroyer sunk in Channel by U-boat. Ten years ago today, Agnes and I had tea in Cranston's, then went to Hippodrome.[86]

Tuesday, 25 September

Tommy went to school today in the motor car at dinner time. Agnes, Hetty and Tommy doing the town in the afternoon. We all went to Palace at night. Big air raid on London: 15 killed, 70 injured. Zepps raid Yorkshire coast, but not much damage done.

Wednesday, 26 September

Dirty wet day. Got exemption card sent me today. I am a free man until 10 December 1917: 'national interests'. Hetty and Agnes went to church at night for the induction of the minister. British 'push' again at Ypres. Battle started at 5.30 this morning. Another air raid over London: six killed, 16 injured. Argentina breaks off relations with Germany.

William McLaren & Company Ltd was a firm of warehousemen in South Hanover Street, in central Glasgow.

Kate Cranston ran four tearooms in Glasgow, all with interiors or furnishings designed by Charles Rennie Mackintosh, with decorative work by his wife, the artist Margaret Macdonald. The Glasgow Hippodrome was attached to Bostock's Zoo in New City Road, north of the city centre. It offered both circus and cinema entertainment.

Thursday, 27 September
Agnes, Hetty and Tommy at church tonight, a social on. I went to Greenlodge. British victory at Ypres: 1,600 prisoners. Costa Rica severs diplomatic relations with Germany. Who's next?

Friday, 28 September
Agnes made plum jam tonight. Russian destroyer mined in the Baltic.

Saturday, 29 September
Hetty has come to the end of her stay, so we all saw her off at Cross Station by 8.12 p.m. train. Air raid on England last night.

Sunday, 30 September

We all went to church today, and heard the new minister. Text was 'The Call to the Christians' (which does not include Germans). After dinner we went out a walk by Pollokshields. We saw the Duke of Connaught inspecting motor cars.[87] Another air raid on London last night. 11 killed, 32 injured.

Monday, 1 October

Our monthly list of visitors started tonight with Hetty Cook. I saw her away. Walked her down to Bridge Street and put her on a yellow car there. Stuttgart (Germany) bombed by French airmen. Big British victory in Mesopotamia; 4,000 Turks captured. Air raid on London last night; nine killed, 42 injured.

Tuesday, 2 October

Another air raid on London last night; 10 killed, 38 injured. During September, British have captured in France 5,296 cursed Germans, 11 guns and 377 machine guns. Fire in munitions work in north of England. 10 lives lost.

Wednesday, 3 October

No air raid on London last night. Lloyd George says we are going to have 'reprisals', and bomb the cursed Huns at home. We will see.

Thursday, 4 October

I went to Greenlodge at night and mended the kitchen easy chair. American troops in Glasgow, but I have seen none yet. Ships sunk this week by U-boats lowest on record. British make another big attack at Ypres.

---

[87] Prince Arthur, Duke of Connaught and Strathearn, was a son of Queen Victoria. After a distinguished military career, he was Governor General of Canada from 1911 to 1916. He was elected Grand Master of the United Grand Lodge of England annually from 1902 to 1939.

Friday 5
(278-87)

Some heavy showers today very cold.

Agnes made Damson Jam tonight, Butter is about 3/6 the pound. Tommy got a very bad cold.

British Capture nearly 5000 Germans in Yesterdays great victory. Hoch, hoch.

British Cruiser "Drake" sunk by U. Boat north of Ireland. 19 lives lost.

Saturday, 6 October

A couple of U-boats sunk in the North Sea by British aeroplanes and destroyers.

Sunday, 7 October

Broke a cup today, so I must break other two articles.[88] Some U-boats sunk by American destroyers in European waters.

Monday, 8 October

Peru and Uruguay break off diplomatic relations with Germany. We are going to get potato bread now.[89]

Tuesday, 9 October

Agnes went down to the wash-house at night. Haig strikes again from Ypres at the Germans. French attacking also. 2,000 prisoners. Got in gas bill today. I see price is advanced another 2d per 1,000.

Wednesday, 10 October

No matches, no sugar, no butter, no tea to be got in Govanhill. These are the times to live in.

Thursday, 11 October

Managed to get two dozen boxes of matches in the town tonight. Great rejoicings. During this year 11 U-boats have been destroyed in the Adriatic.

Friday, 12 October

Took Tommy to the hair merchant at night to thin his crop. Germany says: 'Never, no never, will we give up Alsace-Lorraine.'

---

[88] A common superstition.

[89] The government planned to add more potato flour to the recipe for the War Loaf, to supplement the flour from imported wheat.

Saturday, 13 October

No butter to be got today. British take about 943 prisoners at Ypres. The weather stops operations meantime. Mutiny in Austrian warships.

Sunday, 14 October

Agnes and Tommy went to church. German naval coup in Gulf of Riga. Under cover of the Fleet, Germans landed on some islands there. Russian forts silenced.

Monday, 15 October

Hard frost in the morning. Foggy forenoon. Bright sunny day and pouring wet night. Rung up Mr Cormack and invited him, wife and family for tea on Wednesday night. Agnes made an 'eggless' cake at night.[90] British make a raid on German trenches and kill 200 of the vermin.

Tuesday, 16 October

Coal selling today for 1/11 per bag. Eggs 3/9 per doz. Played Tommy and Agnes at quoits tonight and regret to say I won. Two U-boats sunk in Mediterranean by French. British minesweeper Begonia missing, presumed to be lost with all hands. British armed mercantile cruiser Champagne torpedoed. 56 lives lost. French steamer Medis sunk by torpedo. 250 passengers missing.

[90] These were also known as 'war cakes'.

Wednesday, 17 October

We got our sugar ticket today. All the Cormacks up tonight for tea. Spent the evening with music and cards. Bruges bombed by British airmen. Nancy bombed by British airmen. Essen bombed by French airmen.

Thursday, 18 October

Filled in my sugar ticket tonight. German and Russian Baltic fleets in great naval fight. Russian battleship *Slava* sunk. Russian coast batteries smashed up. U-boat crew mutiny at Ostend. Officers thrown into the sea.

Friday, 19 October

Went to my barber tonight and he cut my hair for a consideration. A year ago on this date Donald Ferguson died.

Saturday, 20 October

Tea 4/- a pound now, and very scarce. Currants scarce too. Big Zepp raid on east coast and London. 34 killed and 56 injured. Zepps get away. German success in North Sea. Fleet of neutral ships, escorted by two British destroyers, attacked by German cruisers. Nine ships sunk, and HMS *Mary Rose* and HMS *Strongbow* sunk with a loss of 135 men.

Sunday, 21 October

I went to church in forenoon. It was communion. Came down the road with Andrew's sister. We all went to church at night. I'll have to attend kirk better. Sat beside an Elder and he asked me was I a stranger. That does it. Great Zeppelin rout. Zepps pass over France. Three destroyed by gunfire and one captured. The French know their business. Waken up, John Bull.

Monday, 22 October

I went to church at night and took a sitting.[91] British and French take a bit out of German lines. Fitzsimmons, the great boxer, dead.[92]

Tuesday, 23 October

Today's scarelines. New French push/ Splendid start today/ Powerful positions attacked/ Big haul of prisoners. German night attack/ British retire short distance/ All other gains maintained. British naval air raid/ Ghent railway bombed/ Zeebrugge mole hit. Ostend bombarded by British warships.

Thursday, 25 October

Got a notice from factor. Rent up 3d a quarter. If I was not a member of the Kirk I would say: 'Curse the factor.'

Friday, 26 October

Wind, rain, snow, hail, lightning. Managed home a few sticks tonight. British advance again at Ypres. French capture 11,000 in the Aisne battle.

Saturday, 27 October

I went to Sam's shop at night and got some necessities of life. Brazil declares war on Germany. Who next?

Sunday, 28 October

On the 28 October 1914 poor Lily died. American troops in front line with French troops. First shot fired.

[91] To 'take a sitting' is to 'occupy a pew'. Thomas may have paid to reserve a seat.

[92] Robert James Fitzsimmons was an English-born New Zealand boxer, who made boxing history as the sport's first three-division world champion.

Monday, 29 October

Willie Mackenzie (home on leave) in seeing us tonight. Italian disaster. Enemy enter Gorizia. Julian front pierced. 100,000 men and 700 guns captured.

Wednesday, 31 October

This is Hallowe'en. We had a dumpling. My niece Lily here for tea. Italy still retreats. German towns bombed by British.

Thursday, 1 November

They are going to put gas up another 4d. What will it come to? 30 Gothas raid London, 10 persons killed, 21 injured.[93]

Friday, 2 November

Duncan gave us a visit tonight. British capture on the Western Front in October: 9,125 Germans, 15 guns, 431 machine guns and 42 trench mortars.

Saturday, 3 November

Germans retreat on the Aisne front. Fruits of recent French victory.

Sunday, 4 November

I went to church in the forenoon, Agnes went in the afternoon. I went out for a walk before tea time. Agnes went to church at night. Naval fight in the Cattegat. 10 German patrol boats and one cruiser sunk. British lose nil. Germans send out a wonderful electric warship off Belgian coast. We sunk it.

---

[93] The Gotha was a twin-engined bomber with a range of 500 miles and a bomb load of up to 1,100lb.

Tuesday, 6 November

Doing the 'working late' trick tonight. British and French troops being rushed to Italy's help.

Wednesday, 7 November

Agnes doing a lot of knitting this weather. Italy still advancing backwards.

Thursday, 8 November

Nellie here at tea time. She and Agnes went to the Pavilion last house.[94] Russian chaos: Kerensky deposed. Russia going to propose peace.

Saturday, 10 November

Agnes' birthday. Very nice day (naturally). More revolutions in Russia. She is going to be a poor ally.

Sunday, 11 November

We had a dumpling today to celebrate Agnes' birthday. I did full justice to it.[95]

Monday, 12 November

Andrew's sister up last night about 10.30 for Agnes. Andrew's wife thought her time was come, so Agnes went over.[96] I went to Sinclair Drive for the nurse. Nothing doing. A false alarm. We retired about 2 a.m. Fire in a Manchester workhouse. 15 old women burned to death.

---

[94] The Pavilion Theatre, in Renfield Street in Glasgow city centre, opened in 1904 as a music hall. It still presents a variety of musical, theatrical and other entertainments.

[95] Thomas has depicted his stomach, which is full of dumpling, as AI, mimicking the army medical code for fully fit, while his chest is still CIII.

[96] Andrew's wife believed her baby was about to be born.

Wednesday, 14 November

We all went out to Sam's house at night. The girls from the shop were there, also William Kirk. Tommy got a new overcoat for school. Nellie made it from an old overcoat of mine. British capture about 6,000 Turks in Palestine.

Thursday, 15 November

Spent the evening at home. Looks as if I would not spend many more. Lowest losses by submarines this week on record. Only six ships sunk. British advance towards Jerusalem.

Friday, 16 November

Civil war in Russia. Thousands killed in Petrograd and Moscow. British 21 miles from Jerusalem. British captures from all fronts since war began: prisoners 160,000, guns 800.

Saturday, 17 November

Agnes very ill. British three miles from Joppa.

Monday, 19 November

Tommy at his old school today (the one that was burned). Agnes still very ill. General Maude dead in Mesopotamia of cholera.[97] British occupy Jaffa (Joppa) in Palestine.

Tuesday, 20 November

Agnes much the same. Five U-boats sunk on Saturday. Germans getting wiped out in East Africa.

---

[97] Lieutenant General Sir Frederick Stanley Maude, the British commander who captured Kut and Baghdad in the spring of this year.

Wednesday, 21 November

Agnes very weak. Great British victory in France near Cambrai. The Great Hindenburg Line rushed by hundreds of 'tanks', followed up by our infantry and cavalry. Advance on 10 miles of front to a depth of five miles. 8,000 Germans captured. USA destroyer sunk.

Thursday, 22 November

Agnes all out at night.

Russia fed up with the war & proposes peace to Germany

Friday, 23 November

Daisy here in the afternoon. A slight improvement in Agnes' condition. British capture another 1,000 prisoners in France.

Saturday, 24 November

Great scarcity of butter. Went out to Ruglen in the afternoon and got my new overcoat (£3 5s). My next overcoat will likely be of a khaki shade.

Sunday, 25 November
Took a turn up before dinner to see Andrew. He is home the weekend. He wears the crossed flags on his sleeve now, being a signaller.[98] U-boat sunk by Yankees. 10,000 prisoners now captured by us in the Cambrai battle.

A German signpost amongst the ruins of Cambrai.

Monday, 26 November
Agnes went over and consulted her doctor about her illness. The verdict was none too cheerful. Andrew and Maxwell up to see me tonight. Maxwell is now a second lieutenant.

Thursday, 29 November
Wild wet day as usual. Got a note today from the military letting me know they would be at home on 13 December. Truce between Germany and Russia.

Saturday, 1 December
I cleaned all the windows in the afternoon. Agnes went out at night and engaged a lady to do a washing. I beat Agnes at Cassino at night.[99] Great German counter-attacks at Cambrai.

---

[98] The Royal Engineers Signal Service was formed in 1908 and provided communications during the First World War. This included motorcycle dispatch riders, semaphore and wireless operators.

[99] Cassino is a card game played with a standard deck, for two or more players. The object is to score 21 points by taking cards.

Monday, 3 December

Tommy opens a bank account at his school. Amount at credit: three pennies. Feeling frivolous, we all go to Greenlodge at night. Agnes feeling much better now. British in sight of Jerusalem.

Tuesday, 4 December

Great snow fall all day long. Tommy got a half holiday. Terrific German losses at Cambrai. East Africa, Germany's last colony, conquered.

Wednesday, 5 December

Being tired of clay pipes, I got a new one of cherry wood for the house. Lull in the Cambrai battle.

Thursday, 6 December

The lady who washes here today. Tram car smash at Queen's Park gate. Three killed, 40 injured.[100] Submarine losses serious again this week. Big air raid on London and coast. Two enemy machines down and crews captured. British air raids into Germany.

Friday, 7 December

We all went to the zoo tonight.[101] *British forced back at Cambrai.*

[100] On 5 December 1917 Glasgow Corporation Tramways Car Number 157, travelling from Netherlee to Kirklee, was turning into Victoria Road opposite Queen's Park gate, when it left the rails and overturned. Three passengers were killed and 56 were injured.

[101] This may have been the Glasgow Hippodrome in New City Road.

A square mile of the port of Halifax, Canada is levelled after the titanic explosion caused by the collision of the Mont Blanc *and the* Imo.

Saturday, 8 December

Terrible catastrophe in Halifax, Canada. Munition ship blown up and half the town. 2,000 killed, 8,000 wounded.[102]

Monday, 10 December

Agnes in town in forenoon with Nellie Hamilton (Mrs Pettigrew). Nellie has been left a house at the coast. British and French troops in front line Italian trenches. Revolution in Portugal. Another rising in Russia. Jerusalem taken by British.

Thursday, 13 December

Nice dry day. British losses heavy this week by the pirates. 21 boats down. Cuba declares war on Austria-Hungary.

Saturday, 15 December

Went to the Govanhill Baths in the afternoon. Got our new sugar application forms from our grocer today.

102 The French munitions ship *Mont-Blanc* collided with the Norwegian *Imo* in Halifax harbour, starting a fire that led to the largest man-made explosion until the atomic age. The town of Halifax was devastated.

DECEMBER, 1917.

Monday 17

(351-14)

Very Cold day Hard frost. Ill soon be skating So that Tommy would not fall on the Slippy pavement Agnes took him to school Agnes fell and suffered various injuries.

Christmas Cleaning in our house tonight Agnes dusted down Kitchen and Cleaned the "wedgewood" dinner service. I polished the silver covers, etc. and the golden jam-pan. will do more anon.

17/12/07 Agnes at Jennie Duncan's marriage party.

Tuesday 18

(352-13)

Frost completely away
dirty wet day

Gave the kitchen Clock its annual polish tonight.

We were dazzled by the result.

Bad day for us at sea. British Convoy sunk with destroyer. German destroyer raid off the tyne.
14 Ships altogether down.
Britannia rule the wave
(and do it now)

Friday, 21 December

The minister up for a little tonight accompanied by the Elder.

Saturday, 22 December

Agnes and Tommy went to town. They presented me with a scarf for my Christmas. Long life to them.

Sunday, 23 December

My father here in the afternoon. British armed steamer *Stephen Furness* sunk by U-boat in the Irish Channel. 101 lives lost.

Monday, 24 December

Agnes consulted her doctor and got another bottle. Presented Tommy with Dometo building blocks.[103] A. Baxter Junior presented me with a new pipe today.[104] British advances in Palestine.

Tuesday, 25 December

I got away today at 11 a.m. I took a walk round Rutherglen in the afternoon. Had a talk there with Alice Fraser. We got a few Xmas cards today. Tommy got from Coatbridge a pair of stockings [socks] and a brace of handkerchiefs.

Wednesday, 26 December

Got away at 5 p.m. I went straight out to Sam's for my tea. Agnes and Tommy there before me. We all then went to the church and listened to Sam's choir's rendering of the divine *Messiah*.

[103] Dometo was a construction kit with wooden interlocking bricks, which had a tongue and groove connection between the rows.

[104] One of the partners in the business that employed Thomas.

Thursday, 27 December

Was speaking to Frank Ruth in town today. He says he goes into the army on 4 January. My oh my. No butter or margarine to be got anywhere today. Agnes in the wash-house today and at night she went to baths and was akin to godliness. She saw a fire in Allison Street so I went out to see it, but it was out by this time. Sir John Jellicoe, First Sea Lord, 'retires'[105]. In his place, Admiral Wemyss.

Friday, 28 December

Agnes, being favoured of the gods, got ½lb of margarine and ½lb of butter. Western Front snow bound. Three British destroyers sunk by mine or torpedo off Dutch coast. 193 lives lost.

Saturday, 29 December

Agnes called to see Nellie Hamilton at night and had to get doctor for her. The great event is coming. Tommy got a new pair of slippers from Mrs Carmichael tonight for his Ne'erday.

Sunday, 30 December

After tea Agnes went up to see how Andrew's wife was getting on. The event was over. A son born at 2 a.m. British advance in Palestine.

Monday, 31 December

On holiday today. Took a walk out to Ruglen. Into Sam's shop and from thence gave Greenlodge Terrace a look up. Josephine gave me a cake of shortbread and some chocolates. Saw a lot of whisky queues, and butter queues. Great French victory in Italy. ,300 prisoners.

[105] Former Admiral of the Fleet and First Sea Lord Sir John Jellicoe was dismissed on Christmas Eve by Eric Geddes, the new First Lord of the Admiralty, after three years in command of the British fleet. He went on to serve as Governor General of New Zealand from 1920 to 1924.

NEWS

1918

Tuesday, 1 January

A Guid New Year. We opened the ball by first-fittin' the Carmichaels. After a sleep we got up, dressed etc. and got the 2.51 train from the Cross to Coatbridge. We spent the afternoon in the various bosoms of the Crozier family. Had a nice day, and then away for our train. The 9.20 p.m. train very busy, so we went class the one. Guatemala destroyed by an earthquake. 2,500 lives lost. Two British vessels torpedoed and sunk. HM minesweeping sloop *Arbutus* and HM armed boarding steamer *Grive*.[1]

Wednesday, 2 January

Went to my work at 10 a.m. and away again at 1.45. We all went to the Palace at night. Peace talks broken up between Germany and Russia. British have captured on Western Front during 1917: 74,349 prisoners. Hoch!

Thursday, 3 January

Fine day. Andrew home on leave so he gave us a look up at night. Submarine losses heavy this week: 18 big ships down, and three smaller ones.

Friday, 4 January

On to our sugar rations today. One and a half pounds to do a week.

Saturday, 5 January

Got a note from the tribunal letting me know that they would consider next Friday why I should not be in the army. Here's luck! Tommy and I out in afternoon to Ruglen.

[1] The *Arbutus* was sunk on 16 December 1917, and the *Grive* on 24 December 1917. The censor may have been holding back news until the Christmas season was over.

[2] It is likely that the weather, rather than an excess of entertainment, made the night a wild one.

[3] Singer railway station was named for the adjacent premises of the Singer Manufacturing Company, the world's largest sewing machine factory.

unday, 6 January

After dinner we boarded tram car for Clydebank, and visited enny Roxburgh and her folks. Enjoyed ourselves so well that ve stayed overnight at their earnest request. It was a wild night o I didn't need much coaxing.[2] 25,000 Germans revolt in Russia.

Monday, 7 January

'ravelled in from Singer Station this morning with Kate Roxburgh.[3] Agnes and Tommy spending most of the day there. When I got home at night, Agnes and Tommy just arrived efore me. All of us very well pleased with our little holiday. We erewith accord Mr and Mrs Roxburgh a hearty vote of thanks carried unanimously; loud applause). It looks as if Russia will ght Germany again.

'uesday, 8 January

nvaded at tea time by crowd from Greenlodge Terrace: Pa, osephine, Lily, Isa and Jack. Tommy got a picture book, and osephine presented Agnes with a 'peeny' for state occasions and nyself a new pair of 'gallowses'.[4] Put thermometer outside cullery window at night. It fell to 24°.[5] It is cold!

Wednesday, 9 January

Agnes went to Ibrox after tea time. British hospital ship *Rewa* orpedoed in Bristol Channel.[6] All on board saved except three ascars.[7]

A 'peeny' is a pinny or pinafore and 'gallowses' or galluses are braces for holding up trousers.
'ommy's measurements are in Fahrenheit. The equivalent temperature in Celsius is -4.5°.
'he *Rewa*, heading from Malta to Bristol with wounded from Greece, was torpedoed by the J55 in the Bristol Channel on 4 January 1918. Two crewmen died.
.ascar was a term used to describe a sailor from India or other countries east of the Cape of Good Hope working on a European vessel.

Thursday, 10 January
When I got home at tea time, visitors at the door, Tommy inside by himself. So he did not open in case it might be burglars. Agnes came in shortly afterwards. Germans are digesting ours and American peace terms, which they don't like.

Friday, 11 January
I appeared before the Tribunal today, with our lawyer. They heard me for one minute, then told me to go and be 'graded', in other words get medically examined once again. Here's luck! The daft wife upstairs set the house on fire today. We go the water.

Saturday, 12 January
Jenny Roxburgh here today. We toasted ourselves in the room. She gave Tommy a box of chocolates. Great scarcity of beef now

Sunday, 13 January
Duncan here at night. The tank Julian arrives today from Edinburgh to collect money for War Loan.[8] Edinburgh collected £4,342,825 in a week. British destroyer Racoon founders in snow storm off north coast of Ireland with all on board.

[8] During 1918, HM Tank Number 113, also known as 'Julian', was taken on a tour of the country and people were encouraged to throw spare change into the 'tank bank' or buy National War Bonds and War Savings Certificates from the tank staff to raise funds to prosecute the war against Germany.

Monday, 14 January

The arctic weather continues. Tried the temperature this morning. It was below 18°[9] – don't know how much as my thermometer stops there. Agnes baked a cake for tomorrow night. The tank took up its position this forenoon in the square for a week to collect a few million pounds.[10] It gave a display in the Green of demolishing trenches, barbed wire etc.[11]

Tuesday, 15 January

Snow lying very deep now. The Clyde frozen over. Sam, Nellie and John here at night. Very hard to get coal now. Coal men refuse to carry coal up. Cuss them. Great queues at the tank today. Yarmouth bombed by U-boat. Karlsruhe bombed by British airmen.

Coalman with cart.

Wednesday, 16 January

Got a note from the military that they would be pleased to examine me once more from a medical point of view on the 26th at 11 a.m. prompt once again. Here's luck! Agnes and Mrs Carmichael carried up a hundredweight of coal today in clothes baskets. In three days the tank has drawn £5,000,000, the record so far. British aviators drop tons of bombs on German factories.

9 The equivalent temperature in Celsius is -8°.
10 The square was George Square, the main civic square in central Glasgow, in front of the City Chambers, the seat of the local authority.
11 The Green was Glasgow Green, a large park at the south of the city centre.

Thursday, 17 January

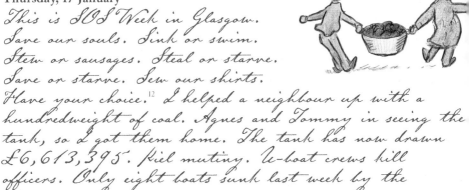

This is SOS Week in Glasgow. Save our souls. Sink or swim. Stew or sausages. Steal or starve. Save or starve. Sew our shirts. Have your choice.[12] I helped a neighbour up with a hundredweight of coal. Agnes and Tommy in seeing the tank, so I got them home. The tank has now drawn £6,613,395. Kiel mutiny. U-boat crews kill officers. Only eight boats sunk last week by the pirates.

Friday, 18 January

Snowed solidly all day. Two British destroyers sunk in storm off Scottish coast. All on board lost, except one man.

Saturday, 19 January

A thaw on this morning. Rain then heavy snow then very heavy rain. The roads in a terrific mess. No men to sweep up. Fitted kitchen gas with a new mantle and nozzle. Tank's total up to last night: £8,671,658. A record!

Sunday, 20 January

Dull mild day. Some heavy rain. Lit a fire in room and made myself comfortable. Agnes took a turn over to see Nellie Hamilton and her baby. Glasgow beats all records with tank drawings. Total for week £14,503,714. Other totals: Birmingham £6,703,439; Edinburgh £4,764,639; Manchester £4,450,029; Bradford £4,050,000; Newcastle £3,932,324; Liverpool £2,060,512; Sheffield £1,297,698.

[12] SOS Week, which was held across Britain, exhorted the population to save or starve. This was the last gasp of a voluntary food conservation policy, which was soon replaced by rationing.

Monday, 21 January

Got a letter from the military today. Bless the military!! British naval victory in Dardanelles. Cruiser *Breslau* sunk and battleship *Goeben* beached. Strikes in Austria. War works all closed. Demonstrations against Germany.

Tuesday, 22 January

Had to go to military headquarters today with some information they desired. Crisis in Austria. 1,200,000 workers on strike. They actually want to stop the war!

Wednesday, 23 January

I got two boxes of matches in town today. Agnes went over at night to see how Andrew's baby was keeping. British airmen bomb German towns.

PROVISIONS.
SOLD OUT OF EVERYTHING
"S.O.S."
Provisions very scarce now.
no beef
no butter
no sugar
no margarine
no tea
no "nuffin".

Thursday, 24 January

May Crozier and Hetty Cook here at night. Seven boats sunk by the pirates last week. British airmen bombing away at the Goeben.

Friday, 25 January

Mrs Gordon here in the afternoon to see if I'm in the 'sojers' yet. I'm not. Germany defiant yet. Refuses the Allies' peace terms. We will maybe get on with the war now.

Saturday, 26 January

I went up to Sauchiehall Lane to be overhauled by the Medical Board. They marched a dozen of us to an Orange Lodge in Cathedral Street and studied my anatomy there. Not having the development of Sandow, I was passed 'Grade 3'.[13] *I don't suppose I'll have to fight. We all went to the Majestic at night.*

Sunday, 27 January

I went to Divine Service in the forenoon. After dinner I went as far as Govan and saw the boats. The boats are all 'camouflaged' in a wonderful manner. Like this. The food controller says that in one week in December the Germans sunk 3,000,000 lbs of bacon and 4,000,000 of cheese. Got strafe the Huns.

[13] Eugen Sandow (1867-1925) was a pioneering bodybuilder of the Victorian era.

Monday, 28 January

Dirty wet day. Agnes in the wash-house. Tommy had a bit of a cold so he stayed in and watched the house. Cunard Liner *Andania* torpedoed north coast of Ireland, but got towed to port.[14]

Tuesday, 29 January

Provisions getting scarce, so I hunted the town today and got ¼lb of tea, ¼lb of cheese and ½lb of margarine, total cost 2/6. Big German air raid on London. 47 killed, 169 injured. German aeroplane down in flames. Berlin workers strike. 100,000 out.

Wednesday, 30 January

We all went to Sam's house at night. Another air raid on London. Three killed, 10 injured. 750,000 strikers out in Berlin, so they say. The Clyde workers want peace or they 'down tools'.[15]

Shocked air-raid victims make their way to shelter in London.

Thursday, 31 January

As my shaving brush is getting bald-headed, I got a new one today for 1/6. Agnes did a pile of ironing at night. Big shipping losses last week. 15 boats down. Mutiny and strikes all over Germany. Air raid over Paris.

Friday, 1 February

Meant to put varnish on the soles of my boots, but couldn't get the shiny stuff in Govanhill.[16] It is evidently as scarce as beef or matches. Berlin in a state of siege owing to the strike. Between 20,000 and 30,000 deserters in Switzerland from the various armies. Some of them British.

---

[14] Seven people lost their lives.

[15] The Clyde Workers Committee, which was campaigning for a 40-hour working week, extended its demands to calling for peace. This was partly a reaction to the government's Military Service Bill, introduced in January 1918, which proposed moving men from the munitions factories to the trenches.

[16] The varnish, as well as making his boots watertight, was, like the studs he has already applied, intended to stop the leather soles from wearing down, so lengthening the life of his boots.

Saturday, 2 February

We all went out in the afternoon. I got some varnish and a box of matches. Great joy. Put a coat of varnish on Tommy's boots to make them watertight. British captures for January: 171 prisoners, seven machine guns and three trench mortars. Rebellion crushed in Germany.

Sunday, 3 February

Took Tommy down to the docks after dinner and let him see the pie-bald boats.[17] When we got home Agnes was dressed ready for Kirk. She went herself. In her absence, Andrew (the 'sojer') dropped in. His son and heir was Christened at Kirk today, so he had got leave for a day. His advice to me: 'Keep out the army.'

Monday, 4 February

I tried to get lard (what you need to make apple cakes with) but got none in the town. We were delighted when Jenny Roxburgh came in at 9 p.m. She is nursing a sister in Maryhill. I saw her all the way home. Two British aviators get 10 years penal in Germany for dropping tracts.

Tuesday, 5 February

Went into the library at Miller Street for some godly literature. Got a little note this morning from the City of Glasgow Local Tribunal. Notice of hearing to be considered at the place and date indicated. Nature of application or of question raised: G39 L40 R1. Date, Friday, 8 February 1918. 2 p.m. At 249 George Street in Committee Room 204.[18] Now we know what to do.

[17] The boats painted in camouflage designs.
[18] The address is a side entrance to the City Chambers.

Wednesday, 6 February

Dirty, wet, cold day. To brighten up our lives we took seats in the Palace tonight, situated in the Gorbals. Agnes got a quarter pound of real butter today. Britain threatens stern reprisals on Germany if she does not give proper treatment to the captured aviators. Since the war began Germany has murdered by air raids and U-boats 14,120 British civilians including women and children.

Thursday, 7 February

Received today from the Ministry of Food an application form for food tickets. We are going to be starved. I have to fill up aforesaid form. *Tuscania* (Anchor Line) sunk: great Clyde liner torpedoed off Irish coast. 2,000 American troops aboard. 209 on missing list. 2,187 persons saved.

Friday, 8 February

I went to the Tribunal today and the military man wanted to make me a clerk but I got exemption. What they call 'conditional exemption'.[19] Great relief in the home circle. U-boat that torpedoed the *Tuscania* meets a like fate by a British destroyer.

Saturday, 9 February

At 11 p.m. Agnes was presented, as a slight token of esteem, with a nice silk blouse by Mrs Carmichael, the 'munitioneer'.[20] Lord Jellicoe warns us that we are in for a bad three or four months with the U-boats. He's a cheery bloke.

---

19 Thomas' exemption from being called up was conditional on him continuing to be employed in work of national importance. It was up to him, or his employer's lawyer, to argue that Thomas' job met this definition.

20 Mrs Carmichael is evidently working in a munitions factory.

Sunday, 10 February

After breakfast, Agnes and Tommy went to church. Germany seems to be massing troops on Western Front.

Monday, 11 February

Horse flesh is now an official ration. Ora pro nobis. Russia throws up the sponge. All Russian armies demobilised. So Roumania is left in the lurch.

Tuesday, 12 February

I got a love letter from Jenny Roxburgh today saying they were coming out on Saturday. HM destroyer *Boxer* sunk by collision in Channel last Friday. One boy lost. (An old destroyer dated 1894.) Wilson warns Germany: 'America will never turn back.'

Wednesday, 13 February

Got a note from the Tribunal this morning telling me to join the Volunteers. We went to the Palace at night.

Thursday, 14 February

Got our food ticket today for butter or margarine, and tea.[21] Now we are going to starve. To fulfil the majesty of the law, I went out tonight to join the Volunteers. Not being a 'one' man, they let me off.[22] Nothing doing. Cleaned the windows when I came home. Heavy losses this week by the U-boats. 19 boats sunk.

---

[21] The food ticket, or ration card, allowed each household to buy small amounts of meat, sugar butter and eggs each week. Bread was not rationed.

[22] Thomas was not a 'one', he was a CIII (or C3), at the bottom of the medical scale.

Friday, 15 February

Very busy tonight. Polished the jam-maker and parlour pokers etc. Washed the lobby floor. Agnes put curtains on room windows. Bolo, the arch-traitor in France, sentenced to die.[23] British captures last year: 168 heavy howitzers, 68 heavy guns, 438 field guns, 1,055 trench mortars, 2,843 machine guns.

Saturday, 16 February

Rose this morning at 5.20 and washed the blinking floor. Jenny Roxburgh and her three sisters here at 3.30 p.m. We had a lively time. I saw them all off by 10.17 tram from the Cross. German submarine fires a few shells into Dover. One child killed. German destroyers raid the Straits of Dover, sink eight trawlers and drifters and kill 30 of our men. The war is costing us £6,384,000 per day.

Sunday, 17 February

Dull, cold day. After breakfast I took a seven-mile walk in the country by Ruglen and Croftfoot. We favoured Ibrox at night with our company. Air raid on London: 11 killed, four injured.

Monday, 18 February

Was delighted ? to get a 'phone message from Lily that she and her Ma would be here at night. Lily here at tea time and Josephine on or about 8 p.m. I saw them to the car about 10.30 p.m. We start on our beef ration card today. Another air raid on London. 19 killed and 34 injured. Germany again at war with Russia.

---

[23] Paul Bolo, a career criminal, was found guilty of obtaining funds from Germany to set up a pacifist movement in France.

Tuesday, 19 February
Broke a few sticks at night. Another air raid on London gets turned back.

Wednesday, 20 February
We all went to the Palace tonight. British air raids into Germany. German patrol warship strikes mine in Baltic. Crew drowned. Germany wants indemnity from Russia of £800,000,000.

Thursday, 21 February
Oiled our ancient sewing machine thoroughly and filled a few spools. Broke some sticks, also a small hammer. Last week's U-boat losses: 15 boats down, 12 large steamers and three small. British advance from Jerusalem, four miles from Jericho. Our mercantile losses last year - 1,302 ships; 824 over 1,600 tons, 296 under 1,600 tons, 182 fishing boats. 666 unsuccessful attacks. D... the Germans.

Friday, 22 February
Mended the wee hammer I broke last night. Washed floor tonight. General Allenby reports that Jericho was occupied by us yesterday morning. Cavalry reach Jordan. Germans advancing through Russia. Italian air squadrons bomb Innsbruck.

Saturday, 23 February

All Ibrox here about 6 p.m. After tea Mrs Gordon, Mrs Livingstone and the Misses Gordon favoured the company with a few songs, the accompaniment being tastefully rendered by TCL. Number of recruits accepted for service in the army during 1916 was 1,190,075.

The Livingstone family was musical, and often entertained one another with renditions of popular songs such as this one by Irving Berlin.

Sunday, 24 February

Wild wet day. I did not go over the door-step today. Sunday is a day of rest anyway. Between 5 December 1917 and 19 February 1918, British airmen have raided German territory 20 times and dropped bombs on the beast to the weight of 48,706 pounds.

Monday, 25 February

Russia surrenders abjectly. Humiliating peace.

Tuesday, 26 February

Agnes spending the day in the wash-house. Tommy taking photographs now (of a kind). Germany making for Petrograd.

Wednesday, 27 February

We all went to the Palace to see the pictures. Got a note in letter box when we got home. Sam had evidently tried to get in. Sorry! Union Castle Liner *Glenart Castle* (hospital ship) sunk in Bristol Channel by U-boat. 150 lives lost.

Friday, 1 March

Took a run out to the shop to see Sam at night to arrange about the concert etc. Japan to watch over Allied interests in the Far East.

Saturday, 2 March

In the afternoon I took Tommy by the hand and we walked out to Rutherglen. I saw my tailor on the possibility of a new pair of 'culottes' for myself. Our captures during February on Western Front: 312 prisoners and 20 machine guns. German torpedo boat and two minesweepers sunk by mines in North Sea.

Sunday, 3 March

After dinner I took a walk through Queen's Park. Russian capital removed to Moscow. Bolsheviks reported to have seized Vladivostok.

Monday, 4 March

The Prince of Wales in Glasgow for a few days.[24] *I have not yet clapped his back.*

Tuesday, 5 March

We all at Sam's for our tea, then we went to his concert in the Town Hall. Tommy lost his first tooth today, one of the bottom set.

Wednesday, 6 March

The 'City Hall' commandeered by the Food Control Committee.[25] Armed Allan liner *Calgarian* torpedoed off the Irish coast. 48 lives lost. Cork steamer *Kenmare* torpedoed. 29 lives lost. The great Irish patriot, John Redmond, dead.[26]

[24] The Prince of Wales was to become Edward VIII.

[25] The City Hall in Candleriggs, central Glasgow, was composed of a large hall that was used for public meetings and concerts and a number of smaller halls. The halls stood above the city's fruit and vegetable market.

[26] John Redmond (1856-1918) was an Irish nationalist politician, barrister, Westminster MP and leader of the Irish Parliamentary Party from 1900 until his death. He was regarded as a moderate and conciliatory politician.

1918

Thursday, 7 March

Dull day, and most bitter cold wind. Shipping losses serious this week. 18 boats down. Roumania out of the war. Forced to make peace on Germany's terms. Who next? 20,000 skilled men from the army to be sent to build ships.

Friday, 8 March

Tommy had a holiday today. 'God bless the Prince of Wales.' Japan landing troops at Vladivostock. Air raid on London. About 21 killed and 50 injured.

Saturday, 9 March

Tea scarce this week. So is tobacco. I went into town tonight for some literature. At last, heavy fighting on Western Front. Big attacks on British north-east of Ypres. Air raid on Paris. Nine killed. British advance again in Palestine.

Sunday, 10 March

Rose at 7 a.m. Gave Agnes a cup of tea and had a smoke. As it was raining hard, I went back to bed. After dinner I walked through Queen's Park, Maxwell Park and Bellahouston Park, and took car home from the Toll.[27] British airmen drop bombs on Mainz, on the Rhine.

Monday, 11 March

Went to the Govanhill Baths at night and came back in a more godly frame of body. Some shops have actually no tobacco now. Margarine is more plentiful. We are at war. Things lively at Western Front. Stuttgart bombed by British airmen.

---

[27] Paisley Road Toll.

Tuesday, 12 March

We entertain tomorrow night, so Agnes did some baking, and I cleaned spoons etc. Big air raid on Paris. 100 killed (including 66 in a panic by suffocation). 79 injured.

Wednesday, 13 March

A British airship passed over Glasgow today, which I saw. It was like a Zeppelin. Tommy also saw it from the school. Hetty and May here when I got home. Sam, Nellie and Willie Kirk came later. We had a night of song. I got four boxes of matches today. Zepp raid on Hull. Big British air raid on Germany (Coblenz) also on Bruges.

Thursday, 14 March

Agnes not up to the mark tonight. She retired shortly after 9 p.m. U-boat menace: 18 ships sunk this week. Zepp at Hartlepool. Five lives lost, nine injured. Air fight in North Sea. Two British machines attack and defeat five German planes. Freiburg (Germany) bombed by British airmen.

Saturday, 16 March

This is Irish Flag Day. We all went out in the afternoon and looked at the shops and thought it would be nice to have a lot of money.

Sunday, 17 March

This is the Day of Saint Pat, of a rotten country.[26] After dinner I walked into town and took car to Clydebank. Walked along to Dalmuir. I saw an aeroplane flying about. At the canal I watched about a dozen aeroplanes lying in a field. Just as the aviator was going up, heavy rain came on and he stayed down, and I came home. British airmen again bomb Germany.

[26] St Patrick is the patron saint of Ireland. His feast day is on 17 March.

Monday, 18 March

The merchant shipping position is very serious. Too many boats being sunk and not enough being built. Serious times ahead. British airmen raid Germany. British net loss in shipping by U-boats to 31 December 1917 is 20%. Net deficit per month 120,000 tons.

Wednesday, 20 March

Got our new meat tickets today. Being sort of absent-minded I paid gas bill today. We all went to Palace at night to be cheered up. Fight between British and German seaplanes in Heligoland Bight. We won.

Thursday, 21 March

Nice warm day, but terribly blowy. Tommy and Agnes out a walk with the Cormacks at night. They have got a 'plot'.[29]
Sea fight off Dunkirk. British and French victory. Five German destroyers sunk. We lose none.

Friday, 22 March

World's shipping loses to end of 1917:

British	7,079,492
Foreign	4,748,080
	11,827,572 tons

At last! The great German offensive begins. British fiercely attacked on a 50-mile front.

[29] The Cormack family has begun renting an allotment, possibly in Queen's Park.

Saturday, 23 March

By order of the government I put all the clocks an hour forward towards midnight. The great battle goes on. The Kaiser in command. Germans claim 25,000 British prisoners and 400 guns. British line broken near St Quentin.

Sunday, 24 March

After dinner I had a stroll by the Clyde at Shieldhall. I saw a submarine and an American warship in the docks. British pressed back from the St Quentin front. Great slaughter of Germans. British cross the Jordan in Palestine.

Monday, 25 March

Agnes got a new hat today. Tobacco getting very scarce. The firing of the guns of the big battle heard at Dover. Furious fighting at Bapaume. A million Germans flung into the battle. French army into the fight now. Germans report 30,000 prisoners and 600 guns now taken. Paris bombarded by a big gun 75 miles away!

Tuesday, 26 March

Got one ounce of 'thick black' today from a tobacconist as a favour. Lull in the big battle. Germans hurrying forward fresh divisions. French hotly engaged. Noyon given up. British lose Bapaume. British destroyer sunk by collision. British minesweeping sloop mined. 66 lives lost. Metz and Cologne bombed by British.

Wednesday, 27 March

Took Tommy at night to Sweeney Todd.[30] He got a balloon. German attacks weakening. British reserves arriving on field. German losses are estimated about 400,000. Great British air triumph. In five days we knock down 256 German machines. We lose 32.

Thursday, 28 March

Tommy got his Easter holidays today. Somme battle renewed. Whole front ablaze. British line still intact. We are now on tea and butter rations. We get 4½oz of tea per week.

Friday, 29 March

Dull cold day. Duncan here at night. British holding up the Germans. Great British victory in Mesopotamia. Turkish army wiped out, 5,000 prisoners.

Saturday, 30 March

On my way home from work I met Isa and Jack going to the station. Jack was going to Rothesay with his uncle Sam Ferguson. I saw them to the station. Went out to my tailor in afternoon and got my new trousers. I ordered a new suit also. It is going to be very dear. German long-range gun shells Paris. 75 killed in a church. Big German defeat at Arras.

Sunday, 31 March

Seeing as it is Easter Sunday we had ham and eggs for breakfast. We all went to church in afternoon. Before tea time we took car to Shieldhall and saw all the strange looking boats in the docks.[31] Battle raging south of the Somme. Germans claim 70,000 prisoners now and 11,000 guns. British advance in Palestine.

[30] The barber.
[31] The boats were painted in camouflage patterns.

Monday, 1 April

I have a holiday today. We all took train at 2.20 p.m. from the Cross to Coatbridge. Hetty Cook was there. Fierce German attacks south of the Somme. British advance north of Albert. Moreuil recaptured by the French, Canadian cavalry and British infantry. Russia recaptures Odessa from the Germans.

Tuesday, 2 April

The 'Curfew' Act comes into force tonight.[32] Great anti-conscription riots in Quebec, troops fire on mob. Four killed. British boarding steamer *Tithonus* torpedoed and sunk. Paris again shelled.

Thursday, 4 April

Heavy rainfall on Western Front.

Friday, 5 April

Went to my hair artist tonight and got some hair removed. German offensive resumed. Very heavy fighting for Amiens. British stand firm.

Saturday, 6 April

Cold day. Some heavy showers. British bomb Luxemburg.

[32] The Board of Trade introduced a Curfew Order to reduce fuel use. Under the order, restaurants had to put out their lights at 10 p.m., theatres had to be dark after 10.30 p.m. and shop fronts should show no lights. The order lasted until December 1918.

[33] The Military Service Bill proposed that the Director-General of National Service would have the power to cancel any certificates of exemption granted on occupational grounds.

Sunday, 7 April

Sam and Nellie here at night. Sam thinks he is as good as in the army now. Nearly all exemptions are to be withdrawn by the new 'Manpower' Bill.[33]

Monday, 8 April

Bought a soft collar today.[34] I am going to reduce the laundry bill. Filled in the ticket that allows us so many ounces of ham per week. This is War Weapons Week: Glasgow intends to raise £2½ million to buy a super dreadnought.[35]

Tuesday, 9 April

Nice bright afternoon. Saw the most wonderful sight I ever saw. A dozen aeroplanes giving a display over Glasgow, looping the loop etc. Agnes and Tommy also saw them at Govanhill.

Wednesday, 10 April

Saw the captured German gun in the square today.[36] We went to the Palace at night. Great German attack launched between La Bassée and Armentières. British forced back. 'Manpower' Bill introduced last night.

Thursday, 11 April

Got our lum swept today and a taste of oil on the 'whirly'. Saw another display of aviation today. Great battle raging on the whole front. British lose Armentières.

---

[34] Most office workers wore shirts with detachable collars. Stiff collars were cleaned and starched outside of the house, while soft collars could be cleaned at home.

[35] War Weapons Week was held throughout Britain from 8 to 13 April and people were encouraged to buy National War Bonds (sold in denominations from £5 to £5,000) or War Savings Certificates (15/6).

[36] George Square.

Saturday, 13 April

Cold, wet day. In the afternoon we all went to the square to see the aeroplanes. We saw the square, but the aeroplanes did not appear. We admired the captured German 'aviatik', listened to the bands and watched the procession, and then home to tea, likewise to thaw.[37] Position on Western Front very serious. The crisis seems at hand now. Haig's order to the British Army: 'With our backs to the wall every position to be held to the last man, and there must be no retirement.'[38] Gothas raid Paris: 26 killed, 72 injured. Zepps raid England: five killed. Allies raid Zeebrugge.

Sunday, 14 April

After dinner I had a walk through Queen's Park to Pollokshaws, then on to Kennishead and Thornliebank and Giffnock and car home. Very cold day. Terrific battle. Great German losses. Allied line unbroken.

Monday, 15 April

Tommy got a penny from me for some wonderful new 'peary' he was dying for.[39] I could get no tobacco in town today. Glasgow's total for War Weapons Week was £3,000,000. British lose again Neuve Eglise. Fierce fights at Merville.

Tuesday, 16 April

Managed to get one ounce of thick black today, so I bought a brace of clay pipes. British Fleet sweeps the Cattegat. Ten German trawlers sunk. Great fire in Friedrichshafen (Germany). Gotha factory destroyed. 30 squadrons of aeroplanes destroyed. Hallelujah.

---

[37] The Aviatik was a reconnaissance aircraft built in Germany and Austria-Hungary during the First World War. It was captured and displayed in George Square.

[38] Haig's Special Order of the Day, issued in response to the German Spring offensives, urged the British Army to 'fight it out' and insisted that 'Victory will belong to the side which holds out the longest'.

[39] A 'peary', usually spelled 'peery', was a spinning top, set in motion with a whip or cord. See illustration on page 11.

Wednesday, 17 April

Got word today that [Claude] Maxwell is wounded in the Big Battle. Shrapnel in the head.

Thursday, 18 April

Agnes and Mrs Carmichael at the Royal tonight.[40] *I saw German prisoners today. Germans take Passchendaele Ridge and Malern. British line still intact.*

Friday, 19 April

Was greatly upset today to hear that James Crichton was killed in action. He fell on 21 March. He is the first of our staff to go. 'Manpower' Act now the law of the land. Conscriptions for Ireland and all fit men up to 51 to join up. Germans heavily repulsed at Givenchy.

Saturday, 20 April

Agnes started a new dodge with the sugar allowance. I get a dish with ½ lb, she gets one and Tommy gets one and it has to do a week.

Agnes
bought
new
Corsets
today.

---

[40] The Theatre Royal, in Hope Street, central Glasgow, offered both comedy and drama. It is now the home of Scottish Opera.

Sunday, 21 April

Agnes went to church but she did not get in. Maybe it was overcrowded and maybe she was late. After dinner I walked down the Clyde to Renfrew. Saw the submarine 'K.7' at Govan Dock has a coat of 'camouflage' paint.[41] I crossed over the ferry at Renfrew and home by Partick. Agnes and Tommy at church tonight. Great uproar over Ireland and the Conscription Act.

Monday, 22 April

Germans still keeping quiet.

Tuesday, 23 April

New budget out. Tobacco is going to be dear. Oh help! Great naval raid by British to bottle up the U-boat bases. Zeebrugge bottled up by old cruisers and submarines filled with cement and sunk. Ostend treated same way, though not so successfully.

Wednesday, 24 April

Agnes spring cleaning the bathroom tonight.

[41] K-class submarines were steam-propelled, and were intended to operate with the battle fleet. K.7 was built by HM Dockyard in Devonport and commissioned in July 1917.

Friday, 26 April
The third great battle going on. Germans get a footing on Kemmel Hill.

Saturday, 27 April
We all went to Queen's Park in the afternoon. Nellie Hamilton and her small child up for a little at night. Having thoughts of making jam, I took a walk over to Sam's shop and managed 'quatre livres de sucre'.[42] No cheese to be got today. British lose Kemmel but do well south of the Somme.

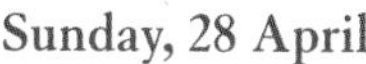

Sunday, 28 April
Tommy and I went to the Art Galleries. We got no dinner today as the sausages spoke back to us when we looked at them.[43]

Monday, 29 April
Paid today 8½d for an ounce of thick black and ½d for a box of matches. I never did like the Kaiser. British gain at Festubert.

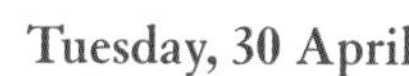

Tuesday, 30 April
I walked out to Ruglen tonight. Up Mill Street, over Cathkin and back by Burnside. Car from Town Hall home. German bid for Ypres most bloodily repulsed.

Wednesday 1 May
Went to the tooth doctor before tea time and got my teeth faked up. Mount Kemmel heavily shelled by the Allies.

---

[42] Four pounds of sugar.
[43] The sausages had gone off. Always a problem for people in the days before domestic fridges.

Thursday, 2 May

Agnes and Tommy out at Ruglen seeing Nellie. Tommy got an old barrow of John's, with a 'game' wheel.[44] In their absence, Willie Mackenzie in for five minutes for a final goodbye. He is soon for the front.

Friday, 3 May

Mended the wheel of the barrow that belongs to Tommy.

Saturday, 4 May

No cheese this weekend yet. We are to be allowed less beef and more ham. Quiet on the Western Front.

Sunday, 5 May

Lovely sunny warm forenoon, so I dressed in my best, deserted my well-beloved wife and family and walked over Cathkin Braes via East Kilbride Road. Came back by Mill Street and went into the cemetery and had a seat beside poor Lily's grave. How different things might have been.

Monday, 6 May

I got a telephone message from Lily that her grandma was dead, and I'm to go to the funeral.[45] Agnes made rhubarb jam. Sebastopol taken by the Germans.

Tuesday, 7 May

Germans take over the Russian Black Sea fleet.

Wednesday, 8 May

Bought a black tie today.

[44] 'Game', pronounced 'gammy', means crooked, broken or dislocated.
[45] Only men attended the burial part of the funeral at this time.

Thursday, 9 May

Took a half holiday. Went over to Greenlodge after dinner, met Sam and Duncan there. We all went to Riddrie and attended the funeral. Took a walk round by Pollokshields at night. Watched the female soldiers drilling and other warlike articles.

Friday, 10 May

Another great naval raid by British on the submarine base. Ostend blocked. *Vindictive* filled with cement and sunk in channel. Over 500,000 American troops now in France.

Saturday, 11 May

We all out for a walk in the afternoon, and looked at the shops, admiring the things we can't buy. At night I went over to Sam's shop. Got a little butter and cheese and some sugar to make jam with.

Sunday, 12 May

Rose at 7 a.m. Went out to Ruglen by Ruglen Road and the Green and back by Toryglen. Came back invigorated at 9 a.m. for my breakfast. After dinner we all went to Pollok Estate and basked in the sunshine. We are rationed now for butter and margarine. Now ¼lb of butter and ½lb of the grease has to do us a week.

Illustration of an American kissing his wife goodbye as he leaves to join the war in Europe, from Le Petit Journal, *1918.*

Thursday, 16 May

Great Italian naval raid. Pola harbour entered. Austrian battleship torpedoed. 12,500 men of the British merchant mercantile marine have been killed by enemy action so far.

Friday, 17 May

Our kitchen gets whitewashed tomorrow. I reverently took down the kitchen clock. Agnes washed our priceless dinner service. British air raid into Germany (Saarbrücken).

Saturday, 18 May

Was not away from my work till after 2 p.m. The man McCort had the kitchen whitewashed when I got home, then Agnes and I girded up our respective loins, and washed paint, windows, floors etc. for the rest of the day.

Sunday, 19 May

Another nice day. Agnes feeling tired so she rested today. I took a walk to Queen's and Bellahouston parks in the afternoon. British aviators make a big raid into Germany (Cologne). 39 killed, 95 injured.

Monday, 20 May

Agnes starts an offensive on the room.[46] Great German air raid over London. 44 killed, 179 injured, seven Gothas destroyed.

[45] In other words, Agnes began spring-cleaning the parlour..

1918

Tuesday, 21 May

This is a holiday so I did no work. I took down the Old Masters in the room in the forenoon, then went out for a stroll. After dinner we all went out. Boarded car at Eglinton Toll, went out to Giffnock, walked through by the quarries to Cathcart and got car home. After tea we went to the Palace. Another British raid into Germany (Landau).

Wednesday, 22 May

Met my niece Lily in town, took her home with me. We sat in the room and had a little music. I walked Lily home. 1,000 German aeroplanes downed by the British during the last two months.

Friday, 24 May

Agnes finished the room tonight. Heaven be praised. Tommy got a new pair of sand shoes today. Germans make a highly successful air raid on a British hospital in France. Hundreds killed and injured.

Saturday, 25 May

Rained all day. Got my gamp recovered today for 7/6.[47] After tea we went to town to get Tommy a new blazer. Troopship *Moldavia* torpedoed. 56 Yankees missing. Cork Steam Packet Co. steamer *Innis Carra* torpedoed off Irish coast. 30 lives lost.

Sunday, 26 May

I went to the Park of the Queen in the afternoon. After tea, I took Agnes and the family a walk out to Rutherglen. We gave Sam a look-up in the passing, but as he was out, we had to look down again. We meandered through the Overtoun Park and then carred home.[48]

---

[47] A gamp is an umbrella.
[48] Thomas means that he and his family travelled home by tramcar.

Monday, 27 May

Agnes went to the Royal Infirmary to see Jenny Roxburgh. Poor Jenny was operated on last Friday. Miss Fraser also went, so Agnes had a crack with her old boss. After tea, Agnes and Tommy went down to Clydebank. Germans open new offensive this morning in British and French sectors between Rheims and Soissons and Locre and Voormezeele.

Tuesday, 28 May

The great German push continues. They make between Soissons and Rheims. They cross the Aisne.

The final German offensive of the war began in March 1918, when the Central Powers attacked the Allies at St Quentin. The German forces, with additional units newly arrived from the Eastern Front, hoped to break the Anglo-French line, and at first made great advances. The Allies regrouped under the French military strategist General Ferdinand Foch and introduced 300,000 troops who had been held in Britain against the threat of invasion. The Germans continued to advance, and Paris was again under threat. The Allies contained the danger, however, and the Germans were halted.

In July 1918, General Foch commanded a combined force of American and French troops against the beleaguered Germans and, in what became known as the Second Battle of the Marne, drove them back across the River Marne. This was the beginning of the end, as the Allies battled the Germans back along the entire length of the Western Front.

Wednesday, 29 May

Gave Mr Carmichael a little assistance with his new waxcloth, then I took Agnes and Tommy to the Palace. Agnes at infirmary in afternoon seeing Jenny. Germans sweep on.

Thursday, 30 May

Agnes dwelling in the wash-house and back green all day. I rose early this morning, walked out to Ruglen, Mill Street, Croftfoot and back by Mount Florida. Germans capture Soissons but held up at Rheims. They claim 25,000 prisoners.

Saturday, 1 June

Another fine sunny day. We all went out to Ruglen in the afternoon and had a seat in the Overtoun Park. Germans reach the Marne and 50 miles from Paris. Rheims still holding out. Germans claim now 45,000 prisoners and 400 guns. British air raid on Zeebrugge and Bruges docks. Another British hospital bombed in France by the Huns. Some WAACs killed.[49]

Sunday, 2 June

Another day of great heat and sunshine. Went over Cathkin before breakfast and back by Croftfoot and Mount Florida. After dinner we all went out the Carmunnock Road and back by Cathcart. After tea we had a seat in Queen's Park and watched the girls. We are all quite sunburnt. Germans advance still further.

Monday, 3 June

German advance held up. Gotha raid on Paris. On and after today, postage on letters costs 1½d and postcards 1d. We are at war.

---

[49] WAAC was the Women's Auxiliary Army Corps, established in January 1917 as a new voluntary service, in which women served as clerks, telephonists, waitresses, cooks and gas-mask instructors.

Tuesday, 4 June

My birthday. Got up early this morning. Toryglen, Ruglen, 100 Acre Dyke and home by Hangingshaws. Agnes and Tommy down at Clydebank in the afternoon. Very bad news. No hope for Jenny, my good old pal. Agnes very upset. Germans over the Marne. And thrown back again. 150 American war vessels in European waters, manned by 35 to 40,000 men.

Wednesday, 5 June

Hotter than ever today. Sunshine all day. Agnes met me in town and I got a pair of boots at three times the pre-war price. Agnes got a pair of slippers (4/6). After tea we all went to the Palace. American troops doing well in France.

Thursday, 6 June

We all went to [Claude] Maxwell's house in Langside. He home on sick leave after being wounded. He goes back next week. Miss Maxwell (his sister) is a teacher in Tommy's school. U-boats appear off American coast. 14 boats (20,000 tons) sunk.

Saturday, 8 June

Went out in the afternoon to my tailor and got my suit. It will cost just twice what I used to pay.

Sunday, 9 June

Josephine and Pa arrived at 4.30 p.m. Agnes not eating very well just now. A month at the coast would be a good idea. These worrying times are trying to her.

Monday, 10 June

I spent the night repairing the big chair. This is the 'anniversary', for better or worse. German offensive renewed between Montdidier and Noyon.

Thursday, 13 June

Paid the Corporation Gas robbers their bill today for my share of their bad gas. Agnes down at Clydebank at night to see Jenny Roxburgh. Absolutely no hope for Jenny.

Friday, 14 June

Some heavy showers. Agnes got me two ounces of 'thick black'. Germans held up again. Four Rhine towns bombed by British airmen.

Sunday, 16 June

Very dull day. Put on my new suit, new boots and soft hat, so dressed like a gentleman I went to church. Communion on. After dinner we all went out to Sam's house.

Monday, 17 June

With the permission of my dearly beloved I took a walk at evening to wit through Maxwell and Queen's Park. Tommy got a penny today from the headmistress of his school for getting high marks for all his lessons. Good boy!

Tuesday, 18 June

Rose at 5.30 a.m. this morning and went to Queen's Park. Some rain fell. Dull, nasty day. Agnes spent it in the wash-house, so it rained at frequent intervals. Great British naval air raids on Zeebrugge, Ostend, Bruges etc.

Wednesday, 19 June

Agnes is not keeping in the best of health just now. We'll need to see about some holidays. I doctored a few boots with studs etc. Big German attack on Rheims turned into a bad defeat for the Huns.

Thursday, 20 June

When I got home, Agnes went down to Clydebank to see Jenny. I always dread the worst when she comes home. Tommy did some painting during the evening. Agnes got home at 10.30. Poor Jenny has not got long now. She suffers greatly.

Saturday, 22 June

Would have been a nice day if it had not rained so frequently, if it had been warmer, and if the wind had not been so violent. Sat at the fire and made ourselves comfortable.

Sunday, 23 June

Rose at 6 a.m. and had a walk over Cathkin. After dinner we met Sam, Nellie and Wee John and William Kirk at Jamaica Street, took car to Bishopbriggs and walked to Cadder Church. After the service, they came back with us for tea.

Tuesday, 25 June

Fine day, but not warm enough yet. Coal now 5/- per bag, and we need a fire every day yet.

Wednesday, 26 June

Agnes went down to Clydebank after tea time. Jenny slowly sinking, but cheerier tonight.

Thursday, 27 June

900,000 American troops now in France.

Friday, 28 June

Tommy got his summer holidays today. I filled in the new Ration Books at night. Paris raided by German aeroplanes. 11 killed.

Saturday, 29 June

Nice day and more like summer. We all went to the Majestic at night.
Agnes saw an airship today and Tommy saw two aeroplanes. I saw nothing.

Sunday, 30 June

Rose at 6 a.m., took a walk out to Ruglen and back by Carmunnock Road. Got home at 9.30 for my breakfast. We all went to the West End Park, a band performance being on.[50] Tremendous crowd, so we did not wait.

Monday, 1 July

Very dull, depressing sort of day. Great British air raids on Rhine towns.

[50] The West End Park is now known as Kelvingrove Park. The park played host to the 1888 International Exhibition, the 1901 International Exhibition and the 1911 Scottish Exhibition. Like Queen's Park, it was designed by Sir Joseph Paxton.

Tuesday, 2 July

Took Tommy out at night for a walk, 100 Acre Dyke, came back by Mount Florida. Carried some water for Mr Cormack's plot. Another U-boat crime. Hospital ship *Llandovery Castle* torpedoed, 234 lives lost. Disaster in England. Shell factory blown up, 100 lives lost.

Thursday, 4 July

British air raids on Metz and Coblenz. This is the day we fly 'Old Glory'.

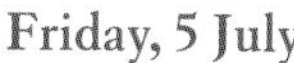

Friday, 5 July

Influenza epidemic spreading all over the country. What they call the 'Spanish Influenza'.[51] Sultan of Turkey dead.

Sunday, 7 July

I went down to Govan and the docks to see all the wonderful boats. Influenza seems everywhere, even among the troops.

Monday, 8 July

In the forenoon, Jean Crozier and Jane McGregor here with the shocking news of May's death. All the Coatbridge girls at Lamlash on holiday and confined to bed with influenza, and Meg very seriously so. Poor May had gone down last Friday, feeling ill, developed pneumonia and died this morning about 3 a.m. It is an awful shock to us. Jean in a state of collapse. Agnes going to Coatbridge, so she went out to Ruglen to see about leaving Tommy there. We both feel very upset at the sad news.

---

[51] The Spanish flu pandemic of 1918-19 was one of the most devastating epidemics in recorded history. Roughly a third of the world's population was infected by the virus, which killed an estimated 50 million people. The disease progressed extremely rapidly and, unusually, was particularly fatal among young adults.

Tuesday, 9 July

Wet, dark, dismal day. Agnes took Tommy out to Nellie this morning and left him there, then went to Coatbridge herself. Don't know when she will be back. Felt very dumped tonight, so I went out to Ruglen to see how Tommy was doing. Sam off his work today with the influenza, evidently. Got home at midnight. The influenza evidently at Greenlodge. Isa has had it.

Wednesday, 10 July

Terrible day of heavy showers. Feel out of sorts altogether today. Took a run out to Greenlodge at night. Josephine and Lily both confined to bed with the influenza. Home at 9.45 p.m. No news yet from Agnes. Looking forward to yet dreading tomorrow.

Thursday, 11 July

Very nice weather today. Left my work at 10 a.m. Went to Coatbridge for the funeral. Was there about 1 p.m. Got Jean McGregor from the station. Poor May laid at rest in Old Monklands Cemetery. After dinner at the hotel, Agnes and I went home. We got home about 6.30 p.m. and then walked out to Ruglen to bring Tommy home. As usual, Sam was playing bowls. We got home about midnight. It has been a sad, sad week. Even as I write this I can hardly believe I'll never see May again.

Friday, 12 July

This is Fair Friday. I got away at 1.15 p.m. May's untimely death is too fresh in my mind to think much of the Fair holiday.

Saturday, 13 July

Fair Saturday, so I have a holiday. Went out before breakfast, Queen's Park etc. Agnes thinks she is taking the 'Spanish Influenza' as her legs feel very wobbly. I took a walk through the shows on the Green, then called up for a little at Greenlodge. Only my niece Lily in. She is getting better of the influenza.

Monday, 15 July

Fair Monday, so I am still on holiday. I was out at 6.30 a.m. for a walk, but the rain came on extra so I went back again. Before dinner I took a run out to Ruglen and had a look-in at the Bowling Green. Spoke to Dan Hamilton, an old school mate. He is just newly discharged from the army after three years in France. I came back by Croftfoot and Cathcart. Great German offensive launched against the French on 55-mile front east and west of Rheims.

Wednesday, 17 July

The plumber here in the morning destroying the woodwork and sorting the plumbing. Kate Roxburgh here at tea time. Battle resumed for Rheims. Great German losses. Americans regain lost ground. Japanese naval disaster. Battleship *Kawachi* blown up, 700 lives lost.

Friday, 19 July

Agnes went out tonight to Ruglen. I cleaned all the kitchen brasses and put Tommy to bed. French and Americans still advance. 16,000 enemy taken.

Saturday, 20 July

Dull depressing day. Agnes got a postcard from Kate Roxburgh. Jenny is much worse. After tea Agnes went down to Clydebank. I took Tommy out a walk to Maxwell Park. Agnes got home 1 p.m. Poor Jenny very ill indeed. The end can't be far off. Good progress being made with Franco-American counter-offensive. 17,000 men and 360 guns captured. Scottish troops capture Méteren, in the Bailleul sector.

Sunday, 21 July

Very wet morning, but turned out a lovely warm day. I took a walk to Paisley and Renfrew in the afternoon. Germans retreat across the Marne. Great French advance. Grand Fleet and seaplanes bomb Zepp nests off the Jutland coast.

Monday, 22 July

Feel my throat a trifle sore. Nellie Hamilton up for a few hours at dinner time. Andrew laid up in hospital at Norwich with neuritis.[52] Influenza scourge: 62 deaths last week in Glasgow. 14 from influenza and 48 from pneumonia following influenza.

[52] Neuritis is the general inflammation of the peripheral nervous system.

[53] La Musique du Premier Zouave, the leading Zouave band of the French Army, visited London on 12 July 1918. The 80 Zouaves, described as being fresh from the battle front, may also have played in other cities. The Zouaves were French light infantrymen, recruited from the Algerian Kabyle tribe of Zouaoua.

Tuesday, 23 July

Dull, depressing wet day. Agnes went down to Clydebank at night to see Jenny. Yankee soldiers beginning to appear in the streets today. Saw the famous Zouave Band in the square today.[53]

Wednesday, 24 July

Swallowing quinine pellets all day to ease my throat.[54] White Star liner Justicia torpedoed. 13 lives lost. 400 passengers landed on Irish coast.

Thursday, 25 July

My throat seems easier now. Big munition strike in England.[55] American troops arriving in France 300,000 per month.

Friday, 26 July

We went to Queen's Park at night and heard the famous Zouave Band. Enormous crowd. Some of the Zouaves came round with collecting boxes for the French Red Cross. Tommy put in a donation and the Zouave patted his cheek. Great delight of Tommy. Eggs 5/- per dozen now. At beginning of war, tonnage of the British navy was 2,500,000. It is now 8,000,000.

Saturday, 27 July

Very nice day. In the afternoon I took a stroll to Langside Library. After tea we all went to Maxwell Park and home by Queen's Park. I got a clay pipe but no tobacco. Fresh progress by Allies on the Marne. 1,800 more prisoners. Cabinet's ultimatum to the strikers: 'Work or fight!'[56]

[54] Quinine was a popular remedy for sore throats, mouth ulcers, influenza and headaches.
[55] After the munitions workers of Coventry and Birmingham went on strike, the National Engineering and Allied Trades' Council decided to extend the strike if there was no settlement before 30 July.
[56] On 26 July, the government warned the striking workers that after 29 July, they must either return to work or go into military service.

Monday, 29 July

We all visited our poor relations at Greenlodge Terrace. Duncan not back yet from his holidays in Ireland. There is a notice from the military waiting for him, calling him up 31 July. Hard lines. Munition strike ended. Strikers prefer to make £10 to £20 a week to going to the trenches, blast them.

Tuesday, 30 July

Deaths from influenza [in Glasgow] last week were 25, pneumonia 28, total 53. Capture of Sergy by Americans. Scottish successes at Soissons.

Thursday, 1 August

Agnes went down to Clydebank at night. Lily telephoned me today that Duncan left last night for London. He is in the Army Service Corps and has to learn motor driving. Got half an ounce of 'thick black' today. German defeat at Rheims. Signs of further retreat. Kaiser's war boast: 'Not afraid of America's Army'.

Friday, 2 August

Thought I had not locked the office safe so Tommy and I walked in at night. It was a false alarm. I showed Tommy a 'Yankee' soldier or 'doughboy'.[57] Marne advance. New push last night. Ridge captured. One and a half million American troops in Europe now. Britain has loaned the Allies £1,402,000,000.

Saturday, 3 August

After dinner we had a seat in Queen's Park. An aeroplane flew about. Great Allied victory: Soissons regained. Advance on 25-mile front for three miles.

[57] A 'doughboy' was slang for an American infantryman.

Sunday, 4 August

After tea, we all went up to the Cormacks. Mr Cormack's brother had no 'thick black' so I gave him a couple of inches. This is the Great War anniversary.

Monday, 5 August

Tommy got his weekly new pair of shoes. Paris shelled again by the long-range gun.[58] Since the beginning of the war, Great Britain has raised for the army 6,250,000 men, India 1,250,000 and the Colonies 1,000,000. 1,500,000 men are in the British navy over and above this.

Wednesday, 7 August

Agnes and Tommy came into town with me at dinner time as they were going to Clydebank. Jenny not so well. Tommy got half-a-crown from Jenny for his birthday (which is on Friday). Covered Tommy's new shoes with studs to see if they would last a week or two.

Thursday, 8 August

Tommy in bed all day with a bad cold. We had all to go out to Sam's tonight, so Agnes went herself. I stayed at home with Tommy, wrote up my diary, broke sticks and laid aside some lumps of coal for the lean time to come. Great new offensive: Haig leads two armies, British Fourth Army and French First Army. Advance on wide front in Amiens region. Hundreds of tanks in action.

[58] The Paris Gun, also known as the 'Kaiser Wilhelm Geschütz' (Emperor William Gun), was the largest piece of artillery used during the war. It was an oversized railway gun made by Krupp. The gun could propel a 210lb shell 81 miles.

Friday, 9 August

This is Tommy's birthday. The cherub is now seven years old. Long may his lum reek.[59] We had a dumpling to celebrate.

Saturday, 10 August

We bought Tommy a boat to sail at Rothesay for his birthday. Allies rapid advance. 24,000 prisoners taken. Montdidier taken.

Sunday, 11 August

We went down to Clydebank [in the] afternoon via Renfrew Ferry. Poor Jenny very far gone and low-spirited. I'm afraid the end is drawing near. She bade me 'Good-bye'. The Allied advance continues. Thousands of prisoners and hundreds of guns captured.

Wednesday, 14 August

Working late at night. When I got home we had a wild time of packing bags. It was great. Victory at Amiens now complete. 30,344 prisoners in a week.

Thursday, 15 August

Saw my well-beloved and Tommy away by 10.40 a.m. train to Rothesay via Wemyss Bay. Sam also there seeing Nellie and John off. Felt sort of unsettled at night. Went up to Mr Cormack's plot and helped with pea-pods. Then went up and had tea with him and his better half. Wish it was Saturday.

Friday, 16 August

Got a letter from Agnes, which pleased me greatly, showing she had arrived safely. She tells me to bring down a pot of jam. I go to the grocer. No jam. Here's luck.

---

[59] A Scottish blessing: long may his chimney smoke.

1918

Saturday, 17 August

This is the day I get my holidays, so the weather is very dull. Met Sam at Central Station about 6 p.m. We got 6.15 p.m. train to Wemyss Bay and arrived at Rothesay 9 p.m. per the good ship Iona.[60] *Rained in buckets all the time.*

Sunday, 18 August

Rained practically all day. We walked to Port Bannatyne before dinner. After dinner we went to Ascog and back by the country. After tea Agnes, Nellie and Isa out for a little. Sam, Jenny and I sat in. Looks as if I would get sunburnt.

Monday, 19 August

Nice forenoon. Sam and I saw Isa off by early boat before breakfast. After breakfast Sam and I walked to Craigmore. We went to the Empire at night.[61] British advance south of Ypres. 900,000 British have been killed in the war so far.

Tuesday, 20 August

Poured all day. Sam and I fished out in the bay for a couple of hours. We got five wee fish. After dinner we all went to Port Bannatyne, took out a boat for an hour and a half, and fished. NBG. After tea we all adjourned to the Palace to see the pictures.[62]

[60] The passenger steamer *Iona*, operated by David MacBrayne, was built on the Clyde in 1864 by J. & G. Thomson.

[61] The Empire was a theatre in Rothesay.

[62] The Palace cinema stood near the pier in the centre of Rothesay. From 1913, it was owned by James Gillespie Snr, who made and showed films of local events, such as Highland games.

Wednesday, 21 August

Dull sort of day, but dry. Before breakfast Sam and I walked to Ascog and back. After breakfast we all went to Ettrick Bay and had a picnic. Big crowd going back in the car. We had to wait in a queue. When we got home and had a decent tea we took a walk Craigmore way. New French advance between Oise and Aisne. 10,000 prisoners. British advance in wide front on Ancre.

Thursday, 22 August

Dull day. Very stormy and some rain. Before breakfast Sam and I climbed the Barone Hill. After breakfast Sam and I went up to the bowling green for a little. After dinner we all went to Loch Fad. Went out in a small boat. We landed and gathered brambles. At night Sam and I went to a very third-rate music hall and listened to some attempts at singing etc. British attack continues.

Friday, 23 August

Nice warm sunny day so we thought we would take a sail. We spent the day at Millport and made our tea on the rocks. We got back about 7 p.m.

Saturday, 24 August

Dull weather and heavy showers. Sam and I out fishing before breakfast. Coal men very independent here, so I had to go out myself and wheel a hundredweight of the precious stuff. The situation saved. I then took Tommy out for a little in a small boat. After dinner I walked to Ascog and back by the Loch. After tea we all went out in a boat and examined the submarine, mine-layers and other devilish instruments.[63] 14,000 prisoners taken by British in 3 days.

[63] The deep waters of the Clyde estuary were used for ship and submarine tests and exercises.

13th after Trinity. Sunday **25**
(237-128)

Warm day Terrific showers at intervals.

Before breakfast Sam & I went as far as the place where females dance up & down in the water

LADIES BATHING STATION.

NO LOITERING

In fore noon Sam, Ina, Jenny & I out for a walk after dinner we all went out by Ascog. We saw the submarine making for Rothesay We came back by Skippers Wood and got caught in a most unholy Cloud burst.

British nearing Bapaume.

AUGUST, 1918.

Monday **26**

(238-127)

Fine day but heavy rain after dinner. Sam & I saw Ina & Jenny off by early boat. Then we took a walk to Craigmore and watched some of the female sex splash about. In the forenoon Sam & I fished for a brace of hour. After dinner we all took motor to Mount Stuart & walked back to Ascog and motored home. We spent the evening at the "Palace"

British strike new blow in the "Scarpe" sector. 20000 prisoners in 4 days.

Tuesday, 27 August

Rain poured solid hard all day long. Sam and I played casino all forenoon and after dinner we went out in a boat fishing for two hours. We got soaked through, and had to change our garments. At 7 p.m. we saw Sam off in the boat (his holidays are up) then we returned to the 'De Luxe'.[64] British advance goes on. Great struggle on Somme. High Wood won. Anzacs reach Bapaume.

Wednesday, 28 August

Great rejoicings. Nice sunny day, but very breezy. In the forenoon I walked to Kerrycroy. Got lost in Knocknicol Wood and then struck into the Moor Road and got home by Loch Ascog. After dinner we all had a seat near Ascog. After tea we went up Canada Hill and home by Ascog.[65] New British gains on Somme and Scarpe fronts.

Thursday, 29 August

Dull, windy, sunny, showery, and pouring wet night. Am not well today. Sort of sick and can eat nothing. Consternation. Took a small walk before breakfast then in forenoon Tommy and I went through the Skipper Wood and had a seat at Craigmore. After dinner we all took car to Port Bannatyne and had a seat about a mile past it.[66] I was not well enough to enjoy it. At night I sat in. Agnes and Nellie went out for a walk and got a soaking. British push eastwards. The Hindenburg Line in peril.

---

[64] Thomas' and his family's accommodation was unlikely to have been in the Hotel de Luxe category.

[65] Canada Hill, according to local legend, got its name because locals used to gather there to watch emigrant ships travelling from the Clyde to North America.

[66] The Rothesay Tramways Company ran electric trams from Rothesay to Port Bannatyne and on to Ettrick Bay.

Friday, 30 August

Fine forenoon. Blustery afternoon and heavy showers. I am feeling all right again and eating as a Christian man ought to. Went out by Ascog in the forenoon. In the afternoon we all went to Barone Hill but did not get up as heavy rain came on. We went to the Palace at night. Fresh British advance. Bullecourt and Combles won. French enter Noyon. Police strike in London.

Saturday, 31 August

Very windy and some heavy showers in the forenoon. After breakfast I took Tommy and John out in a boat. Could hardly row back it was so wild. After dinner I took a walk to Canada Hill and back by Craigmore. On my way back saw Agnes and Nellie waiting on Ina, then we all went up for tea. I loitered on the Esplanade towards evening. Very cold at night. Ina took Tommy to the 'pictures'.

Entertainment

Thomas was writing before the days of radio, which arrived in Scotland in the early 1920s, and all the entertainment in the Livingstone house had to be supplied by its inhabitants. Thomas and his family are keen singers, and Thomas himself plays the piano. His brother Sam leads a choir in Rutherglen, and Thomas often sits in public parks and listens to bands playing there. The family would also have heard the popular singers of the day in the music halls, and the silent films shown in the city's early cinemas would at times have been accompanied by music. Many phrases used in the diary derive from hymns and popular songs or poems. In March 1916 Thomas writes, 'To "keep the Home Fires burning" I broke some wood tonight', quoting 'Keep The Home Fires Burning', a hugely popular wartime song written by Ivor Novello and Lena Ford in 1914. In September 1918, he recorded 'a terrific downpour of rain from early morn till dewy night'. The last six words are from 'The Nymph's Song to Hylas' by William Morris:

I know a little garden-close
Set thick with lily and red rose,
Where I would wander if I might
From dewy dawn to dewy night,
And have one with me wandering.

The theatres in Thomas' day mainly offered variety or music hall programmes, mixing comedians, singers, jugglers, plate-spinners, stage magicians, escapologists, dancers and other performers in a show held together by a master of ceremonies. Among the singers popular in Scotland at the time were Harry Lauder, whose songs became Scottish staples for half a century or more, and Will Fyffe, who wrote the city's national anthem, 'I Belong to Glasgow'. The cinemas, or 'picture theatres' as they were called, showed short, silent, black and white films, often made by stars of the stage, including Charlie Chaplin, who is mentioned twice in the diaries.

"The One and Only"
Charlie Chaplin
His Signature
In his First Million Dollar Picture
"A DOG'S LIFE"
A "First National" Attraction

The reading room at the Anderston library in Macintyre Street.

The range of theatrical entertainments still being offered at the height of the war can be seen from the advertisement columns of the Glasgow Herald on Wednesday 20 June 1917. Under the heading 'popular entertainments', there are four listings for the Glasgow Coliseum, the Alhambra, the Pavilion and the Empire. The Coliseum, twice nightly at 6.55 p.m. and 9 p.m., presented 'the latest London Hippodrome revue', Zig-Zag, with an 'unprecedented star cast', a 'superb beauty chorus of over 60' and an 'augmented orchestra'. The revue was described as 'a gorgeous spectacle and musical feast for eye and ear'. The Alhambra, 'the resort of the elite' had two performances of a musical called Keep to the Right, while the Pavilion - billing itself as 'Scotland's premier vaudeville theatre' - had a musical comedy called Blind Man's Bluff. The Empire was presenting Joy-Land, which featured 60 'Joy-Belles', presumably female dancers.

Thomas is a keen visitor to the municipal libraries of Glasgow, and mentions the Langside, Gorbals, Pollokshields and other branches as well as the flagship Stirling's Library in Miller Street, a few streets away from his place of work. He is coy about what books he borrows, referring to 'religious literature' and 'improving literature', but his ironic sense of humour is surely disguising a taste for a much wider selection of subjects, not all of which would please readers of only religious or improving works. Glasgow's municipal library system began with an enabling parliamentary act in 1899, which empowered the Glasgow Corporation to borrow £100,000 and levy one penny on the rates to set up a free lending library service.[67] The first city library opened in the working-class Gorbals district in 1901, and by 1907 there were 12 branch libraries. Andrew Carnegie, the Scots-born American industrialist and philanthropist, gave more than £100,000 to the city to support the library service. Stirling's Library became part of the municipal system in 1912, after being set up in 1791 under the terms of the will of Walter Stirling, a Glasgow merchant,

[67] Before council tax, people paid 'rates' to a local authority. These were based on the 'rateable' value of a person's house, which was calculated by the district assessor as the annual rent that the property could be let for in the open market on a particular date. The council set rates as a certain number of pence for each pound of value, so if one's house was assessed as having a rateable value of £20, and the local rate was set at 5/- to the pound, one would pay £5 a year to the council in return for local services. After the council added a penny to the rate, in this instance one would have paid an extra 20d (1/8d).

The Juvenile Reading Room at Govanhill Library.

but never really thriving as a charitable concern. By 1914 the city had 21 public libraries.

Thomas also visits the Art Galleries at Kelvingrove, another educational and entertaining facility provided by the Glasgow Corporation. There, he would have seen portraits of the royal family from the seventeenth century to his own day; a number of 'Tassie medallions', three-dimensional cameo portraits cast in a glass paste; oil paintings by many of the Old Masters of Europe and the leading painters of Scotland and England. Many of the paintings were bequeathed to Glasgow by the great and good of the city, the families who had made money from shipbuilding, locomotive construction, hewing coal and iron and smelting steel. Kelvingrove, fat upon the profits of its benefactors, was not a minority interest: more than two million people visited the galleries in 1921.

Glasgow was once complimented as being 'a very Tokyo for tea rooms', in part reflecting the vigorous and determined temperance movement that swept the city in Victorian and Edwardian times. Tea rooms also provided a safe and respectable space for women to meet in the city centre. The grande dame of tea rooms in Glasgow was Catherine Cranston, sometimes called Katie Cranston but more usually Miss Cranston. Thomas and Agnes visited one of her tea rooms, probably the branch in Sauchiehall Street, before they were married. Miss Cranston employed George Walton and Charles Rennie Mackintosh, two of the most prominent architects and designers of the period, to design her tearooms both outside and in, right down to the last teaspoon. A menu board from 1911, hand painted by Mackintosh, lists 'This day's specialities': Creamed sole and tomato, 10d; Fried filleted flounder and caper sauce, 9d; Two potted herring with salad, 6d; Wiltshire bacon and poached egg, 9d; Cold roast chicken and bacon, 1/-.

For many people in Glasgow, then as now, football was more than just entertainment, it was a way of life, almost a religion. Thomas, who mentions going to Hampden Park stadium only once, does not seem to have been much of a football fan. But the sport, while not as commercialised and taking up far less media space than it does now, played a prominent part in Glasgow life. In the early twentieth century, the Glasgow teams - Queen's Park, Clyde, Third Lanark, Partick Thistle, Rangers and Celtic - had recently invested large sums of money in improving and enlarging their grounds, and Hampden, home of Queen's Park, was also the national stadium. The stadium, which was built in 1903, had a capacity of 125,000 in Thomas' day. It was the largest stadium in the world until 1950, and still holds the record for the largest crowd for a football match in Europe, set in 1937 when 149,415 people watched Scotland play England in the British Home Championship. Now all-seated, its capacity is a paltry 52,000.

Footballers were not excused military duties, of course, and many players were quick to enlist. Every member of Heart of Midlothian football club volunteered on 26 November 1914. Home International matches were suspended for the duration of the war, the Scottish Cup was shelved and, as fuel supplies became scarce, Scottish League matches were confined to clubs in the central belt of the country.

Hampden Park, Glasgow during an international match between Scotland and England in 1910.

Sunday, 1 September

Wet morning but turned out very nice day, but sort of stormy. Took a walk to Kerrycroy in forenoon and back by the road that winds by Loch Ascog. In the afternoon we all climbed the Barone Hill and then did the Loch Fad Walk. We got home about 8 p.m. Did some packing up. We go home tomorrow.

Monday, 2 September

Nice day. At an unearthly hour Ina and I boarded the old tub *Benmore*.[68] She left at 6.50 a.m. Was in my work about 9.30 a.m. Went home at dinner time and opened up the house and sorted out the correspondence. No calling-up notice! Agnes and Tommy got home after 2 p.m. Hindenburg Line broken for two miles. Canadian success at Arras-Cambrai Road.

Tuesday, 3 September

Getting settled down now. Cleaned all the windows and washed the Rothesay dirt off my feet. Great British victory. Hindenburg Line broken for about six miles. Enemy retreat on whole front.

Wednesday, 4 September

Tommy resumed his scholastic duties today. Agnes went down at night to see Jenny. Poor Jenny far gone. British and French forging ahead. British nearing Lille and Cambrai. Germans completely defeated.

[68] The passenger steamer *Benmore* was operated by John Williamson. It was built by T. Seath of Rutherglen in 1876.

Saturday, 7 September

I went to the Stirling's Library in afternoon. After tea we took a 'hurl' in the car to Cathcart and back. Agnes not well at all. I am very disappointed at the result of our holidays. The rain, long walks and bag lifting has done Agnes no good.

Sunday, 8 September

Agnes worse today. Seems to be her old trouble back again. French victory in the Somme. Five mile advance. St Quentin Canal crossed. British still pushing back the Germans. British captured 19,000 Germans last week.

Monday, 9 September

Coal position going to be very serious this winter. Wonder what we will keep in the bunker?

Wednesday, 11 September

Agnes not well this morning. Looks like the influenza. She improved later on in the day, in fact, she made plum jam tonight. The plums came from Kilcreggan.[69] We got in another bag of coal today. Hoarding it in a mild sort of way. British lines pushed forward at Gouzancourt Ridge. French two miles from La Fère. Great Allied success in Siberia.

[69] Kilcreggan is a village on the north side of the Clyde estuary.

Thursday, 12 September
Went down to Ibrox tonight, with the case we had on loan from them. Anarchy in Russia. Fire and murder in Petrograd. Ex-Czar's family reported murdered. Great American attack launched at Verdun today. Germans falling back.

Czar Nicholas II under arrest in Siberia, 1917.

Sunday, 15 September
Very dull, cold and windy. In afternoon it developed into a wild wet day. We did not go out. Made ourselves comfortable and read good books etc. British advance at St Basle. New French advance south of St Quentin.

Tuesday, 17 September
Agnes ironed all my soft collars of divers colours. Offensive started in the Balkans by French, Serbs and Greeks in 12-mile front for a depth of five miles. 4,000 Bulgars captured.

Wednesday, 18 September

We had a woman to do the wash-house trick today. Great applause from Agnes. Govanhill coal men on strike. New British attack towards St Quentin.

Thursday, 19 September

Agnes went down to Clydebank at night. Owing to the coal shortage, we speculated today in some peat. I sawed the blocks in two at night to fit the grate. Terrific fighting, further big gains by British in new advance. 8,000 prisoners. Bulgarian rout. Allies gain 12 miles.

Saturday, 21 September

Tommy completely all out. No appetite, sick, headache, tired, sneezing, restless. Kept him in bed all day. I went for doctor about 9.30 but it was too late. Tommy feverish and delirious during the night, so we took turn about sitting up. I've got a dose of the cold myself. Great British victory in Palestine. 3,000 Turks captured.

Sunday, 22 September
Tommy not any better. He can't eat yet. As the doctor did not come, I went out to his house in Cathcart at tea time. He thinks Tommy has influenza and will come tomorrow. He gave me a line for three powders, which I duly got in a chemist. A worrying sort of weekend. Allies advancing on all fronts.

Monday, 23 September
Doctor Gardiner up today. Tommy has got the influenza. To be kept in bed. Milk diet etc. His temperature is high. The great battle for Cambrai and St Quentin goes on. Serbs advance 40 miles. Great victory in Palestine. Entire Turkish army there captured. British cavalry reach Nazareth.

Tuesday, 24 September
Tommy seems more like himself today, but still in bed. The Bulgarian rout continues. Serbians have advanced over 40 miles. Turkish rout continues in Palestine. Haifa and Acre entered.

Wednesday, 25 September
Doctor up. Tommy much improved and temperature normal. Don't feel well myself tonight. I'm up the blinking pole. Sat at the fire and enjoyed myself. Think Tommy has 'smitted'me.[70]

[70] Thomas is playing with words here: 'smitted' is an invented form of 'smite', and the sense is that Tommy has smitten him with the cold germs.

Thursday, 26 September

Stayed in bed all day. I can't be feeling well. Serbs still advancing. British troops invade Bulgaria. Palestine lost to the Turks. 45,000 captured to date.

Friday, 27 September

Got tired lying in bed so went to my work today. Feeling not so bad but my nose ran awful at night. Tommy improving. Ella Gordon here at night. Fresh British advance on a wide front near Cambrai. Franco-American attack on 40-mile front in Champagne. 16,000 prisoners. Serbs have advanced miles altogether and captured 10,000 prisoners. British and French troops storm heights in south Bulgaria.

Saturday, 28 September

Terrific day of rain. Tommy up for a little. I am not well.
Above written by Agnes.[71] I will now take up the pen. My nose running awful all day. Second British Army and Belgian army begin attack this morning in Flanders. 10,000 prisoners taken by British on Cambrai front, and 18,000 by Americans and French in Champagne. Bulgaria sues for an armistice.

[71] Agnes has captured in a few words three of Thomas' diary-writing obsessions: the weather, his family and the illnesses they endured.

Sunday, 29 September

Nice sort of day. I'm either getting better or just taking the influenza so stayed in bed all day. Took a dose of castor oil. Josephine and Pa here at evening. Put all the clocks back one hour tonight. 'Summer time' ended. British two miles from Cambrai and have now taken 12,000 prisoners.

Monday, 30 September

Nice day, and this is the autumn holiday. Not feeling any better, so stayed in bed till 4 p.m. Played Tommy and Agnes an exciting game of Ludo. Agnes in the wash-house doing her 'white things'. Ten years ago on this holiday, Agnes and I went to Kilmun. Bulgaria out of the war. Unconditional surrender to Allies' terms. A fatal blow to Germany. British on the outskirts of Cambrai.

Tuesday, 1 October

Went to my work. Feeling not bad now. Agnes in wash-house all day. Nellie Hamilton (Andrew's wife) and her wee boy here at tea time. Hostilities cease today with Bulgaria. Germans fighting desperately to retain Cambrai.

Working week

Thomas worked for Paterson, Baxter and Company, linen and sailcloth manufacturers, of 170 Ingram Street, in central Glasgow. They had other offices in Leeds, London, Cape Town, Oslo and Copenhagen. The firm, which at the time of the diaries was owned by Alexander Baxter, traded from 1880 to 1964. Thomas' office sat at the heart of what is now called the Merchant City, a revitalised and redeveloped area filled with up-market shops, restaurants, hairdressers, bars and flats. In Thomas' time it was far less grand. William Power, writing in 1922, referred to the area as the 'werrus' or warehouse region, dominated by wholesalers of cloth and clothing, household goods and fruits and vegetables.[72]

In the 1910s, the majority of people in Glasgow were employed in physical labour, whether riveting together the hulls of great ships, packing shells for the front or working the machines that made textiles, tools, tramcars or tobacco. Thomas was among the elite of the working class: as a clerk he was paid monthly rather than weekly, his work did not involve physical exertion, and he was unlikely to be injured in the course of his employment. He had leisure time to visit the library, walk in the country, or enjoy a family sing-song. He could afford a piano, and had money for trips to the theatre and cinema, and holidays in Rothesay on the Isle of Bute in the Clyde estuary, or in the north of Ireland.

As a mercantile clerk, Thomas was a junior member of the business community in the city, not the industrial working class. The centrepiece of the Glasgow business community at the time of Thomas' diaries was the Royal Exchange, sitting in the centre of Royal Exchange Square.

One of the buildings in Royal Exchange Square, Glasgow's centre of commerce.

[72] William Power, 'Glasgow To-Day', *The Book of Glasgow* (Glasgow: Alex Macdougall, 1922), p. 81.

This building, which faces along Ingram Street, would have been familiar to Thomas from the outside. If he had penetrated its impressive portals, what would he have found? G. B. Primrose described the business of the Royal Exchange as he knew it in 1922:

> If you are wishing to build an ocean liner, go into the Royal Exchange and you will meet members of several firms willing to make the steel plates for it. If you are wanting timber for its decks or sheets for its ventilators, you will almost instantly knock up against the people who can provide these needs. Perhaps you have a cargo of coal to send to south America. In the Royal Exchange you will find many men eager to ship it for you. Or perhaps you yourself are a shipowner, and are looking for a cargo. There is no place you are more likely to pick it up than on the floor of the Royal Exchange.[73]

The other nexuses of power in the city were the Glasgow Stock Exchange in St George's Place, where shares were bought and sold, and the Corn Exchange in Hope Street and its near neighbour the Central Hotel, where grain trading and other agricultural business were conducted.

Thomas may not have moved in quite these circles, but he did wear a suit and a bowler hat, which marked him out as someone who did not make his living by the sweat of his brow. The workers wore flat caps, as Thomas did in his leisure time, but for work he donned the bowler that indicated his status among the business and administrative classes.

Thomas' working week, like that of most people who worked in offices or banks, ran from 8 a.m. to 6 p.m. from Monday to Friday, with a 'dinner hour' in the middle of the day, and from 8 a.m. to 1 p.m. on Saturdays. Christmas Day, unless it fell on a Sunday, was just another working day. Banks, insurance companies and some offices that did business with England would be closed, but most offices, markets, factories and shops would be open as usual. New Year's Eve, better known in Scotland as Hogmanay, marked the beginning of a two-day holiday during which people held family reunions, gave presents and visited friends and neighbours.

Agnes' working week was perhaps less structured than her husband's, though no less busy. His office job was not physically strenuous and his contribution to the household tasks was generally limited to joinery, painting, washing the windows, polishing brass pans and doorknobs and taking part in spring cleaning. Agnes' week, however, involved at least one full day of heavy manual labour in the unpleasant surroundings of the communal wash-house. With no electrical appliances to make life easier, nor rubber gloves to protect her hands, this would have involved soaking the household's clothing, bedding, towels, curtains, wash-cloths and other textiles in a wash-tub with hot water and soap, scrubbing them by hand on a washboard, then rinsing them and putting them through a mangle before hanging them to dry, either on the washing lines in the back green or on the kitchen pulley. This was heavy, backbreaking work, and Agnes often followed it up with an evening ironing, pressing hot and heavy tools that had been heated on the

[73] G.B. Primrose, 'Business Life in Glasgow', *The Book of Glasgow* (Glasgow: Alex Macdougall), 1922, p. 210.

range across damp clothing or bedding until they were smooth and dry.

Whatever illnesses Agnes was otherwise susceptible to, this weekly ordeal would surely have exhausted and weakened her. And while Thomas was willing to help with some of the routine household chores, Agnes did the bulk of the domestic work. In addition to looking after the family's washing and ironing, she would have shopped every day for perishable foods and cooked all meals from scratch, as well as making her own home bread and jam. She had a sewing machine to help repair clothes, but even so the weight and bulkiness of many of the family's clothes would have made this heavy work. And once a week it was her turn to wash the communal stairs leading to the family home, using a stiff brush, harsh soap and hot water.

Thomas was also on hand to help with the spring and autumn cleaning, when he and Agnes would carry their carpets and mattresses outside to beat the dust out of them, and both of them were involved in re-painting their house when the need arose. With all other domestic tasks, however, when Agnes was too ill to work her female relatives stepped in to the breach. Driving trams and packing shells may increasingly have been women's work, but so was washing, cleaning and cooking.

Wednesday, 2 October

Rain fell gently all day long. Agnes in dire distress all day long with neuralgia. St Quentin taken by the French. Terrific battle for Cambrai. Damascus occupied by British.

Friday, 4 October

After tea time Agnes had a lie down, the pain in her face and head so severe. All out, hors de combat, dead to the world, up the pole, non compos mentis.[74] I put Tommy to bed and sewed a button on my nether garments. British and Italian warships raid Durazzo, Austrian naval base, and destroy fortifications etc. Italian offensive in Albania. Haig captures 4,000 Germans at St Quentin.

Saturday, 5 October

Agnes' head a little easier. Agnes went into Bow's at night and came home with a waxcloth affair for the hearth and a candlestick. We are going to give up the gas. King Ferdinand abdicates the Bulgarian throne. Germans show signs of retreat from Belgian coast. The German army is smashing up.

Sunday, 6 October

Terrific rain all day and wind blowing a thousand miles an hour We did not go out. About 7 p.m. Kate Roxburgh came up to see how we all were. She gave Tommy a bunch of grapes from Jenny. Poor Jenny is suffering constant pain now. More victories. Germans again retreating on British, American and French fronts. British about four miles from Lille.

[74] All these synonymous terms indicate the same thing: that Agnes is utterly exhausted and unable to take part in daily life.

Monday, 7 October

Wrote to Duncan tonight and we made up a parcel of food for him, as they evidently don't feed him in the army. Put some canvas up side of scullery window to lessen the wind coming in. Germany sues America for an armistice to discuss peace.

Tuesday, 8 October

Went myself at night to Greenlodge and had a musical evening. Got home at 1.15 a.m. Agnes in desperation with neuralgia. Got very little sleep. Great British offensive on 20-mile front launched today between Cambrai and St Quentin.

Wednesday, 9 October

The Spanish Influenza getting serious in Glasgow. Agnes got some neuralgia powders today which eased the pain somewhat. Fall of Cambrai. British enter today. Enemy still retiring. President Wilson replies to Germany: 'Must quit invaded territory.'

Thursday, 10 October

Another vile day of rain. Agnes and Tommy in town in the afternoon. At night Agnes went down to Clydebank to see Jenny. British making headway in Cambrai Battle. Yesterday's victory: 12,000 prisoners. 200 guns. In seven weeks' fighting, British have taken 110,000 prisoners and 1,200 guns. German army faced with disaster.

Friday, 11 October

Tommy got out to play today. I went to Langside Library at night. British capture Le Cateau. Argonne Forest won by American troops. French make progress on Chemin des Danes. Big Japanese liner *Hirano Maru* torpedoed off Irish coast, 201 lives lost. Irish mail steamer *Leinster* torpedoed off Irish coast, 600 lives lost. American steamer *Ticonderoga* torpedoed, 10 officers and 200 enlisted men lost.

Saturday, 12 October

We are to be allowed only one hundredweight of coal per week. My oh my. British past Le Cateau, now making for Douai. Great German retreat now started from Belgian coast to Verdun.

Sunday, 13 October

Took a walk into town in afternoon to see if there was any excitement over the 'peace' proposals. I saw no signs. In the evening we did a little singing. I thought I heard the neighbours going for the police or the fire brigade, so we gave it over. Germany says it agrees to Wilson's peace terms.

Tuesday, 15 October

Dull day. Some rain at times. Agnes in the wash-house. Put some patches of waxcloth in scullery at night. 310 deaths in Glasgow last week from influenza. 10,000 prisoners taken in great battle in Flanders. American troops advancing north of Verdun. Socialists in Germany demanding Kaiser's abdication. Wilson replies to Germany's peace proposals: 'Armistice on battle field.'

Wednesday, 16 October

Very nice day. Played Tommy at quoits tonight. Agnes ironed and otherwise enjoyed herself. In Flanders offensive we have captured 12,000 prisoners in last couple of days. Menin taken and now on road to Courtrai. Durazzo (Albania) captured by Italians.

Thursday, 17 October

The good weather continues. Father here at tea time. Says he came here to get warm as they have no coal in Greenlodge. Agnes went down to Clydebank to see Jenny. Lille taken. A British triumph. Heavy blow to Germany. Belgians capture Turnhout and are making for Bruges. New attack launched today by British on Bohain-le-Cateau front. Wild scenes in Berlin. Looks like revolution.

Friday, 18 October

Dirty wet day. Got a note from our Hun-factor increasing our rent to £4 per quarter. We take Ostend, Tourcoing and Roubaix. Belgian cavalry near Bruges. French cavalry near Thielt. The Germans would like to 'negotiate'.

Saturday, 19 October

Dirty wet day. Tommy needs a new pair of gloves, so Agnes took him into town at night and got him a pair. Allies sweeping on. Bruges cleared of the enemy. Entire Belgian coast abandoned by Germans. Belgians reoccupy Zeebrugge. British capture Thielt.

Sunday, 20 October

Dull, dry day. Agnes and I both at church in forenoon (communion). Tommy stayed at home all by his little self. In the afternoon we took a walk through Queen's Park, Shawlands and home by Cathcart. Having left some music at Greenlodge we all went there at night and had to walk home. America answers Austria's peace appeal: 'No negotiations or armistice.'

Monday, 21 October

Agnes and Tommy out at Coatbridge in the afternoon. I went to the Cross Station and met them there at 9.50 p.m. and escorted them home. Big British victory, River Selle. Heavy fighting. French break through Hunding Line. British army fighting a battle on 40-mile front. German reply received. Negotiations wanted etc. etc. Steamer *Dundalk* torpedoed between Liverpool and Ireland. 16 lives lost.

Tuesday, 22 October

Given up the 'clay' so I bought a new species of pipe yesterday. British closing in on Tournai and Valenciennes. French and Belgian forces launch attack in direction of Ghent. In the eastern theatre of war, Allied forces reach the Danube. British airmen bombing Germany. Good-oh.

1918

Wednesday, 23 October

My niece Lily here at tea time with her boy, Private John Martin ASC (home on leave from France). We had a great night. They left after 11 p.m. Tommy started school again. Big British attack on Cateau-Solesmes front launched this morning. Franco-Serbian forces take about 3,000 prisoners. In the last three months, Germany has lost 5,000 guns.

Scottish soldiers home from France.

Thursday, 24 October

Agnes went down to Clydebank after tea time. Influenza very bad in Glasgow just now. Hard fighting Oise to the Scheldt. Germans well hammered. Mons next. Wilson's reply to Germany. Armistice conditions: no negotiations with Germany's present rulers. Demand for surrender.

Friday, 25 October

Father here about 8 p.m. I saw him home and had to walk back. Tommy got a bad cold once more.

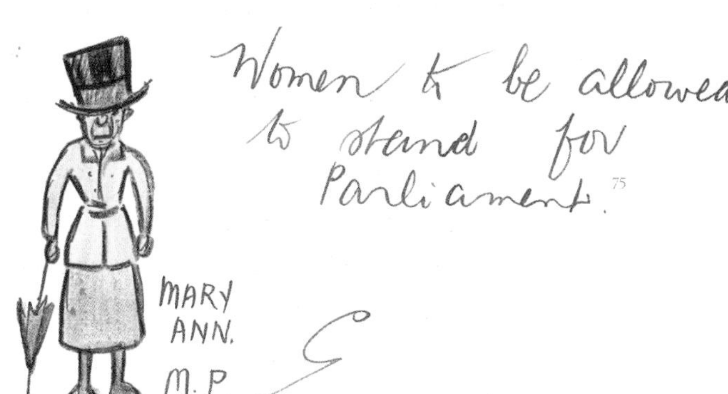

Women to be allowed to stand for Parliament.[75]
MARY ANN. M.P.

[75] On 21 November 1918, the Parliamentary Qualification of Women Act received Royal Assent. This allowed women over the age of 30 to stand for the Westminster parliament.

Sunday, 27 October

Nice sunny day. In the afternoon I took a walk by Pollokshields, Dumbreck Road and back by Maxwell Park and Pollokshaws. We saw three aeroplanes today. British closing in on Valenciennes. British airmen still putting the fear of death into German towns.

Monday, 28 October

Our Kirk is going to be renovated, so there was a female up at night to see what we were going to do in the matter. We donated. Tommy saw three aeroplanes today. Great British and Italian offensive started against Austria. Four years ago today, Lily died.

Tuesday, 29 October

Agnes in wash-house all day and ironed all night. British enter Valenciennes. Germans still fighting in parts of it. Austria wants an armistice. So does Turkey.

Thursday, 31 October

This is Hallowe'en, so Tommy lit his lantern. We did not dook.[76] C'est la guerre.[77] Another ally lost to Germany. Turkey surrenders to Britain. Fighting ceases at noon today. Armistice signed. Austria next?

Friday, 1 November

Agnes washed the stairs at night and I cleaned the brasses. Agnes got three ounces of 'thick black' for me today. Eggs are now about 6/6 per dozen (not per 100). 300,000 British troops now available from Turkey.

---

[76] Dooking (or bobbing) for apples is a traditional Hallowe'en game. A tub is filled with water and apples put into it. Players try to catch one of the floating apples in their teeth, without using their hands. Thomas and his family may not have played this game because there were no apples to be had.

[77] It's the war.

Saturday, 2 November

Seeing the war is nearly over, we went to the Cinerama at night. More Allied advance in France. Thousands of prisoners. British take Valenciennes. Break-up of Austrian empire. Hungary in revolt. Republic in Budapest. Riots all over Germany. King of Bulgaria abdicated. Peasant ministry formed.

Monday, 4 November

Agnes spent the evening sewing and I did the usual sweet idleness. Austria out of the war. Armistice signed yesterday. Germany's doom sealed.

Tuesday, 5 November

Nellie Hamilton and her baby here at tea time. Agnes went down to Clydebank at night. This is the month gas rationing starts: 9,000 cubic feet per annum. Italy's victory now complete. Austro-Hungarian army destroyed. 500,000 prisoners and 5,000 guns. The great advance in France continues.

Wednesday, 6 November

We all went to Greenlodge at night as Duncan is home on leave. While we were sitting in the room enjoying ourselves, a telegram came from the military recalling him back to England on the mortal spot. Consternation. British five miles from Mons. French capture Guise.

Thursday, 7 November

Dirty wet day. Fell this morning and nearly broke every bone in my blinking body. I survived. German rout continues. Ghent evacuated. Americans into Sedan. We are getting near the end now. Mutiny in warships at Kiel. Revolt in Hamburg.

Friday, 8 November

German army cut in two. Sedan completely conquered by Americans and French. German peace delegates on the road. They get 72 hours to make up their minds to accept armistice terms. Fighting to continue till then. Mutiny spreads all over German fleet. Revolution in Cologne and Bremen.

Saturday, 9 November

We played Ludo at night. France nearly cleared now of the Germans. Revolution in Germany. Kaiser abdicates.

Sunday, 10 November

This is Agnes' birthday. 'Many of them,' say I. Took a walk into town in afternoon to see if any war news.

Monday, 11 November

Fine sunny day, but cold. Got a telephone message this morning from Mr Roxburgh that poor Jenny died at an early hour this morning. We have lost a very dear friend. She will visit us no more. We will miss her sadly. At last, the Great War is over. Germany vanquished, the Kaiser a fugitive in Holland. Armistice signed at 5 a.m., all hostilities ceased at 11 a.m. This is the greatest day in history of the world. I got away at 1 p.m. Great scenes in Glasgow. Took Agnes and Tommy into town in afternoon to see the sights. City packed.

Tuesday, 12 November

Agnes went down to Clydebank in afternoon. In her absence, Tommy fell and knocked bits off himself, including one of his front teeth. Andrew's sister up about 10 p.m. letting us know Andrew was home on leave. World at peace. Allies' great task done. Germany staggered by our terms: 30 warships and 50 destroyers to be given up. Hoch hoch! Kaiser interned in Holland. Recruiting for army stopped. Shading of lights done away with.

Wednesday, 13 November

Agnes in wash-house today. Left my work early and went down to Clydebank to attend poor Jenny's funeral. We laid her to rest in the Western Necropolis. It was a wrench when I turned away, but surely we will meet again. Went straight back to my work, and worked late.

Sleep on my beloved, sleep, and take thy rest;
Lay down thy head upon thy saviour's breast;
We love thee well, but Jesus loves thee best - Goodnight.[78]

Thursday, 14 November

Nice sunny day. Working late at night, then I went out to see Andrew, who is home on leave from hospital.

Saturday, 16 November

Agnes in town in the afternoon. I sat in, too comfortable to go out.

Sunday, 17 November

Foggy sort of day. We did not go out at all, not even to the Kirk. Allies' march into Germany starts today. The German force in East Africa surrenders. Von Tirpitz a fugitive in Switzerland.

Monday, 18 November

Working late tonight. Agnes and Tommy over at Hickman Street tonight. Brussels now free of Germans. Revolution in Berlin. Two German warships sunk with all on board by the rebels.

[78] This is the opening verse of the hymn 'The Christian's Good Night' written by Ira Sankey and Sarah Doudney. It has passed into the modern folk repertoire and been recorded by, among others, the Incredible String Band and the Grateful Dead.

Thursday, 21 November

Nice sunny day. I have got a sore neck, a sore nose, and something has been in my eye all day. 'Sorrow, sorrow, without relief.'[79] Agnes' throat is giving her bother. I worked late tonight. German High Seas Fleet surrenders to Admiral Beatty today. Sic transit etc.[80]

Friday, 22 November

Navy's great day. Historic scene in the Forth. German flag hauled down at 2.57 p.m. and not to be hoisted again. Nine battleships, seven light cruisers, five battle cruisers and 50 destroyers of German High Seas Battle Fleet and more to follow. All surrendered without a blow. U-boats continue to surrender at Harwich.

The German battleship Hindenburg *surrenders at Scapa Flow, in Orkney, as seen from a British ship.*

[79] 'Sorrow, without relief' is a phrase from the poem 'The Debt' by African-American poet Paul Laurence Dunbar.

[80] The Latin phrase 'Sic transit gloria mundi' means: 'And so passes the glory of the world.'

Saturday, 23 November

Having an uneasy conscience, I went out to Ruglen in the afternoon and paid my tailor all the money I owed him. Agnes got a very bad cold indeed. The surrendered German fleet off to Scapa Flow. 50 U-boats have so far surrendered.

Sunday, 24 November

Agnes in bed all day until evening. I went out in the morning for eggs, but eggs were evidently extinct in Glasgow this morning. So I made breakfast without them. Andrew's wife heaved in towards afternoon, and Hetty Cook came in about 5 p.m. She stays in Pollokshields now.

Monday, 25 November

Agnes keeping a little better. Tommy is now in the 'first standard'.[81] Agnes broke the kitchen window today, and it a newly put in pane of glass. Terrible. French army enters Strasburg. British troops reach German frontier.

Tuesday, 26 November

Got a shock today. Saw a shop saying: 'Thick black for sale.' I got two ounces. British fleet sails for Kiel.

[81] The 'first standard' was the best-performing class in each school year.

Wednesday, 27 November

Working late at night. When I got home the lady from the Kirk was in getting cash for the Kirk. The darkening shade is now off our stair gas, seeing that Germany is no more. I filled in our fuel rationing paper. According to it, I'm to get 24,000 cubic feet of gas in a year. The other notice said 9,000. Something wrong, somewhere, so I interviewed the gas expert. He says the larger amount is correct. It's 'quare'.[82] We are getting white bread now.[83]

Thursday, 28 November

Agnes not keeping well at all just now. The King visits France. Vive le Roi! Other 27 U-boats surrendered yesterday at Harwich. 114 now surrendered. Belgium now clear of the Germans.

Friday, 29 November

Agnes not keeping any better. I cleaned all the windows. The paint is now off our one and only lamppost in Morgan Street. 'Let it shine.'[84] Ex-Kaiser to be demanded from Holland. Austrian casualties in the war: four million (800,000 killed). 1,100 Jews massacred at Lemberg.

Saturday, 30 November

I took a walk over to Sam's shop and had a crack with him. Agnes not keeping much better. This is St Andrew's Day, so I ought to don the kilt, but I didn't. Anarchy all over Germany. The Kaiser renounces the throne.

[82] An Irish phrase, literally 'it's queer', meaning odd or puzzling.
[83] Supplies of wheat were restored after the U-boat menace was banished, and bread could once again be made with processed white flour.
[84] Possibly from the chorus of the spiritual song 'This Little Light of Mine'.

Monday, 2 December

Agnes went and consulted the man of medicine at night. He gave her a bottle. She is Grade 3, very much so.[85] He says he may have to come up for an examination. Tommy seems to have the cold. British and American troops now in German territory.

Tuesday, 3 December

Saw a most unholy mob of Bolsheviks in town today. It was a procession of some of our enlightened citizens welcoming home [Maclean] from jail.[86] He is standing for Parliament for the Gorbals.[87] Heaven help us all! Seeing that the war is over, we went to the Cinerama at night. After about a fortnight's search I managed to get a gill bottle of 'emergency medicine'.[88] It cost 2/- and is poor, weak and emasculated stuff. But it will do.

Thursday, 5 December

We engaged a lady to do our washing today. I went at night to a political meeting in Dixon Halls with Mr Cormack. A Labour meeting, it was, which does not necessarily mean that I'll vote for him. Agnes not looking well at all tonight.

Friday, 6 December

Dirty wet day. I have got a bad cold. Covered my boots with pieces of iron to make them last longer. Bolshevikism reigns supreme in Germany. The entire Turkish fleet now surrendered.

[85] Thomas is referring to the military's scale of medical fitness. He, of course, was graded as CIII.

[86] Following the armistice, the Marxist educator John Maclean was freed from jail, where he was serving a five-year sentence for sedition. He was given a hero's welcome. The event was celebrated in the song 'The Ballad of John Maclean' by Glaswegian singer Matt McGinn, and in a poem, 'The John Maclean March', by Hamish Henderson.

[87] John Maclean contested the Gorbals seat as the official Labour candidate in December 1918.

[88] Whisky.

Sunday, 8 December

Nice dry day. Agnes very ill during the night. I went for the doctor this morning. He duly arrived and examined her, but evidently went away as wise as he came. Agnes' cousin, Hetty Cook, here about 5.30. James is in the army and home on leave. He has two gold wound stripes.[89] Agnes got up about 6 p.m. to help entertain. They departed about 10.30.

Tuesday, 10 December

Dirty wet day. My watch ceases work as from today. 'No tick.'[90] Josephine up at night seeing Agnes. I saw her away as far as Govan Street about 10.30. She tells me that Pa is very ill. The doctor says it is cancer. I did not tell Agnes, knowing the sad state of her nerves.

Wednesday, 11 December

Cold, foggy day. Hoar frost lying on everything. Tommy seems to have a bad cold. The doctor up seeing Agnes. His diagnosis not so favourable as I hoped for. The bloodthirsty man thinks he may have to operate. So cheery.

Thursday, 12 December

Wet sort of day. Being a man of wealth I bought a new watch today (15/6). Tommy's cold worse. Agnes not so well. James Cook and his sister Hetty here for tea. We had a nice time. Five captured German guns in George Square.

Friday, 13 December

Dirty wet day, but very mild. I went round to the doctor at night for his special bottle of brew for Agnes. Tommy in bed all day. He has ear-ache. No appetite, bad cough, no interest in anything. I'm beginning to get melancholy.

[89] These were small, gold-coloured, vertical stripes sewn on to the lower left sleeve.

[90] Notices in shops, bars etc. proclaiming 'no tick' indicated that goods and services would not be offered on credit. Thomas is aiming for a pun here.

Saturday, 14 December

Very cold, raw day. This is the day we vote in the Parliamentary Election. Agnes voted for the first time. Females have now 'the vote'. Agnes feeling not so bad today, but very tired at night. The world has lost 15 million tons of shipping by U-boats.

Tuesday, 17 December

Bright frosty day. Lily phoned me today to say that Father had seen the professor and the trouble was not so bad as feared. He has to undergo a slight operation. Mrs Cormack dropped in at night and talked drivel for two solid hours. Tommy spotted a beetle. I swotted the beetle then plastered up some bits of the press to discourage any more.

Most women in Britain were accorded the vote by the Representation of the People Act that was passed in February 1918. This allowed practically all men to vote, regardless of their property qualifications, and gave the vote to women over 30 who met minimum property qualifications. At the time, the Act was seen as a political necessity. The war would soon be over, the politicians felt, and they were concerned that the men returning from defending democracy abroad would demand the same for themselves. Women, too, were more likely to be militant after their experiences working in factories and farms, if not in theatres of war. The principle of 'one person, one vote' had to wait until 1928, but the 1918 Act made Britain much more democratic than it had been.

Opposite page *'Alarum' is an older spelling of 'alarm'.*

DECEMBER, 1918.

3rd in Advent. Sunday **15**

(349-16)

Seems a nice sort of day dry and calm

Tommy's big front tooth out today

Josephine & Pa here. Pa seemed cheery enough. I showed him the alarum clock and did some tricks with it

They went away 8 30.

Agnes got up today about 2. p.m. If anything she is a little better.

Alarum clock wont go.

DECEMBER, 1918.

Monday 16

(350-15)

Cold raw day Heavy rain & hail showers

Seeing that the weather is cold I got 2 winter Semmits (12/- each)

agnes not so bad today

Spent the night investigating the "clock-that-wont-go".

managed so far that it goes lying down.

16/12/08. G. Ferguson & I out at Mary's house tonight.

Thursday, 19 December

Very cold day, hard frost. Agnes went to the wash-house today!!!!!!! Which filled me with gloomy forebodings. Got the wee clock to go tonight (maybe). Ten years ago today, I gave Agnes her engagement ring. Great rejoicings.

Friday, 20 December

Agnes went to the doctor tonight and got another bottle. She not so well tonight. She does too much and I do too little, which is a most unsatisfactory arrangement. I had a bad headache today and not very well generally. Poles invade Prussia.

Saturday, 21 December

Sam in to see me at the business today. He left Father at the Royal Infirmary and I have to go for him in the afternoon. After dinner I went to that place and took Pa to Greenlodge in a cab as he was very shaky. Got home myself about 7 p.m. Entire Austrian navy now in the hands of the Allies.

Sunday, 22 December

Snow fell most all day. Took a turn over to Greenlodge to see my father. He is in a most nervous condition. I got home 8 p.m

Tuesday, 24 December

Tommy got his holidays today, I went away at 4.30. Andrew's wife here in the afternoon letting us know that her man was home on leave. Tommy hung up his stockings, so I did the necessary Father Noel trick. We got a few cards.

Opposite page *'Semmit' is a Scots word for vest or undershirt.*

Wednesday, 25 December

Peace on Earth. Thank God. The first Christmas since 1913 in which we could say it. I left my work about 11 a.m. We all went to the Cinerama in the afternoon. At night I took a turn over to Greenlodge to see how Pa was keeping.

Thursday, 26 December

Agnes baked a New Year cake today. We all went over to Andrew's house at night. We talked to the wee chap and managed to pass the rest of the time playing cards.

Friday, 27 December

Cold wet day. Hetty Cook rung me up today telling me she was married. Wish I was the man (pro tem).[91] The Food Controller is allowing me an extra ¼lb sugar per head for this week, seeing it is the festive season.

Saturday, 28 December

Very nice day. Left my work at 9.30 a.m. and went out to Greenlodge for my father. We got to the infirmary at 10.30 a.m. We got out from the doleful place at 1 p.m. Pa came out more cheerful than when he went in. I saw him back to Greenlodge, took a cup of tea and then home. At night I took a turn over to Dalmarnock and saw Sam. On my way home I met Josephine at Bridgeton Cross. She not feeling well, so I took her on the tram to the foot of James Street. Home myself 10 p.m.

[91] The Latin phrase 'pro tem' means 'for the time being'. Thomas may mean 'temporarily'.

Sunday, 29 December

Very wet day. None of us out at all. Agnes made a dumpling today. Oh my! I addressed tonight a few tokens of love and esteem to our various friends in the shape of New Year cards. This is the last Sunday of a very sad year.

Monday, 30 December

Dirty wet cold day. Agnes went over to doctor at night. Went to the baths tonight and took the 1918 dirt off. I'll start the new year with a clean skin, if nothing else. Got the alarum clock going not so bad now. Clocks is clocks these times. Used to get them for 2/6. Cheapest now is about 21/-.

Tuesday, 31 December

Nice day, with a touch of frost. Got away at 1 p.m. Took a turn over in the afternoon to see my father, but got no one in, so I had a look in at the People's Palace. We did not go out at night, but sat and waited for the New Year coming. So ends the year 1918. The year of peace, but a year I will always look back on with deep regret.

I see the fairest flowers fade,
The rosy cheek grow pale;
The awful wreck disease has made,
The strongest mortals fail.
They also speak to me of death
In language strong and clear.
Thy life is going with each breath
- Eternity is near.[92]

[92] Poem or song not identified.

British Navy Casualties
for the Great War 39,760
33,367 killed
5,183 wounded
missing 47
prisoners & interned 1,175

British merchant
seamen casualties
14,661 killed
3,295 prisoners

Austrian casualties
in the war
4 million
(800,000 killed)

American losses
in the war
dead 9,158
wounded 189,955
missing 14,290
prisoners 2,705

British military casualties
in the Great War
(not complete yet)
3,049,991
killed 660,000
wounded 2 million
prisoners, missing, etc.
350,000
of whom 80,000
are considered killed

German losses
in the Great War
1,600,000 killed
103,000 missing
618,000 prisoners
4,064,000 wounded

Serbian casualties 322,000

French casualties in this war
1,831,600 (?) of whom
1,071,300 are killed

Italian losses in war
1,430,130 of whom
467,900 are killed.

1933 and 1950

1933

Sunday 23 April

Looked a nice day but I did not go out. Sat in and read and read & had an occasional smoke and generally made myself a nuisance.

Agnes and Tommy went to Church in the forenoon my throat not quite right yet

Monday 24 April

Nice warm sunny day but a dull wet night. My throat a wee bit tight but otherwise

Iris well. Agnes spent a busy night whitewashing etc. the "loft".
Tommy took our "wireless" to the shop that does our radio-wants, to get it all wired over again.

With these few remarks I will now close this diary and never write in it again. I have kept it faithfully for 20 odd years. It has seen many changes and dire events, and as for the future, I hesitate.

So, Amen.

see over —

Mon. 27 Feb. 1950.

Agnes my darling wife & sweetheart, died early this morning.

"At the going down of the sun and in the morning, I will remember her."

Wee Tommy the sailor aged around two or three years at a Glasgow photographers studio.

Not so Wee Tommy in his usual attire of kilt, possibly in the grounds of Glasgow University.

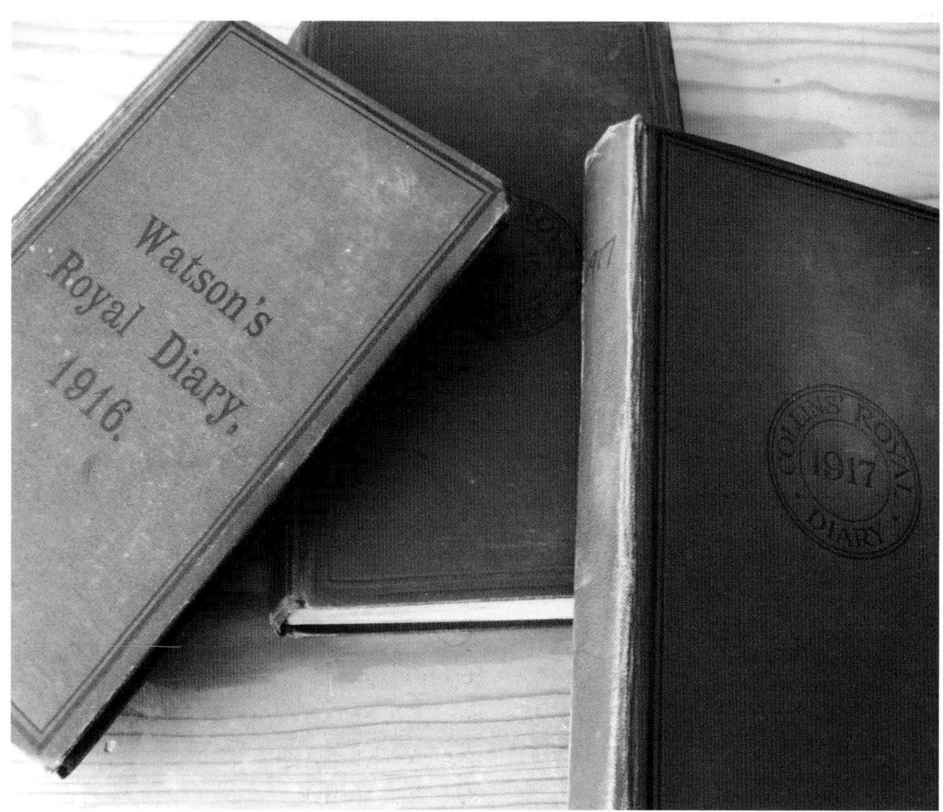

The diaries

Picture credits

Every effort has been made to trace the owners of copyright material produced herein, but if any have been inadvertently overlooked, the publishers would be pleased to make the necessary arrangements at the first opportunity.

Getty Images / Hulton Archive:
Pages: 47, 49, 57, 61 (Popperfoto), 66, 73, 81, 115, 123, 141, 142, 155, 161, 190, 216, 217, 221, 223, 239 (Popperfoto), 248, 249 (Time & Life Pictures), 254, 259, 260, 277 (Time & Life Pictures), 297, 336, 339 (Popperfoto), 355, 361.

Mary Evans Picture Library:
Pages: 53, 60, 63 (Onslow Auctions Limited), 70, 91 (Alfred Leete/Illustrated LondonNews), 106 (Onslow Auctions Limited), 118-119 (Illustrated London News), 129 (left, centre and right: Joyce Dennys), 162 (Rue des Archives/Tallandier), 180, 188, 189 (Illustrated London News), 215, 255 (Illustrated London News), 275 (Rue des Archives/Tallandier), 291, 311, 342 (AISA Media).

Virtual Mitchell Collection / Glasgow City Council:
Pages: 5, 7, 9, 32, 33, 100, 146, 200, 208, 236, 238, 287, 337, 338, 347.

©The Estate of Thomas Cairns Livingstone 2008
Pages: 378, 379, 380.

All other illustrations taken from the original diaries of Thomas Cairns Livingstone.

If you have further information specific to the people and places that Thomas Cairns Livingstone has written about in these diaries, please contact:

tommyswar@harpercollins.co.uk

Or write to:

Tommy's War
Harper Press
77-85 Fulham Palace Road
Hammersmith
London
W6 8JB